OXFORD HISTORICAL SERIES
Editors
V. H. GALBRAITH   J. S. WATSON   R. B. WERNHAM

BRITISH SERIES

Oxford University Press, Amen House, London E.C.4
GLASGOW NEW YORK TORONTO MELBOURNE WELLINGTON
BOMBAY CALCUTTA MADRAS KARACHI KUALA LUMPUR
CAPE TOWN IBADAN NAIROBI ACCRA

© *Oxford University Press 1957*

THE EMBASSY OF
SIR WILLIAM WHITE
AT CONSTANTINOPLE
1886–1891

By

COLIN L. SMITH

OXFORD UNIVERSITY PRESS

1957

Soc
DA
47.9
T8
S5

PRINTED IN GREAT BRITAIN

TO
MY PARENTS

TO
MY PARENTS

PREFACE

IT might be argued that Sir William White requires no further attention from the historian. A biography already exists, and there are numerous general studies of the Near Eastern question which cover the period of his embassy at Constantinople. But the inadequacy of the present biography is alone an ample justification for further research. H. Sutherland Edwards's work, published in 1902, has long been outdated. Moreover, it was written as a personal memoir rather than as a diplomatic study, and the result was the publication of some of White's private letters together with a commentary which made very little use of any of the other materials then available. In contrast to the tedious length with which the earlier and comparatively unimportant period of White's life is treated, the climax of his diplomatic career is dismissed with a briefness which reveals a lack both of material and understanding: less than a fifth of the book is devoted to White's embassy at Constantinople, and one short paragraph is thought sufficient to deal with the events of 1887, the year which witnessed one of the greatest diplomatic crises in Europe before 1914. In such a biography the omissions are more significant than the contents.

References to White in other works are vague and sketchy: brief pen-portraits in the biographies of his contemporaries, and occasional mentions in the footnotes of scholarly monographs record his abilities and acknowledge his greatness, but fall short of giving a satisfactory explanation for his success as an ambassador. 'If the time ever comes', wrote Dr. Washburn of the Robert College, in 1909, 'when the government allows the publication of his private papers, which it took possession of after his death, it will be the most interesting of books.'[1] This challenge, thrown down over forty years ago, has yet to be taken up.

All of White's official correspondence and many of his private papers may now be seen at the Public Record Office. The correspondence of many of those who were closely

---

[1] G. Washburn, *Fifty Years in Constantinople, and Recollections of Robert College*, p. 220.

acquainted with him can also be inspected either there or in the British Museum, and, in addition to these unpublished sources, there are printed collections of documents from the archives of most of the great European powers and several well-documented biographies and monographs on the period. I owe a special debt of gratitude, however, to the present Lord Salisbury and the authorities at Christ Church who have allowed me to make use of the private papers of the third Marquis of Salisbury, and, above all, to White's grandson, the late Captain William de Geijer, who made available to me a collection of his grandfather's private papers and newspaper cuttings that has remained in the possession of his family. These, and the series of talks I had with Captain de Geijer until his death in April 1954, gave me an invaluable insight into his grandfather's ideas and character.

It would be almost impossible to name all those who have helped and encouraged me to write this book, but I feel I should mention Professor W. N. Medlicott, who originally introduced me to my subject when I was a student at the then University College of the South West, Exeter; Professor Dame Lillian M. Penson, at whose seminars I first learnt the technique of historical research; the Warden and Fellows of St. Antony's College, who enabled me to continue my studies at Oxford, and Mr. A. J. P. Taylor of Magdalen College, who supervised my work during its final stages and encouraged me to get my thesis published. I should also like to express my gratitude to Miss Agatha Ramm, M.A., formerly of Bedford College, London, and now at Somerville College, Oxford, who has been ready at all times to give me frank criticism and sound advice. Finally, I wish to thank Mr. Steven Watson of Christ Church for all the help he has given me in getting this book through the press.

C. L. S.

CONTENTS

LIST OF ABBREVIATIONS	xi
I. THE MAN AND THE PROBLEM	1
II. ROSEBERY AND THORNTON	41
III. THE FIRST MEDITERRANEAN AGREEMENT (*February–March* 1887)	47
IV. THE SECOND MEDITERRANEAN AGREEMENT (*December* 1887)	83
V. THE PROBLEM OF ASIA MINOR	109
VI. THE END OF AN EMBASSY, 1888–91	134

APPENDIX I
  (1) *Memorandum by Sir William White, dated 27 June 1885*   158
  (2) *White to Salisbury, Private Letter, dated 4 July 1885*   159

APPENDIX II
  (1) *White to Salisbury, Private and Confidential Letter, dated 22 September 1885*   161
  (2) *Salisbury to White, Private Letter, dated 24 September 1885*   162

APPENDIX III
  Salisbury to White, Private and Secret Letter, dated 20 April 1887   163

APPENDIX IV
  (1) *Memorandum by Sir William White entitled: 'Remarks applying to different British schemes for the construction of Turkish Railways in Asia', dated 25 July 1887*   164
  (2) *White to Salisbury, Private Letter, dated 16 October 1888*   167

BIBLIOGRAPHY	168
INDEX	181

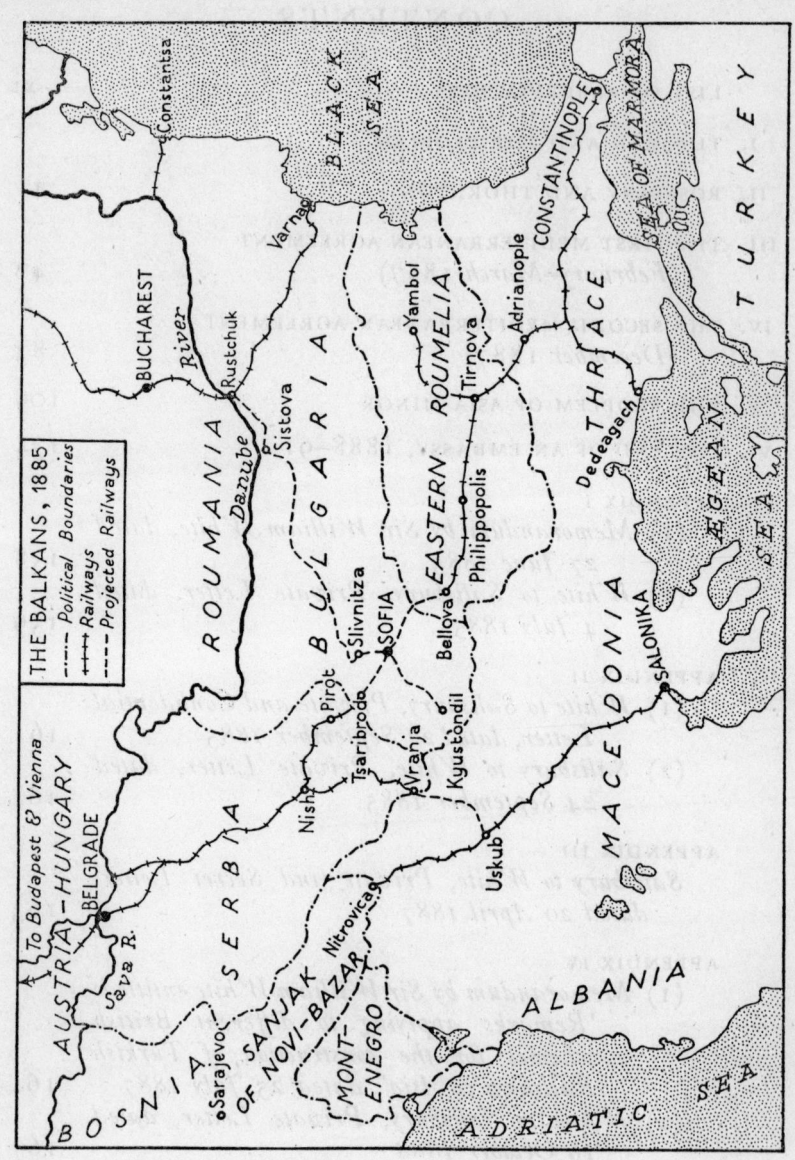

LIST OF ABBREVIATIONS

A. & P.	*Accounts and Papers* (Blue Books).
D.D.F.	*Documents Diplomatiques Français, 1871–1914*, 1st series, vols. v–vi, vi *bis*, vii–ix (Paris, 1933–9).
E.H.R.	*English Historical Review.*
F.O.	Foreign Office Papers and Embassy Archives in the Public Record Office.
G.P.	*Die Grosse Politik der europäischen Kabinette, 1871–1914*, edited by J. Lepsius, A. M. Bartholdy, and F. Thimme, vols. iii–ix, xiv. 2 (Berlin, 1927).
P.P.	*Parliamentary Papers.*
P.R.O.	Public Record Office.

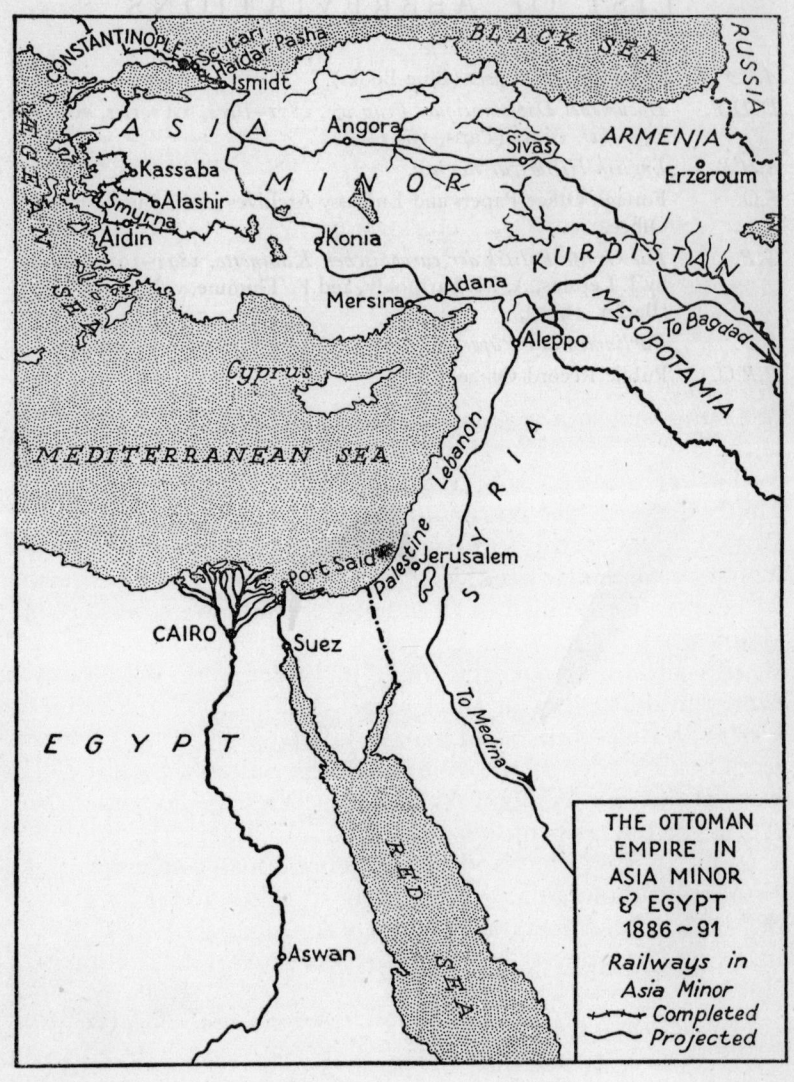

I

THE MAN AND THE PROBLEM

ABDUL HAMID II disliked British ambassadors. During the first eight years of his rule the British embassy at Pera changed hands no less than four times, and each change was marked by a deterioration in Anglo-Turkish relations. In 1867, when Sir Henry Elliot was appointed ambassador at Constantinople, Turkey still regarded Great Britain as her natural and traditional ally, but when he left that capital, ten years later, the relations between the two Powers were severely strained, and he himself was suspect for the part he was supposed to have played in the deposition and 'suicide' of the Sultan Abdul Aziz.[1] Elliot's successors only added fuel to Turkey's hatred and suspicion of her former friend: Sir Henry Layard was 'torn out' of the Sultan's heart;[2] Lord Goschen was never forgiven for employing harsh phrases which permanently rankled in his mind;[3] and Lord Dufferin was cursed for being a devil incarnate.[4] Such was the state of affairs when Sir Edward Thornton was officially appointed as British ambassador to the Porte in December 1884. However, the difficulties of the Central Asian problem detained him at St. Petersburg, and, temporarily at least, he was spared from being added to the long list of the Sultan's enemies.[5] It was left to Sir William White, sent to Constantinople in April 1885 as Thornton's *locum tenens*, to inherit the Sultan's accumulated wrath. 'God knows what sinister schemes this Imperial monomaniac . . . is likely to think I can be guilty of', he confided to Granville soon after his arrival.[6] White had good reason to be apprehensive: many a diplomatic

---

[1] White to Granville, Private, 30 May 1885, P.R.O. 30/29/191; Sir E. Pears, *Life of Abdul Hamid*, pp. 34–59.
[2] A. Vambéry, *The Story of My Struggles*, ii. 365.
[3] Dufferin to Granville, Private, 21 Mar. 1882, P.R.O. 30/29/190; White to Salisbury, Copy of Private and Confidential Tel., 28 Aug. 1889, F.O. 364/6.
[4] Salisbury to White, Private, 10 May 1889, F.O. 364/1; Sir A. Lyall, *The Life of the Marquis of Dufferin and Ava*, ii. 24; H. Nicolson, *Lord Carnock*, pp. 38–43.
[5] Lord E. Fitzmaurice, *The Life of Granville George Leveson Gower, Second Earl Granville*, ii. 365.
[6] White to Granville, Private, 30 May 1885, P.R.O. 30/29/191.

reputation had perished at Constantinople, and his own was about to be put to that exacting test.

William Arthur White was born at Pulawy in Poland on 13 February 1824. The many years which he spent in Poland during the early period of his life, and the fact that his mother and maternal grandmother held land there, gave rise to rumours that he was of Polish origin. In fact, both his parents were British: his father, who came from a family of Dutch extraction which had settled for several generations on the Isle of Man, had served in both the Consular and Colonial Services and had ended his career as the Governor of Trinidad; his mother was the daughter of General William Neville Gardiner whose mission as British Minister at Warsaw had ended abruptly in 1795 with the Third Partition of Poland.

White was educated at King William's College, Isle of Man, and Trinity College, Cambridge. He does not seem to have excelled at scholarly pursuits, and his firm adhesion to the Roman Catholic faith deprived him of the opportunity of taking a bachelor's degree. His real education came later. He left Cambridge in 1843 and joined his mother in Poland where he undertook the management of the small family estates. It was there that he acquired the first-hand knowledge of eastern European languages and politics which was to serve him in good stead throughout his official career.

White's career in the Consular and Diplomatic Services may briefly be summarized as follows. He entered the Consular Service as a clerk to the Consul-General at Warsaw in 1857, became Vice-Consul four years later, and acted as Consul-General for the greater part of 1862 and 1863. He was appointed Consul at Danzig in November 1864, and there he was able to add to his experience by looking after French as well as British interests during the Franco-Prussian war. Transferred to Serbia as Agent and Consul-General at Belgrade in February 1875, he found that he was dealing more and more with political rather than commercial questions, and in the December of the following year he was selected by Derby to assist Salisbury as *adlatus* at the Constantinople Conference. His useful work during that mission earned him a C.B. in March 1878, and secured his promo-

THE MAN AND THE PROBLEM

tion to the legation at Bucharest in the following July. He received his credentials as Envoy Extraordinary and Minister Plenipotentiary to the Roumanian government in March 1879, but he was unable to present them until February 1880, when Great Britain officially recognized Roumania as an independent state. In March 1885, White was created K.C.M.G. for his services in Roumania, and a month later he was chosen by Granville to fill the temporary vacancy at Constantinople.[1]

But a catalogue of honours and distinctions such as that to be found under White's name in the Foreign Office List does not take into account the numerous disadvantages which he had to overcome in the course of his unconventional career, nor does it reveal those personal qualities which enabled him to break almost every rule, written or unwritten, for the attainment of high rank in the Diplomatic Service.

The first great barrier to White's advancement was the sharp social and professional distinction which was drawn between the Diplomatic and Consular Services at the time when he embarked upon his official career. There seemed to be no hope that White, an obscure clerk in an eastern European consulate, would ever reach ambassadorial heights and enjoy the princely splendour of the Embassy House at Pera. In the middle of the nineteenth century English society still moved in narrow and exclusive circles, and family connexions were still considered to be a useful supplement to ability in most branches of the government. The Diplomatic Service, although slowly becoming more formal and professional, had not completely lost its character of previous times when it had been organized 'to combine, as far as possible, the satisfactory maintenance of international relations with the social convenience and advantage of the upper classes of the community'.[2] The career of Lord Augustus Loftus proved that it was still possible for a 'pompous blockhead' to reach the

---

[1] For brief accounts of White's career see H. S. Edwards, *Sir William White*; *Dictionary of National Biography*, xxi. 84–85; W. N. Medlicott, 'Corrections to the Dictionary of National Biography on Sir William White', *Bulletin of the Institute of Historical Research*, v. 58–59; *The Foreign Office List*, 1891, p. 211; *The Times*, 31 Dec. 1891; 1–2 Jan. 1892.

[2] P.P. (1861), vi, *Report from the Select Committee on Diplomatic Service*, p. 9; cf. also p. 211.

top ranks of the diplomatic profession and become ambassador to Prussia—provided he had the necessary connexions.[1]

The Consular Service was the poor relation of its diplomatic counterpart; its members could not expect to be promoted beyond the rank of Agent and Consul-General. When he appeared before the Select Committee on Diplomatic Service of 1861, Hammond, the Permanent Under-Secretary at the Foreign Office, maintained that it was undesirable to encourage consuls to become diplomats: instead of attempting to gain distinction by dealing with political questions, they should confine themselves to their more humble, but equally useful, consular duties.[2] Nor was this official attitude towards the Consular Service extinct in the 'eighties: in the summer of 1885 Graves regarded it as an unusual honour that he—a member of the 'despised Consular Service'—should be left even temporarily in charge of the British agency at Philippopolis;[3] and, earlier in the same year, White's new colleagues at Constantinople did not let him forget that he had once been a mere consul.[4]

White's second great handicap was his failure to get off to an early start in official life. He did not enter the Consular Service until he was thirty-three, and that in itself was sufficient to put him at a serious disadvantage in an era when promotion largely depended upon seniority and was notoriously slow. But, in spite of his late beginning, he rose steadily in the consular ranks and created a precedent in Europe by transferring to the Diplomatic Service. Even the refusal of two offers of promotion in the course of a single year did not halt his advancement: in December 1884 Granville was unable to tempt him to move from Bucharest to a more lucrative post either at Rio de Janeiro or Buenos Aires, and, ten months later, neither a panegyric by Salisbury on the future importance of the Far East, nor the friendly persuasions of Morier, induced him to accept the legation at Peking. Although he was aware that a diplomat in his early sixties was

---

[1] R. J. Sontag, *Germany and England, Background of Conflict, 1848–94*, p. 26.
[2] *P.P.* (1861), vi, *Report from the Select Committee on Diplomatic Service*, p. 72.
[3] Sir R. Graves, *Storm Centres of the Near East: Personal Memoirs, 1879–1929*, p. 77.
[4] J. M. von Radowitz, *Aufzeichnungen und Erinnerungen*, ii. 254; Lord Hardinge of Penshurst, *Old Diplomacy*, pp. 40–41.

taking a great risk in letting such opportunities slip by, he preferred to remain in the Balkans where he could make full use of his wide knowledge and experience of that area. The ultimate reward for his discerning self-sacrifice was a temporary appointment at Constantinople.[1]

Finally, the fact that White was a staunch Roman Catholic added perhaps yet another obstacle to his advancement at the outset of his career. However, his firm adhesion to the faith which had denied him the right to take a degree at Cambridge eventually earned him the distinction of being the first Roman Catholic since the Reformation to reach full ambassadorial rank in the service of Great Britain.[2]

White's chances of becoming an ambassador seemed to be smaller than those of the average nineteenth-century consul who looked forward to dealing with political rather than purely commercial correspondence. Yet nothing deterred him, and gradually he broke down all the formidable barriers which stood in the way of his attainment of high rank: some collapsed before the storm of his forceful personality, and those which remained were undermined by his unusual abilities. Tall and sturdy, with a massive forehead and a flowing white beard, he made an immediate and lasting impression upon all who met him. His individual accent, variously described as Scottish, Irish, and 'foreign', added to the effect of his booming voice which penetrated even the thickest door and made him known to the Turks as 'the Bosphorus Bull'.[3] After making White's acquaintance in Serbia, W. E. Forster described him as 'a tall, stout, most cordial, cheery Scotchman'.[4] 'A polar bear if ever I saw one,' commented Sir Charles Dilke, 'always ready to hug his enemies or his friends, and always roaring so as to shake the foundations of your house.'[5] But in White, as Dilke was well aware, strong lungs were uncommonly combined with an acute mind; his

[1] Edwards, pp. 7–13, 217–18.
[2] Ibid., p. 10.
[3] Cf. Sir E. Pears, *Forty Years in Constantinople, 1873–1915*, p. 31; Sir J. Rennell Rodd, *Social and Diplomatic Memoirs, 1884–93*, p. 242; Hardinge of Penshurst, pp. 40–41; 'Our Diplomatists', *Temple Bar*, lxxxiv, No. 335, Oct. 1888.
[4] T. Wemyss Reid, *The Life of the Rt. Hon. W. E. Forster*, ii. 120.
[5] S. Gwynn and G. M. Tuckwell, *The Life of the Rt. Hon. Sir Charles Dilke, Bart., M.P.*, i. 266.

mental alertness and his capacity for hard work were as outstanding as his bluff manner and his powerful physique.[1]

The Prince Consort had once complained that, generally speaking, British diplomats spent most of their time either with their diplomatic colleagues or with a few British residents, and that they consequently knew nothing of the countries to which they were accredited.[2] White was one of the few exceptions which proved the rule: he used his prodigious knowledge of eastern European languages to mix with all ranks of foreign society and to gather first-hand information from both Court and market-place.[3] He cultivated acquaintances as assiduously as he collected detailed information: 'There are few notable places or people you do not know', remarked one of his correspondents.[4] He had entered official life with little money, and with few friends in either the Consular or the Diplomatic Service, but he possessed a rough charm and an ability to speak with authority on Balkan problems which more than compensated for those initial setbacks. Morier, Odo Russell, Dufferin, Elliot, and Layard were among those who soon came to appreciate the value of his knowledge and the soundness of his judgement, and Dilke eagerly turned to him for advice when he contemplated writing the famous series of articles on international affairs which finally appeared in book form under the title of *The Present Position in European Politics*.[5]

White made full use of his many admirers in his struggle for recognition and advancement. For instance, his appointment to Belgrade from a far inferior post at Danzig owed much to Morier who went in for him 'fire and flames', and to Odo Russell who was frequently canvassed to intercede on his behalf at the Foreign Office.[6] As a true 'Hebrew of politics', he received honours and promotions from both political parties, and numbered Salisbury, Granville, and Dilke among

[1] Gwynn and Tuckwell, i. 266; Pears, pp. 136–7.
[2] Sontag, p. 26.
[3] Cf. *The Times*, 31 Dec. 1891; 1–2 Jan. 1892; 'Our Diplomatists', *Temple Bar*, xxxiv, No. 335, Oct. 1888.
[4] Carlingford to White, San Remo, 5 Feb. 1880, Additional White Papers.
[5] Dilke to White, Private, 23 Apr. 1880, Additional White Papers.
[6] Morier to Salisbury, Private, 7 Mar. 1889, Morier Papers; R. Wemyss, *Memoirs and Letters of the Rt. Hon. Sir Robert Morier*, i. 161; Edwards, p. 69.

his friends.¹ Moreover, he was known in Court as well as Cabinet circles. Using Lady Jane Ely, a Lady of the Bedchamber, as an intermediary, he gained valuable access to Queen Victoria. His correspondence with Lady Jane, which stretches over a period of more than twenty years, reveals that his letters were often shown to the Queen: 'I always tell the Queen when I hear from you', she informed him in one postscript,² and on another occasion she assured him that his letters had been 'duly received and shown to the Queen'.³ In fact, White had a talent for 'making the connexion' which even an eighteenth-century Whig would have envied; he was convinced that his personal advancement and the public interest were identical, and was anxious to ensure that his exceptional gifts were not passed by unnoticed and unrewarded.

He also enjoyed outstanding luck. But for this all his personal charm and professional skill might have been wasted. Fortunately, however, he received a whole series of appointments to capitals which were suddenly and unexpectedly thrown into the diplomatic limelight. With the outbreak of the Polish insurrection in 1863 the British Consulate at Warsaw assumed an unforeseen political importance, and White was called upon to perform duties which went far beyond the normal consular limits—duties which attracted the attention of Lord John Russell to 'the intelligent acting Consul-General at Warsaw'.⁴ His transfer from Danzig to Belgrade in February 1875 almost coincided with the beginning of a revolt in Bosnia and Hercegovina, and the knowledge and skill which he displayed during the ensuing international crisis made Derby single him out to serve as *adlatus* to Salisbury at the Constantinople Conference. Salisbury immediately recognized White's abilities, and rewarded him for his work at the conference by securing his promotion to Bucharest.⁵ This move was the most fortunate of White's whole career, for it eventually enabled him to leap the gap which separated the Consular from the Diplomatic Service.

[1] Edwards, pp. 13–15.
[2] Lady Jane Ely to White, Aix les Bains, 14 Apr. 1885, Additional White Papers.
[3] Lady Jane Ely to White, Balmoral, 26 Oct. 1886, Additional White Papers.
[4] S. Walpole, *The Life of Lord John Russell*, ii. 368.
[5] Edwards, pp. 81, 257–8.

In 1880, when the British government officially recognized Roumania as an independent state, he automatically took the rank of Minister and thus became the first British consul serving in Europe to be transferred to the Diplomatic Service.[1] Once again, White found himself at a capital which had rapidly increased in diplomatic importance. After the signing of the Berlin Treaty Roumania had become a 'good exercising ground for the Autumn Manœuvres of Diplomacy',[2] and both the Roumano-Jewish problem and the delicate question of Roumanian independence provided White with further opportunities to demonstrate his skill as a diplomat and his understanding of the Near East.[3] Granville did not have far to look when he searched for a *locum tenens* for Sir Edward Thornton in the spring of 1885.[4]

White was about to reach the climax of a unique career. Besides mastering all the intricacies of Balkan politics and becoming acknowledged as an authority upon the problems of that area, he had been able to sweep aside conventions and gate-crash into the top ranks of the diplomatic profession. His qualifications were excellent, but he was going to need all his wide experience and stubborn courage for the task which lay ahead of him at Constantinople.

The Pendjeh[5] crisis was at its height when White took up his appointment as Envoy Extraordinary and Minister Plenipotentiary to the Porte towards the end of April 1885. The frontier skirmish between Russian troops and Afghan tribesmen which had taken place a month earlier had come as the climax of a whole series of Russian incursions into Central Asia including the annexation of Samarkand in 1868, and the occupation of Merv in 1884.[6] During April both Great Britain and Russia pushed ahead with preparations for war: on 21 April the Gladstone government announced its inten-

[1] Edwards, pp. 258–9; S. T. Bindoff, 'The Unreformed Diplomatic Service, 1812–60', *Trans. R. Hist. Soc.*, 4th ser. xvii. 158.
[2] Salisbury to White, Private, 24 Dec. 1879, Additional White Papers.
[3] Edwards, pp. 184–90.
[4] Lord E. Fitzmaurice, *The Life of George Leveson Gower, Second Earl Granville*, ii. 365.
[5] Sometimes spelt 'Penjdeh' or 'Panjdeh'.
[6] Sir P. Sykes, *Sir Mortimer Durand*, pp. 133–50; Fitzmaurice, ii. 407–24.

tion of asking Parliament to vote a credit of eleven million pounds, six and a half millions of which were to be spent on preparations for a conflict with Russia; the Russians closed the port of Vladivostok to foreign shipping by laying mines, and on 26 April the British government retaliated by sending a squadron of warships to occupy Port Hamilton, off the coast of Korea.[1] But in spite of these hostile activities, neither government was ready or willing to fight a war with the other. Since it had come into power, in 1880, the Gladstone government had become involved in disputes all over the world, and these had left Great Britain without a powerful friend on the Continent. And, without allies, a war against Russia would be both futile and costly: futile because it would be impossible for British troops to strike a direct blow at Moscow or St. Petersburg, and costly because what fighting there was would have to take place either on the northern frontiers of India, or in the Crimea, provided Great Britain could gain control over the Straits. Russia was equally reluctant to enter into such a conflict: forced by the Berlin Treaty to give up her gains in the Balkans, she chose a more indirect approach to the problem of increasing her influence over the Porte and securing control of the Straits, and her diplomatic object in Afghanistan, as far as Great Britain was concerned, was to put herself into the advantageous position of being able to exert pressure in south-east Europe when the occasion arose.[2] Indeed, throughout the nineteenth century Russia found that the threat to invade India was an extremely effective bogey to use against Great Britain. 'The strength of the Russians for mischief is not material but moral', wrote W. T. Stead. 'It is based, not upon the proximity of their cannons, but upon the ubiquity of our alarmists.'[3]

The Pendjeh scare should be regarded as a Near Eastern rather than a Central Asian crisis. It taught Granville what he should have learnt already from his relations with Bismarck: that all questions between governments were connected, and that it was impossible to deal with each problem

---

[1] S. Gwynn and G. M. Tuckwell, *The Life of the Rt. Hon. Sir Charles Dilke, Bart., M.P.* ii. 120; Fitzmaurice, ii. 440.
[2] A. Meyendorff, *Correspondance diplomatique de M. de Staal*, i. 18, 41.
[3] W. T. Stead, *The Truth about Russia*, p. 114.

solely upon its own merits. Unlike Salisbury, who was soon to succeed him at the Foreign Office, Granville only slowly realized that nothing could be gained in diplomacy except by purchase or compulsion.[1] He soon discovered, however, that the effects of the Pendjeh incident were not confined to Central Asia: he soon found that it was necessary to look towards Egypt and Constantinople in order to appreciate the full force of its impact upon international affairs.

Coinciding as it did with Anglo-Turkish negotiations about Egypt, the Afghan crisis was immediately linked with the general problem of Anglo-Russian rivalry in the Near East. The Russians suspected that Hassan Fehmi Pasha's mission to London was designed to injure their interests at the Porte, and they therefore made increased efforts to come to some secret understanding with the Sultan about the Straits.[2] Meanwhile, it was rumoured that Granville had also attempted to strike a bargain with the Turks: in return for the opening of the Straits, he was supposed to have offered them a free hand in Egypt and Bulgaria, and the sum of twenty-five million pounds; moreover, he was reported to have threatened to sever completely the connexion between Turkey and Egypt should the Porte refuse to accept his offer.[3] But none of these stories rings true, and there is no evidence to support them in the Foreign Office archives. All that can be established is that Granville urged the Sultan not to take any hasty action or ill-considered step which might jeopardize his independence.[4] As for his threat to separate Egypt from its Turkish suzerain, the grain of truth contained in that rumour seems to have been magnified out of all proportion and confused with the Pendjeh affair. Granville had, in fact, been driven to take extreme measures when he was pressing the Turks to adhere to the Egyptian Financial Convention: exasperated by the repeated delays in the nego-

[1] Lady G. Cecil, *Biographical Studies of the Life and Political Character of Robert, Third Marquis of Salisbury*, p. 54.
[2] Wyndham (chargé d'affaires at Constantinople) to Granville, No. 70 Secret, 7 Feb., F.O. 195/1497; Tel. No. 47, 28 Mar., F.O. 78/3758; White to Granville, No. 246 Confidential, 30 Apr.; No. 262, 11 May 1885, F.O. 78/3751.
[3] *G.P.* vii, No. 1376; J. M. von Radowitz, *Aufzeichnungen und Erinnerungen*, ii. 244 (cited in W. L. Langer, *European Alliances and Alignments, 1871-1890*, p. 314).
[4] Granville to White, No. 145, 27 Apr., F.O. 78/3746; Private, 29 Apr., P.R.O. 30/29/212; White to Granville, No. 246 Confidential, 30 Apr. 1885, F.O. 78/3751.

tiations, he had gone so far as to suggest that both the Turkish ambassador and the Turkish special envoy sent to London to discuss Egyptian affairs might be offered their passports.[1]

As far as Egypt was concerned, the main effect of the Anglo-Russian disagreement about the Afghan frontier was to confirm Gladstone and his colleagues in their decision to remain on the defensive in the Sudan. In spite of the Queen's protests that it would be 'most disastrous' and 'ruinous' to leave Gordon unavenged and the Mahdi uncrushed,[2] Gladstone remained obdurate, pointing out that it would be impossible to launch an attack in the Sudan as long as there might arise on the Afghan frontier 'a case of overruling necessity which might derange any previous plan'.[3]

But far more important than its influence upon the conduct of Great Britain's Egyptian policy was the direct bearing which the Pendjeh crisis had upon the perennial contest between Great Britain and Russia for the control of the Straits. It was this, more than anything else, which turned an Anglo-Russian dispute into an international crisis. In the event of an Anglo-Russian conflict much would depend upon which of those Powers controlled the Straits, and upon the attitude which the other Powers would adopt if either of the combatants attempted to force a passage through the Bosphorus and the Dardanelles.

Bismarck suddenly found himself faced with the problem of committing himself to support either Great Britain or Russia in the approaching struggle. The policy he ultimately adopted, in which he was joined by Russia, Austria-Hungary, and even France, was to exert all his influence at the Porte to insist upon the international character of the principle of the closure of the Straits, and to preserve the neutrality of Turkey.[4] His ostensible reason for taking such action, which was

---

[1] Granville to Wyndham, No. 109A Confidential, 24 Mar., F.O. 78/3745; Wyndham to Granville, No. 185 Confidential, 3 Apr. 1885, F.O. 78/3750.
[2] Queen Victoria to Gladstone, 14 Mar. 1885 (printed in G. E. Buckle, *The Letters of Queen Victoria*, 2nd ser., iii. 628).
[3] Gladstone to Queen Victoria, 15 Mar. 1885 (printed in ibid. 628–9).
[4] *G.P.* iv. No. 765; Wyndham to Granville, No. 216 Very Confidential; No. 223 Very Confidential, 17 Apr.; No. 227 Very Confidential, 18 Apr. 1885, F.O. 78/4272.

eagerly proclaimed in several quarters, was his desire to preserve peace, or at least to localize any Anglo-Russian conflict.[1] But this was not his only motive for following such a course; he also used the crisis to demonstrate the solidarity of the Three Emperors' Alliance, renewed at Skiernevice in March 1884. Never again did the Three Emperors' Alliance work so effectively as it did throughout the Pendjeh crisis; never again was Bismarck able to put up such a convincing display of his power over European politics as upon this occasion when he simultaneously showed Russia the value of his friendship, and Great Britain the penalty of his ill will.[2] Even if it is assumed that Bismarck was primarily motivated by a desire to avert or localize any hostilities between Great Britain and Russia, his advice to the Porte that the Straits should be kept closed to ships of war in the event of such a struggle was directed against British rather than Russian interests: in what he described as 'le duel de la baleine et de l'éléphant',[3] he was depriving the British whale of the opportunity of making its way into the Black Sea while allowing the Russian elephant to roam at will on the northern frontiers of India. Thus both at London and at Constantinople there was a growing conviction that Germany and her associates favoured Russia against Great Britain, and that Turkey was unable to resist the will of such a formidable combination of Powers.[4] 'He [Bismarck] is sensitively anxious to avoid giving Russia any grounds for suspicion that he is on *too good* relations with England at the present moment', Scott reported from Berlin early in April.[5] And, at Constantinople, after pointing out that the Sultan looked up to Germany more than any other Power, White went on to observe: 'The German

---

[1] *G.P.* iv. No. 777 (Bismarck to the Emperor William I, 27 May 1885); J. V. Fuller, *Bismarck's Diplomacy at its Zenith*, p. 13.

[2] *G.P.* iv. No. 765; B. Nolde, *L'Alliance franco-russe*, pp. 313–14.

[3] C. de Freycinet, *Souvenirs, 1878–1893*, p. 303.

[4] Wyndham to Granville, Tel. No. 65, 15 Apr., F.O. 78/3758; Scott to Granville, No. 161 Secret, 11 Apr., F.O. 64/1077; Paget to Granville, Tel. No. 10 Secret, 30 Apr., F.O. 7/1082; No. 116 Secret, 27 Apr. 1885, F.O. 7/1077; V. Noack, *Bismarcks Friedenspolitik*, p. 184; O. Becker, *Bismarcks Bundnispolitik*, pp. 63–64.

[5] Scott (chargé d'affaires at Berlin) to Granville, Private, 4 Apr. (printed in P. Knaplund, *Letters from the Berlin Embassy, 1871–1874, 1880–1885*, Annual Report of the American Historical Association, 1942, ii. 394); No. 161 Secret, 11 Apr. 1885, F.O. 64/1077.

Empires act always in concert on Eastern Questions, and one would certainly not take any course without previous consultation with the other. Both are moreover bound to Russia, by certain engagements, since the interview at Skiernevice.'[1]

Early in May, when Great Britain and Russia finally agreed to submit their claims to an arbitrator, the most serious phase of the Pendjeh crisis was over. The two governments eventually dispensed with the services of an arbitrator and entered into direct negotiations about the delimitation of the Afghan frontier, and it was left to Salisbury to bring them to a close and sign the agreement of 10 September 1885.[2]

White had spent only a fortnight at his new post when the Pendjeh affair ended as an international crisis and was once more transformed into a frontier dispute. He had had no time to establish himself at Constantinople and to enter wholeheartedly into the diplomatic struggle about the closure of the Straits in the event of war. But in spite of such handicaps, he had learnt much from the Pendjeh crisis: it had convinced him that another clash with Russia was in the offing and had made him determined to prevent Russia from gaining the advantage on the Bosphorus for a second time; above all, it had shown him that Russia would continue to exert a strong influence over the Sultan, and that the Sultan would continue to yield to most of her demands, as long as she was supported by Germany and her associates.[3] Within less than six months he was to be given the opportunity of taking a much more active part in Near Eastern politics and proving how well he had learnt these lessons.

In the late summer and early autumn of 1885 international tension appeared to have given way to a period of calm, and leave-taking became uppermost in the thoughts of European sovereigns and diplomats. Early in September the Tsar and the Russian imperial family visited Copenhagen, where they were joined by the Prince of Wales and King George of Greece; Salisbury retired to the Châlet Cecil at Puys; Giers

[1] White to Granville, No. 249 Very Confidential, 1 May 1885, F.O. 78/3751.
[2] Sir P. Sykes, *Sir Mortimer Durand*, p. 147; W. L. Langer, *European Alliances and Alignments, 1871–1890*, p. 315.
[3] White to Granville, No. 249 Very Confidential, 1 May 1885, F.O. 78/3751.

went holidaying in the Tyrol, and the Foreign Office at St. Petersburg, with Vlangaly left in charge, was reduced to being a diplomatic *poste restante*. European diplomats in the Near East followed the example of their superiors: Lascelles left Sofia for England, Radowitz was on leave from the German embassy at Constantinople, and, in the prolonged absence of Sir Edward Thornton, White remained in charge of the British embassy there as 'Envoy Extraordinary and Minister Plenipotentiary'.[1]

It could scarcely be perceived that the atmosphere of crisis with which the year had opened was soon to be revived. Anglo-German relations were no longer severely strained by colonial disputes, and Bismarck seemed more eager to work in harmony with Salisbury and his Conservative government than with Granville and the Gladstone administration.[2] Since the fall of the Ferry government at the end of March and France's abandonment of her colonial *détente* with Germany, Anglo-French relations had similarly improved.[3] Even the tension in Great Britain's relations with Russia, so acute immediately after the Pendjeh incident, had been eased by the work of the Afghan Boundary Commission.[4] Salisbury, though cautious and rarely optimistic, did not paint an unduly gloomy picture of the European situation early in August: 'We seem to be fairly good friends with the German Power. France is not unfriendly. Russia of course will do us mischief if she can.'[5] In an era when a complete absence of Anglo-Russian friction would have been considered abnormal, the prospects were promising for a period of calm.

Such illusions were rudely shattered by the *coup d'état* at Philippopolis on 18 September 1885. The Eastern Roumelian government was overthrown by mutinous troops, and the Turkish governor-general was sent packing over the Turkish frontier. Once their success was assured, the leaders of the revolution set up a provisional government, proclaimed the union of Eastern Roumelia with Bulgaria, and called for its Prince to take the lead in the revolt. Prince Alexander was

---

[1] Edwards, p. 232; Sir R. Graves, *Storm Centres of the Near East*, p. 64.
[2] *G.P.* iv, Nos. 779–83; Langer, p. 316.
[3] Lord Newton, *Lord Lyons*, ii. 356.
[4] Langer, p. 315.
[5] Salisbury to White, Private, 5 Aug. 1885, F.O. 364/1.

in an obvious dilemma: if he joined in the revolution he could be sure that the Russians would seek to destroy him; if he refused to take any part in it his position in Bulgaria would become impossible and the loss of his throne inevitable. Putting his present security before any future retribution, he finally accepted the *fait accompli* from Tirnovo and entered Philippopolis on 21 September.¹ The Bulgarian settlement, so laboriously constructed at Berlin only seven years earlier, had been upset in a few hours by a handful of revolutionaries, and Europe was threatened with yet another Near Eastern crisis. Confused by the suddenness of the outbreak, the Great Powers were quick to suspect each other of participation in the Eastern Roumelian plot and correspondingly slow to adapt their policies to meet the needs of the new situation.

Bismarck, faced with the first serious crisis to threaten the Three Emperors' Alliance since its formation in 1881, feared that the outbreak might jeopardize the friendly relationship existing between the Emperor Francis Joseph and the Tsar Alexander III—a relationship which had been reasserted less than a month previously at the Kremsier meeting.² His main object was neither to support nor oppose the union of Bulgaria and Eastern Roumelia, but to prevent the revolutionary movement spreading into Macedonia, and to ensure that the final settlement arose from friendly discussions between the Three Empires.³ With such ends in view, he advised the Turkish government to appeal to the Tsar to disavow the movement and pressed the Austro-Hungarian government to make similar representations at the Porte.⁴ On 21 September he asked Salisbury to follow suit, even suggesting, a day later, that a British naval demonstration, perhaps at the Piraeus, might give the Sultan the moral support he required.⁵

---

¹ *A. & P.*, Turkey No. 1 (1886), lxxv [C-4612], 25; E. C. Corti, *Alexander von Battenberg: Sein Kampf mit den Zaren und Bismarck*, p. 193; A. G. H. Beaman, *Stambuloff*, pp. 58-59.
² W. N. Medlicott, 'The Powers and the Unification of the Two Bulgarias', *E.H.R.* liv. 283.
³ Malet to Salisbury, Tel. No. 74, 22 Sept. 1885, F.O. 64/1081; cf. *G.P.* v, No. 959 (Bismarck to the Emperor William I, 9 Oct. 1885).
⁴ Malet to Salisbury, Tel. No. 72, 21 Sept. 1885, F.O. 64/1081.
⁵ Malet to Salisbury, Tel. No. 72, 21 Sept.; Tel. No. 74, 22 Sept. 1885, F.O. 64/1081.

But once he had taken these first steps, Bismarck confined himself to expressing a vague wish for a conference to 'drown the question in ink'.[1]

Because it had confronted Europe with the San Stefano Treaty in March 1878, and because it had championed a 'big Bulgaria' at the Congress of Berlin, the Russian government might have been expected to rejoice at the union of the two Bulgarias and to welcome the nullification of the provisions of the Berlin Treaty which it had been forced to accept seven years earlier. But guardians are often over-attentive, and protégés are notoriously ungrateful. Even before the arrival of Prince Alexander of Battenberg upon the Bulgarian political scene in 1879, the Bulgarians quarrelled frequently with the Russian officers and officials responsible for the reorganization of the principality, and in 1881, when he assumed dictatorial powers, Prince Alexander added fuel to the new Tsar's personal hatred towards him, and became the whipping boy upon whom diplomatic, military, and business elements in Russia vented their wrath because of the frustration of their plans to exploit the principality. These fierce disputes between the Russian and Bulgarian governments came to a climax in the autumn of 1883 when the Prince dismissed the Russian generals Kaulbars and Sobolev—an act tantamount to the rejection of pan-Slav influence in Bulgaria. From then onwards, Russian policy was concentrated upon the expulsion of 'the Battenberger' as a prelude to any eventual union of Bulgaria and Eastern Roumelia, and none of Prince Alexander's subsequent attempts to reach a settlement with Russia met with any real success.[2]

Russia, as usual, was torn between conflicting policies: 'The one head of the double-headed eagle', Morier once commented, 'is visible and palpable, the other looms enveloped in darkness.'[3] If he erred in his summing up, it was in over-simplification—in crediting Russian policy with only a dual character. The Tsar, Giers, Nelidov, and the Russian agents in the Balkans—all were prompted by different

---

[1] Malet to Salisbury, Tel. No. 72, 21 Sept. 1885, F.O. 64/1081; J. M. von Radowitz, *Aufzeichnungen und Erinnerungen*, ii. 252.

[2] Langer, pp. 336–45; C. E. Black, *The Establishment of Constitutional Government in Bulgaria*, pp. 142–4.

[3] Morier to Iddesleigh, No. 314 Confidential, 8 Sept. 1886, F.O. 65/1261.

THE MAN AND THE PROBLEM

motives to display varying degrees of hostility towards Prince Alexander of Bulgaria. The Tsar received the news of the Eastern Roumelian revolt with an outburst of anger that could scarcely have been rehearsed, and his personal antipathy to the Prince became an obsession.[1] Giers had not originally shared his master's hatred of the Prince. Indeed, he had always been anxious to come to terms with him, and with that end in view he had met him at Franzensbad in August 1885. It was because Prince Alexander had assured him at that meeting that he had no intention of disturbing the *status quo* in Bulgaria, and because the *coup d'état* at Philippopolis followed so quickly upon that promise, that Giers, convinced that he had been cruelly duped, failed to approach the problems raised by the Eastern Roumelian revolt with his customary coolness and detachment.[2] On the other hand, Nelidov's ideas about Bulgaria seem to have been shaped by professional rather than emotional considerations: he was said to have confided to a friend that there was a 'great future' before him, and that if he could handle the crisis successfully and secure the abdication of the Prince, he might soon leave the Russian embassy at Constantinople and replace Giers at St. Petersburg.[3] Although there is no evidence to suggest that the Tsar, Giers, or even Nelidov purposely wished to re-open the Near Eastern question, there is ample proof that Russian agents in the Balkans worked unceasingly to bring about an insurrection in Eastern Roumelia. Both the Russian consul-general and the Russian military attaché at Philippopolis had been aware of the revolutionaries' plans at least as early as June 1885, for during that month they had attended the secret meeting at which it was decided to raise the standard of revolt in September. They seem to have supported the movement in the double hope that their encouragement might restore the faith of its leaders in Russia, and that the Prince, hesitating to join the revolutionaries, would be swept away by them.[4] But, as both White and Paget

[1] Monson to Salisbury, No. 119 Most Confidential, Copenhagen, 23 Sept. 1885, F.O. 22/469.
[2] Corti, pp. 181-8; General von Schweinitz, *Denkwurdigkeiten des Botschafters*, ii. 299; Langer, pp. 345-6.
[3] White to Morier, 7 Dec. 1885 (printed in Edwards, pp. 231-4).
[4] A. Koch, *Prince Alexander of Bulgaria*, p. 235; Corti, p. 190.

suspected, these Russian biters had been bit when Prince Alexander had desperately associated himself with the movement.¹

Whatever the motive for their opposition to Prince Alexander—whether it was largely personal hatred as with the Tsar, annoyance at apparent betrayal as with Giers, prospects of rapid promotion which seem to have determined Nelidov's attitude, or the frustration of carefully laid plans which largely accounted for the bitter hostility of the local Russian officials in the Balkans—the various forces and personalities which made up the complex pattern of Russian policy were momentarily at one in their determination to reverse the Prince's unexpected success. Thus at the end of September, Katkov, the ardent nationalist leader, was in rare agreement with Giers, a typical representative of the Europeanized bureaucracy at St. Petersburg, about the attitude which the Russian government was to adopt towards Bulgaria.² Only Aksakov, an idealist in his pan-Slavism, urged that Russia should afford Bulgaria protection and leave her own private reckoning until later: Russia should not act as a 'darner in the hole of the Berlin Treaty', but take advantage of the fact that a rent had been made in that settlement.³ The Eastern Roumelian outbreak had caught the Russian government on the wrong foot: Vlangaly, overwhelmed by the added responsibilities which had suddenly been thrust upon him, was unwilling to commit his government to any definite course of action,⁴ but by his drastic measures in recalling all Russian officers from Bulgaria on 22 September, the Tsar clearly indicated the stand that Russia was to take.⁵

Kalnoky was no less embarrassed by the outbreak than the Tsar and Giers. Under the terms of the Three Emperors' Alliance, Austria-Hungary was given the right to claim Russian acquiescence in the annexation of Bosnia and Herce-

¹ White to Salisbury, No. 389 Secret, 22 Sept., F.O. 78/3752; Paget to Salisbury, No. 267 Most Confidential, 24 Sept. 1885, F.O. 7/1079.
² B. Nolde, *L'Alliance franco-russe*, pp. 324–5.
³ Grosvenor (chargé d'affaires at St. Petersburg) to Salisbury, No. 335, 3 Oct. 1885, F.O. 65/1218 (encloses abstract of Aksakov's article in the Russian newspaper *Russ* dated 20 Sept./2 Oct. 1885); cf. Nolde, pp. 325–6.
⁴ Grosvenor to Salisbury, No. 323 Very Confidential; No. 324 Confidential, 23 Sept. 1885, F.O. 65/1218.
⁵ *A. & P.*, Turkey No. 1 (1886), lxxv [C–4612], 6.

govina once the union of the Bulgarias had taken place; furthermore, under the terms of the secret Austro-Serbian Alliance of 1881, she was pledged not to oppose Serbia—indeed to give her diplomatic support to win over the Powers to a favourable attitude—if any opportunity should arise for Serbia to make territorial acquisitions, with the exception of the Sanjak of Novibazar, in the direction of her southern frontier. Austria-Hungary could hardly annex Bosnia and Hercegovina as compensation for the embarrassments of her Russian neighbour in Bulgaria; moreover, such an annexation would arouse Serbian as well as Russian hostility, and the Slav elements within the Empire itself would not easily be reconciled to such a step.[1] Confronted with all these difficulties, Kalnoky was anxious to adopt a cautious and conciliatory policy. Two days after the Eastern Roumelian revolt, he assured Paget that the movement had been organized in Bulgaria, 'but without the connivance or knowledge of either the Emperor or Government of Russia'.[2] He also informed the British ambassador that he was opposed to any isolated action to restore order, and that he had implored the King of Serbia not to intervene.[3] It is significant that Bismarck was not unduly concerned at the conduct of his Austro-Hungarian ally during the opening phase of the crisis: when asked by Malet whether Austria-Hungary or Germany took the lead in deciding questions of policy in the Near East, he had replied that all minor questions were left to Austria-Hungary, but when the peace of Europe was seriously threatened, he 'took the reins into his own hands and was able to hold them'.[4] Meanwhile, at St. Petersburg, Schweinitz was acting on the principle enunciated by Bismarck and advising Wolkenstein, his Austro-Hungarian colleague, to moderate the tone of two telegrams in which Kalnoky had displayed considerable distrust of Russia.[5]

[1] W. N. Medlicott, 'The Powers and the Unification of the Two Bulgarias', *E.H.R.* liv. 71; Paget to Rosebery, No. 116, 12 Mar. 1886, F.O. 7/1094 (contains an excellent review of Austro-Hungarian policy during the autumn and winter of 1885).
[2] *A. & P.*, Turkey No. 1 (1886), lxxv [C–4612], 3; J. V. Fuller, *Bismarck's Diplomacy at its Zenith*, p. 23.
[3] Paget to Salisbury, Tel. No. 19 Most Confidential, 20 Sept. 1885, F.O. 7/1082.
[4] Malet to Salisbury, No. 436 Secret, 22 Sept. 1885, F.O. 64/1079.
[5] General von Schweinitz, ii. 311.

The Three Empires were anxious to end their difficulties by stifling the outbreak in Eastern Roumelia, and at first the other Powers appeared to be unanimous in their support of such a solution. On 22 September Salisbury announced that although Great Britain was not sufficiently interested to justify her acting alone, she was willing to co-operate with the Powers in upholding the Treaty of Berlin.[1] In spite of the efforts of French statesmen to take advantage of historical hindsight and attempt to show that French sympathies were already with Russia in the autumn of 1885,[2] all the correspondence written at the time suggests that the French government was essentially passive in its attitude towards the crisis.[3] Freycinet, who had succeeded Ferry as Minister for Foreign Affairs in April 1885, had as yet no leanings towards the idea of co-operation with Russia; he considered the French government to be only indirectly interested in the issues at stake, and he therefore aimed to keep to the golden mean between complete effacement and any undue initiative;[4] he sought to avoid all complications and steer as quickly as possible towards a localization of the crisis and a general pacification, and he instructed his ambassadors at the main European capitals to this effect on 25 September, giving similar advice to his representatives in Serbia, Roumania, and Greece on the same day.[5] Italy's reaction to the problem was similar to that of France, and on 25 September Depretis informed Salisbury that his government was willing to join in all measures calculated to maintain the *status quo* in the Near East and prevent bloodshed.[6]

On 24 September, two days after he had informed White that Great Britain would co-operate with the other Powers in upholding the Treaty of Berlin, Salisbury came forward with a suggestion which seemed to be utterly inconsistent with his

[1] Salisbury to White, Tel. No. 85A, 22 Sept. 1885, F.O. 78/3757; cf. H. W. V. Temperley and L. M. Penson, *Foundations of British Foreign Policy, 1792–1902*, p. 429.
[2] C. de Freycinet, *Souvenirs, 1878–1893*, pp. 305–6; P. Albin, *La Paix armée*, pp. 243–5. [3] Nolde, pp. 351–2.
[4] French Yellow Book, *Affaires de Roumélie et de Grèce, 1885–1886*, p. 55 (Freycinet to Noailles, 29 Sept. 1885).
[5] *D.D.F.*, 1st ser., vi, No. 71.
[6] *A. & P.*, Turkey No. 1 (1886), lxxv [C–4612], 17.

fierce opposition to a 'big Bulgaria' seven years earlier at Berlin: he advocated a 'personal union' of Bulgaria and Eastern Roumelia under Prince Alexander.[1] Salisbury justified this apparent volte-face by expressing a loud and sudden sympathy for the cause of Balkan nationalism: in a speech at Newport on 7 October he claimed that his attitude towards the situation in Bulgaria was determined by his desire 'to cherish and foster strong self-sustaining nationalities';[2] just over a week later he impressed upon the French ambassador that Great Britain could not associate herself with the destruction of young Christian races in the Balkans, and added in criticism of the attitude adopted by the other Powers—'C'est de la politique comme au Congres de Vérone';[3] finally, he wrote a 'Blue Book' dispatch to White on 2 November, defending his policy at great length and stressing the importance of respecting 'the wish of the people of Bulgaria'.[4]

However, an examination of Salisbury's correspondence with the Queen soon reveals the limits of his sympathy for the Balkan peoples.[5] And, as might be expected, he wrote even more frankly about the subject to White:

> I have not much hope myself that a big Bulgaria will be avoided. It is an evil, and a danger to Turkey. But there seems nowhere the will to stop it: and stopping it would require measures of considerable stringency. The next best thing to hope for is a personal union of the two Bulgarias in Prince Alexander, each retaining otherwise its existing institutions. The institutions of Bulgaria are detestable: it would be hard that Eastern Roumelia should be subjected to them.[6]

But when Serbia and Greece, ever jealous of the success of their Bulgarian rival, made claims for compensation at the expense of Turkey in Macedonia, the limits which Salisbury imposed upon his sympathy for Balkan nationalism became obvious even to those who were not his intimates. At the end of September he urged the Austro-Hungarian government

---

[1] Salisbury to Queen Victoria, 24 Sept. 1885 (printed in G. E. Buckle, *The Letters of Queen Victoria*, 2nd ser., iii. 692; Lady G. Cecil, *The Life of Robert, Marquis of Salisbury*, iii. 241.   [2] *The Times*, 8 Oct. 1885.

[3] *D.D.F.*, 1st ser., vi, No. 94 (Waddington to Freycinet, 16 Oct. 1885).

[4] *A. & P.*, Turkey No. 1 (1886), lxxv [C–4612], 197–9; cf. Temperley and Penson, p. 431.   [5] Buckle, 2nd ser., iii. 690–5.

[6] Salisbury to White, Private, 24 Sept. 1885, Additional White Papers. See Appendix II.

to keep Serbia quiet, if necessary by force, and suggested that if Serbia must have compensation it had better be at the expense of Bulgaria, because a conflict with Bulgaria would not have such serious results as a struggle with Turkey.[1] Greece had no small neighbour at whose expense her claims could be satisfied, and only a naval demonstration by the Powers, envisaged by Salisbury before he left office in February 1886, made her give up the idea of compensation in the spring of that year.[2]

What, then, were the reasons for Salisbury's changed attitude towards the Bulgarian problem?

First, he realized that whereas the 'big Bulgaria' of 1878 might have become entirely dependent on Russia, the united Bulgaria of 1885 was sufficiently anti-Russian to act as a useful barrier against any further Russian advance upon Constantinople by way of the Balkans.[3] At the Congress of Berlin the British government had insisted upon the separation of the two Bulgarias by the Balkan range so that Turkey might be guaranteed military control over an easily defended mountain frontier. But that achievement had been nullified long before Beaconsfield and Salisbury left office in the spring of 1880: the cession of Varna and the Sanjak of Sofia to Bulgaria under the terms of the Berlin Treaty made it possible for an invading army to turn the proposed defences; moreover, the Turkish government was too timid to garrison the Eastern Roumelian frontier directly after the Russian evacuation in August 1879 when Russia could have made no effective protest, and it also failed to make full use of the control over the administration of Eastern Roumelia to which it was entitled by the provisions of the Treaty of Berlin.[4] By 1885, therefore, the stubborn independence of the Bulgarian

[1] Hengelmüller (chargé d'affaires at London) to Kalnoky, No. 51B, 29 Sept.; No. 52, 1 Oct.; Tel. No. 84, 30 Sept. 1885, Austrian Archives (cited in W. N. Medlicott, 'Lord Salisbury and Turkey', *History*, xii, No. 47, 245–6). 'Impress upon H.M. the extreme importance of keeping Servia out of Ottoman territory', Salisbury to Paget, Tel. No. 78, 15 Oct. 1885, F.O. 7/1082; cf. also C. Mijatovich, *The Memoirs of a Balkan Diplomatist*, pp. 48–49.

[2] E. Driault and M. Lhéritier, *Histoire diplomatique de la Grèce*, iv, chapter v, passim; Medlicott, loc. cit.

[3] Buckle, 2nd ser., iii. 690–5; Cecil, iii. 239–42.

[4] W. N. Medlicott, 'Bismarck and the Three Emperors' Alliance, 1881–87', *Trans. R. Hist. Soc.*, 4th ser., xxvii (1945), 67.

people seemed a better guarantee against further Russian incursions into the Balkans than a strategically unsound frontier left unguarded by half-hearted Turks.

Secondly, it must be borne in mind that the fate of Prince Alexander was a subject of great personal concern to Queen Victoria, and that Gladstone's 'Bulgarian Atrocities' campaign was still sufficiently fresh in the public mind to make the Bulgarian national cause a popular one in Great Britain. From the very beginning of the crisis the Queen pressed Salisbury to do all he could to save Prince Alexander from his enemies: she had promised the Prince's father that she would preserve him from deposition, and felt 'quite wretched not to be able to do more to help Sandro'.[1] Moreover, Salisbury and his colleagues were aware that it would be fatal to participate in any intervention in Eastern Roumelia which might be described as suppression at a time when their 'caretaker' government was about to go to the polls. 'This is a terrible business for us, I think, this Eastern Roumelian outbreak,' Churchill confided to a fellow member of the cabinet, 'for I do not imagine that we should dare to assist or even encourage the Turk to recover his province on the eve of a general election, and yet if we leave him in the lurch what worthless allies we shall appear to him.'[2] Meanwhile there was considerable rejoicing in the Liberal camp: Gladstone and Granville gloated over the fact that the *coup d'état* at Philippopolis had at last revealed 'the hollowness of the Beaconsfield and Salisbury triumph' seven years earlier at Berlin,[3] and these sentiments were shared and echoed in the columns of the *Daily News*—'The Treaty of Berlin has broken down', its leader declared a week after the outbreak, 'precisely on those provisions for which the government of Lord Beaconsfield and Lord Salisbury, as its Foreign Minister, were most directly responsible.'[4] But both Gladstone and Granville were relieved to find that they were not in office when the Eastern Roumelian crisis broke out, and the

---

[1] Prince Henry of Battenberg to Prince Alexander of Hesse, 16 Oct. 1885 (printed in E. C. Corti, *The Downfall of Three Dynasties*, p. 310); Buckle, 2nd ser., iii. 690–5.
[2] Churchill to Carnarvon, Private, 21 Sept. 1885, P.R.O. 30/6/55.
[3] Granville to Gladstone, Private, 26 Sept. 1885, Add. MS. 44178.
[4] The *Daily News*, 26 Sept. 1885.

attitude which Salisbury ultimately adopted soon won them over to his support and ensured agreement between the two parties about the conduct of British policy in the Near East.[1]

Finally, it must be remembered that Salisbury knew little of the secret understandings which bound the Three Empires together in their Near Eastern policies, and that he therefore pinned his faith to the idea that Austria-Hungary would act in concert with Great Britain if needs be.[2] Indeed, both his private and official correspondence with White during the first ten days of the crisis shows that he was relying upon assistance from Austria-Hungary to prevent the outbreak from spreading.[3] Furthermore, it seems likely that Salisbury was also encouraged to take the stand he did by the reports which he received from his ambassador at Berlin. Summing up Prince Alexander's chances early in October, Malet expressed the view that they were better than they might appear to be on the surface: even if an alternative prince could be found, the Russian government might find it difficult to impose him upon the Bulgarians, and, far more important, Germany and Austria-Hungary, although openly supporting Russia and pressing for Prince Alexander's retirement, appeared to be playing 'somewhat of a double game', and it could even be suggested that they would be glad 'in their heart of hearts' if the Prince remained on the Bulgarian throne.[4]

A combination of rare insight, force of events, and even an element of inspired ignorance, led Salisbury to reconsider the attitude he was to adopt towards the union of the two Bulgarias. The result was not a 'new course' in Great Britain's Near Eastern policy but a reorientation of the traditional Palmerstonian and Disraelian formula for the maintenance of the integrity of the Ottoman Empire, a readjustment of an old policy to meet the needs of a new situation.

---

[1] Gladstone to Granville, Private, 12 Oct.; Granville to Gladstone, 23 Oct. 1885, Add. MS. 44178.

[2] H. W. V. Temperley and L. M. Penson, *Foundations of British Foreign Policy, 1792–1902*, pp. 430–1.

[3] Salisbury to White, Private, 24 Sept. Additional White Papers; Tel. No. 101, 28 Sept. 1885, F.O. 78/3757.

[4] Malet to Salisbury, Private, 3 Oct. F.O. 343/7; cf. Malet to Salisbury, Private, 24 Oct.; 7 Nov. 1885, F.O. 343/7.

Convinced that Turkey was dead, he was prepared to use a lively Bulgaria to guard the corpse: although ostensibly pro-Bulgarian, his policy remained implicitly pro-Turkish and consistently anti-Russian.[1] When first made known to the Powers on 28 September, Salisbury's revised policy was greeted neither with surprise nor alarm, but when it was upheld in face of the increasing inability of the Austro-Hungarian government to control the ambitions of the Serbs, and the growing fierceness of the Tsar's personal vendetta against Prince Alexander, it aroused serious opposition and revealed the superficial nature of the accord which was supposed to exist between the Powers.[2] Much would depend upon the skill and force of character of the British representative at the forthcoming conference if such a policy were to be successful.

Whereas Salisbury's support of the Bulgarian national cause was founded upon quietly detached self-interest, White's sprang from an intimate knowledge of Balkan politics and a sympathetic understanding of Balkan peoples. Discussing the Eastern Roumelian rising with his friend Morier, he claimed that the newly emancipated races of the Balkans wished 'to breathe free air, and not through Russian nostrils'; he pointed out that the future of European Turkey up to Adrianople was destined to belong to those races, and went on to argue that by fostering their growth into nationhood Great Britain would repeat in the Balkans the successes which Palmerston had achieved in western Europe.[3] However, it is easy to lay too much stress upon the differences in the ideas of White and Salisbury about Balkan politics. It is far more important to remember that White put limits on his support for the cause of Balkan nationalism which closely resembled those imposed by Salisbury. His pleas on behalf of the small Balkan states were warm and genuine, but they were also tempered with caution: his correspondence with

[1] W. N. Medlicott, 'Lord Salisbury and Turkey', *History*, xii, No. 47, 244–7; L. M. Penson, 'The Principles and Methods of Lord Salisbury's Foreign Policy', *Camb. Hist. J.*, v. 94.
[2] W. N. Medlicott, 'The Powers and the Unification of the Two Bulgarias', *E.H.R.* liv. 74–75.
[3] H. S. Edwards, *Sir William White*, pp. 231–4; *The Speaker*, 9 Jan. 1892.

Morier shows that he was an enthusiastic champion of those states in their struggle for independence, but it also reveals that he was only prepared to further their cause 'gradually and with proper restraints'.[1]

An examination of White's attitude to the Bulgarian problem before and after the Eastern Roumelian outbreak demonstrates how great those 'restraints' were. In October 1884, when Prince Alexander had impressed upon him that Russia was the only Power opposed to the unification of the two Bulgarias, White had kept silent in order to avoid giving the Prince any encouragement.[2] Earlier that same year he had described the movement for a united Bulgaria to Granville as 'a *ballon d'essai* merely, without much immediate importance', and when the Bulgarians had sounded him about the effect which the union might have upon European politics, he had tried to discourage them from making the experiment, warning them that they would do well to calculate the cost beforehand because, even if successful, such a step would be sure to open other questions.[3] All this confirms the view that White knew nothing of the revolutionaries' plans. In spite of Bismarck's conviction that the Eastern Roumelian revolt was the result of 'English wire-pulling',[4] and in spite of Morier's suspicion that it was due to 'some action or suggestion' on the part of his own government,[5] there is no evidence to show that White even knew of the existence of the plot by which the Eastern Roumelian government was finally overthrown. The reports which he received from Eastern Roumelia described a state of calm, not an incipient revolution. Late in July—that is, a month after the revolutionaries had met to decide upon the date of the rising—Consul Jones assured him that all was quiet at Philippopolis, and that rumours which depicted Eastern Roumelia as 'seething in the cauldron of Revolution' were to be put down to the unscrupulous tricks of the opposition party.[6] Consul Graves, left in charge at Philippopolis while Lascelles went on leave,

---

[1] Edwards, p. 233.
[2] White to T. H. Sanderson, Private, 19 Oct. 1884, P.R.O. 30/29/184.
[3] White to Granville, Private, 20 Apr. 1884, P.R.O. 30/29/184.
[4] M. Busch, *Bismarck, Some Secret Pages of his History*, iii. 149.
[5] Edwards, pp. 230–1, 234–8.
[6] Jones to White, Private, 25 July 1885, F.O. 364/2.

later admitted that the news of the outbreak came 'like a bolt from the blue'.[1] 'I am shocked', Churchill complained to one of his colleagues in the cabinet, 'at the incapacity of our diplomatic agents in allowing so momentous an event to be prepared and carried out without some word of warning or previous knowledge.'[2] But if any of White's close associates was likely to have been kept informed about the plot, it would have been Dr. Washburn, the American president of Robert College, an educational establishment at Constantinople which was reputed to be one of the main nurseries for Bulgarian nationalists. Long regarded at the Foreign Office as a first class authority on Bulgarian nationalism, he was brought into close contact with the leading figures in Bulgarian politics both by virtue of his official position and his personal support of their cause.[3] He had concluded a two months' visit to Eastern Roumelia only a fortnight before the outbreak, but the revolutionaries appear to have guarded their secret even from him.[4]

White's behaviour during the first week of the Eastern Roumelian crisis proves beyond all doubt that the *coup d'état* at Philippopolis took him completely by surprise, and shows that his reactions to the new situation created there were remarkably similar to those of Salisbury. For the first four or five days he remained guarded and negative in his attitude towards the unionist movement: he did not look upon it as a strong and independent national movement, but as a Russian plot which had misfired,[5] and his main concern was to prevent it spreading into Macedonia.[6] He later admitted that the outbreak was even more 'unprovoked and unjustifiable' than the Serbian war of 1876, for there had been perfect tranquillity in Eastern Roumelia and 'not a single Mussulman Pasha or soldier was to be found in a Province which was

[1] Sir R. Graves, *Storm Centres of the Near East*, pp. 64–65.
[2] Churchill to Carnarvon, Private, 21 Dec. 1885, P.R.O. 30/6/55.
[3] G. Washburn, *Fifty Years in Constantinople, and Recollections of Robert College*, passim; *Dictionary of American Biography*, xix. 500–1.
[4] Wolff to Salisbury, Tel. Private, 21 Sept. 1885, F.O. 78/3824; Washburn, pp. 180–3.
[5] White to Salisbury, No. 389 Secret, 22 Sept. 1885; F.O. 78/3752; White to Salisbury, Private and Confidential, 22 Sept. 1885, Bound Volume No. 43, Salisbury Papers. See Appendix II.
[6] White to Salisbury, No. 388 Very Secret, 22 Sept. 1885, 78/3752.

well-governed by its own Christian natives'. Furthermore, he agreed with Salisbury that the Sultan should have acted promptly and stifled the insurrection: few Turkish troops would have been required, and the Turkish government, which could have invoked its treaty rights in defence of such measures, would have been sure to meet with much sympathy in Europe.[1]

Not until 26 September 1885, when Major Trotter, the military attaché at the embassy, returned to Constantinople from Philippopolis where he had been detained by the outbreak, did White receive a first-hand account of the situation in Eastern Roumelia. Trotter, who had met Prince Alexander in person, assured White that the provisional government had no intention of stirring up trouble in Macedonia unless attacked by the Turks; he impressed upon him that the revolution was 'distinctly *national* and Bulgarian' and directly hostile to Russian interests, and he expressed the view that should the union be maintained under the Prince, a great blow would be struck at Russian influence in the Balkans.[2] Hitherto, White had frowned upon the movement for Bulgarian unity: hitherto, he had put that movement down to the work of 'Moscow Slav Agitating Committees'.[3] But Trotter's account of the political situation in Eastern Roumelia revealed to him that the Russian element within the movement had been expelled more quickly and more thoroughly than he would ever have thought possible, and it seems to have been this, more than anything else, which completely changed his outlook upon the Bulgarian problem. It has been stated that Salisbury was 'preaching to the converted' when he first informed White that he was in favour of a personal union of the two Bulgarias under Prince Alexander,[4] but it should be added that White's 'conversion' had taken place as recently, if not later, than that of his chief.

But White, like Salisbury, was anxious to limit the amount of support which his government should give to the cause of Balkan nationalism. He wanted to rescue Bulgaria not be-

[1] White to Salisbury, No. 407 Very Secret, 29 Sept. 1885, F.O. 78/3753.
[2] Trotter to White, Private, 26 Sept. 1885, F.O. 364/2.
[3] White to Granville, Private, 20 Apr. 1884, P.R.O. 30/29/184.
[4] Lady G. Cecil, *The Life of Robert, Marquis of Salisbury*, iii. 241.

cause he was anti-Turk, but because he was anti-Russian. He wished to postpone rather than hasten the eventual collapse of the Ottoman Empire,[1] and was therefore particularly cautious in the attitude which he adopted towards the aspirations of the Balkan states. For instance, he became alarmed and suspected Russian handiwork when it was rumoured, at the end of 1885, that Greece might settle her difficulties with Bulgaria by entering into an alliance with her based upon a compromise with regard to their rival pretensions in Macedonia.[2] And, in October 1886, when King Milan of Serbia asked him what his views would be about a 'Balkan Confederation' which embraced the idea of territorial acquisitions for Serbia, Bulgaria, and Greece in Macedonia, White condemned the scheme as crude and impractical, and denied ever having favoured such a project—'except in the minds of Russian agents'.[3]

It has been shown that Salisbury and his ambassador at the Porte were equally surprised by the sudden outbreak of the revolt in Eastern Roumelia; that both went through the process of being quickly converted to the idea of upholding the union of the two Bulgarias; that both put strict limits upon the support which they were prepared to give, and that they had much in common in their general approach to Balkan problems. In fact, the only important difference to be detected in their respective attitudes was confined to the period of the first few sittings of the Ambassadors' Conference at Constantinople, when it was White, not Salisbury, who was ready to come to a compromise with the other Powers about Bulgaria.

There was complete agreement between the representatives of the Great Powers at Constantinople when, at an informal meeting on 4 October, they drew up a collective declaration censuring the recent events in Eastern Roumelia and warning the authorities there against any acts of provocation.[4] But this declaration was designed simply to check the movement and avoid further bloodshed, and its main

---

[1] White to Salisbury, No. 485 Confidential, 8 Nov. 1885, F.O. 78/3754.
[2] White to Salisbury, No. 1 Confidential, 1 Jan. 1886, F.O. 78/3868.
[3] White to Iddesleigh, No. 539 Secret, 30 Oct. 1886, F.O. 78/3875.
[4] A. & P., Turkey No. 1 (1886), lxxv [C–4612], 86–88.

result was to postpone any definite pronouncement—and consequently any serious disagreement—about the steps which the Powers were eventually to take in order to solve the problem. However, after the first four formal meetings of the conference on 5, 7, 9, and 12 November, the lines of a fundamental difference of opinion between the Powers had been clearly drawn: Great Britain, protesting that respect should be shown for the wishes of the Bulgarian people, advocated a personal union of the two Bulgarias under Prince Alexander; meanwhile, Russia, with the support of the Triple Alliance Powers, insisted upon a return to the *status quo ante* in Bulgaria. Thus, under the guise of reversed roles, with Great Britain as the champion of Slav independence and Russia as the defender of Ottoman integrity, these traditional rivals continued their unceasing struggle against each other in the Near East.[1]

At this stage of the proceedings it was Salisbury, not White, who refused to hear of any compromise. On 18 October, when Prince Alexander had returned to Sofia from Philippopolis, White tried to impress upon Salisbury that if he remained there and so demonstrated his desire to avoid any further provocation of the Powers, and that if he were to concentrate his attention upon retaining the affections of the Bulgarian people, it might then be possible for the Prince to come to some temporary arrangement with the Powers which would leave the door open for a subsequent reorganization of Eastern Roumelia.[2] White became more and more insistent in his arguments for a compromise as the first few meetings of the conference revealed a growing cleavage between Great Britain and the other Powers. On 7 November, after the second sitting of the conference, he warned Salisbury that there would be an immediate breakdown in the 'European Concert' unless he was permitted to follow 'some middle course'.[3] Two days later, when the third sitting took place, he outlined the form which such a compromise might take: he was even prepared to see an Ottoman commissioner take

---

[1] J. V. Fuller, *Bismarck's Diplomacy at its Zenith*, p. 36; W. L. Langer, *European Alliances and Alignments, 1871–1890*, p. 353.
[2] White to Salisbury, No. 446, 18 Oct. 1885, F.O. 78/3754.
[3] White to Salisbury, No. 485 Confidential, 8 Nov. 1885, F.O. 78/3754.

THE MAN AND THE PROBLEM

temporary charge of the Eastern Roumelian government, for he hoped that Prince Alexander would remain popular with his people, consolidate his position in the Bulgarian principality, and wait until improved circumstances guaranteed a more favourable arrangement.[1] But it was not until the following day that White's appeals for moderation reached their climax. He then stated quite bluntly to Salisbury that unless some attempt were made to meet the wishes of the majority, who were firmly in favour of a return to the *status quo ante* in Eastern Roumelia, the conference was sure to break up and Great Britain's position would become perilous. He maintained that the only hope of saving the situation was to come to an arrangement which would enable the Prince to return to Sofia without any loss of prestige and make him appear as a martyr for the Bulgarian national cause, and went on to argue that the Prince might still have a future in Bulgaria if he acted prudently: the gain of a year might mean much in a Europe which was largely governed by the precarious life of an aged German emperor, and in such circumstances a Turkish special commissioner was to be preferred to a regular Vali at Philippopolis.[2] 'The fear of breaking up the Conference has made me put *de l'eau dans mon vin*', he informed Salisbury, 'and leave many things unsaid to Nelidoff. . . . The experience of 1877 ought to convince us that we can do but little here alone and must bide our time and so ought Prince Alexander.'[3]

But Salisbury did not take his ambassador's advice: anxious though he was that the conference should not break up, he considered even that result preferable to being 'dragged by the Three Empires into sanctioning a policy of armed repression'.[4] In reply to White's frantic appeals for some compromise, he insisted upon 'the importance of gaining time',[5] and instructed him to 'oppose any hasty action or

[1] White to Salisbury, No. 489 Confidential, 9 Nov. 1885, F.O. 78/3754.
[2] White to Salisbury, Tel. Private and Confidential, 10 Nov. 1885, F.O. 364/2; cf. Cecil, iii. 248.
[3] White to Salisbury, Private and Confidential, 10 Nov. 1885, Bound Volume No. 43, Salisbury Papers.
[4] Salisbury to White, Tel. No. 194, 11 Nov. 1885, F.O. 78/3757; cf. Cecil, iii. 248.
[5] Salisbury to White, Tel. Private, 9 Nov., F.O. 364/2; cf. to White, Tel. No. 192, 11 Nov. 1885, F.O. 78/3757.

tendency to hurry on matters'.[1] White was ordered to lure the Russians into openly declaring that they were opposed to the wishes of the Bulgarians and Eastern Roumelians, and to prevent either the breaking up of the conference or the demand being made for an assent to the restoration of the *status quo ante*.[2] Left to himself, White would have sought a peaceful solution of the Bulgarian problem based upon a reasonable compromise; but with Salisbury pushing strongly behind him, he had to resign himself to taking the opposite line, and it is greatly to his credit that he played the part which Salisbury had designed for him with such consummate skill: 'I shall sit mute and attend saying nothing...and shall be exposed to much pressure in the meantime, but I do not mind it.'[3]

It is important to remember that the proceedings of the Ambassadors' Conference were divided into two distinct phases by the three days' battle between the Bulgarians and Serbians at Slivnitza (17–19 November), for this, more than anything else, helps to explain White's conduct at that gathering. In fact, there were two Whites at Constantinople during the period of the conference: the first 'sat mute saying nothing' and helped the Bulgarians by keeping the conference in being, and the second drove home the military advantage which they had gained at Slivnitza by bludgeoning his colleagues into submission:

The door opened, and he marched in; shouldered his way to the table, and deposited on it a large paper packet of sandwiches. Then for hour after hour the crowd outside heard the well-known voice booming through the open window—blurred occasionally by a sandwich—and drowning every proposal or whisper of intrigue, until the Conference, famished and enraged, broke up.[4]

Only events in Bulgaria itself were able to break the deadlock at Constantinople. On 14 November the Serbian government, hoping that Austro-Hungarian sympathy might ultimately take the form of material support, declared war on

[1] Salisbury to White, No. 413, 6 Nov. 1885, F.O. 78/3747.
[2] Salisbury to White, Tel. No. 194, 11 Nov. 1885, F.O. 78/3757.
[3] White to Salisbury, Tel. Private and Confidential, 13 Nov. 1885, F.O. 364/2.
[4] G. Young, *Constantinople*, p. 223; cf. Lord Hardinge of Penshurst, *Old Diplomacy*, pp. 40–41.

THE MAN AND THE PROBLEM

Bulgaria, and it seemed almost certain that Prince Alexander, with his army lately depleted by the withdrawal of its Russian officers, would be soundly beaten by the well-equipped Serbian armies which had been heavily financed in Vienna. But these myths were completely exploded five days later at Slivnitza.[1] Before that battle Prince Alexander had few admirers on the continent: Giers cynically ascribed his popularity in Bulgaria to 'the absence of any real kind of danger', and Monson reported from Copenhagen that it seemed to be 'a *mot d'ordre* that Prince Alexander should be well abused'.[2] Nor were any higher opinions held about the Bulgarians themselves: Count Robilant, the Italian foreign secretary, thought it impossible to take the Bulgarian army, with its sub-lieutenants suddenly promoted to colonels, into serious consideration,[3] and Malet, who did not regard the Bulgarians as a people renowned for their fidelity, feared that they might find the war an excuse to desert their Prince.[4]

But such doubts were quickly dispelled by Prince Alexander's resounding victory over Serbian arms at Slivnitza and his subsequent entry into Serbian territory. The battle of Slivnitza surrounded the *coup de théâtre* at Philippopolis with the rays of military glory: instead of being decried as 'the supposed tool of an anarchic and revolutionary faction', the Prince was hailed as a successful leader who had secured the triumph of the Bulgarian national cause against the greatest odds.[5] '*We* have every reason to admire him,' exclaimed one of Salisbury's subordinates, 'for he certainly would be a Democratic Tory and possibly Member for Birmingham, if he were an Englishman.'[6] And, after the news of the Bulgarian victory had reached him, Salisbury himself assured the Queen that the Balkan issue would really be decided by arms—'if Prince Alexander continues to fight as well as he

---

[1] W. L. Langer, *European Alliances and Alignments, 1871–1890*, p. 354.
[2] Grosvenor (chargé d'affaires at St. Petersburg) to Salisbury, No. 369 Confidential, 28 Oct. F.O. 65/1218; Monson to Salisbury, No. 135 Confidential, 7 Oct. 1885, F.O. 22/469.
[3] Lumley to Salisbury, No. 201 Confidential, 23 Oct. 1885, F.O. 45/524.
[4] Malet to Salisbury, Private, 14 Nov. 1885, F.O. 343/7.
[5] *A. & P.*, Turkey No. 1 (1886), lxxv [C–4612], 372; A. von Huhn, *The Struggle of the Bulgarians for National Independence*, pp. 178–80.
[6] Bourke (Parliamentary Under-Secretary for Foreign Affairs) to Carnarvon, Private, 30 Nov. 1885, P.R.O. 30/6/54.

has hitherto done, it will be impossible for Russia to separate the Bulgarias'.[1]

The military success of the Bulgarians at Slivnitza was quickly turned into diplomatic capital at the conference room in Pera. The Great Powers began to abandon the idea of reverting to the *status quo ante* in Eastern Roumelia, and concentrated their attention upon the formidable task of devising a settlement based upon the acceptance of some form of union between the two Bulgarias.[2] White lived up to his legendary reputation and became much more assertive; at the seventh meeting of the conference on 25 November he accepted the idea of an inquiry by a Turkish special commissioner into questions of order and reform in Eastern Roumelia, but flatly refused to hear of a return to the *status quo ante*.[3] Another deadlock had been reached, and the conference was formally adjourned until 28 November. But in fact it was an adjournment *sine die*, for Giers soon realized that the conference was 'a thing belonging to the past'.[4]

After Slivnitza, even the Russians became aware that it would be impossible to restore the *status quo ante* in Eastern Roumelia. Largely owing to the Tsar's rage at the triumph of a personal enemy and the ambitious scheming of Nelidov, the Russian government had put itself into a false position with regard to Bulgaria from the very beginning of the crisis.[5] But although he was bitterly annoyed at Prince Alexander's apparent treachery, Giers soon showed that he was much more inclined to be moderate about Bulgaria than either the Tsar or Nelidov.[6] Moreover, by the beginning of December he had been able to shake himself free from the control of the pan-Slavist elements in Russia, and he appeared to be confident that he could once more win the Tsar over to a policy of avoiding any rupture with Austria-Hungary and maintaining the uneasy accord which existed between the Three Empires.[7] On 23 December he confessed to Morier that

---

[1] Salisbury to Queen Victoria, 20 Nov. 1885 (printed in Cecil, iii. 251).
[2] Cf. W. N. Medlicott, 'The Powers and the Unification of the Two Bulgarias', *E.H.R.* liv. 282.   [3] *A. & P.*, Turkey No. 1 (1886), lxxv [C–4612], 348–59.
[4] Ibid., pp. 372–3.   [5] *Supra*, pp. 16–18.
[6] Morier to Salisbury, No. 401 Secret, 22 Nov. 1885, F.O. 65/1219.
[7] Morier to Salisbury, No. 423 Secret, 10 Dec. 1885, F.O. 65/1219; B. Nolde, *L'Alliance franco-russe*, pp. 336–7.

there could be no return to the *status quo ante*, and inferred that Prince Alexander was the only possible ruler for the future principality.[1] Salisbury received similar, though more cautiously worded, assurances from Staal a week later.[2] Meanwhile, White noticed that he was no longer forced to struggle against a firmly united opposition at Constantinople: the Sultan appeared to be in favour of reaching a direct understanding with Prince Alexander, and even Nelidov had become much milder in his attitude towards the Prince and seemed less eager for a return to the *status quo ante* in Eastern Roumelia. He concluded from this that the Tsar wanted an ostensible reconciliation with Prince Alexander, and would consent to the union of the two Bulgarias provided that it could be made to appear that the Prince had asked and received his forgiveness, for such a solution might enable Russia to regain some of the influence which she had so recently and unexpectedly lost in Bulgaria.[3]

Meanwhile, public opinion in Germany had swung sharply in favour of the Bulgarian cause.[4] The Crown Prince and Crown Princess were full of praise for Prince Alexander's exploits,[5] and although the aged German emperor remained coldly formal in his attitude towards the Prince, it was suspected that this was for personal rather than political reasons.[6] As for the official policy carried out at the Wilhelmstrasse, the observations which Malet had first made in October about Germany's 'double game' were still valid in the following spring: 'With regard to Prince Alexander', he observed in April 1886, 'I feel sure that the political sentiment with regard to him here is favourable, but great pains are being taken to prevent its being known publicly, for fear of giving umbrage to the Emperor of Russia.'[7]

Germany's diplomatic manœuvres bore out this view. For instance, Hatzfeldt negotiated with Salisbury throughout

[1] Morier to Salisbury, No. 439 Confidential, 23 Dec. 1885, F.O. 65/1219.
[2] Salisbury to Morier, No. 461 Confidential, 30 Dec. 1885, F.O. 65/1215.
[3] White to Salisbury, No. 593 Secret, 23 Dec.; No. 603 Secret, 28 Dec.; No. 605 Confidential, 29 Dec. 1885, F.O. 78/3756.
[4] Scott (chargé d'affaires at Berlin) to Salisbury, No. 626 Very Confidential, 11 Dec. 1885, F.O. 64/1080; von Huhn, pp. 179-80.
[5] E. C. Corti, *The Downfall of Three Dynasties*, pp. 317-18.
[6] Ibid.; cf. Malet to Rosebery, Private, 9 Apr. 1886, F.O. 343/7.
[7] Malet to Rosebery, Private, 9 Apr. 1886, F.O. 343/7.

the December of 1885 in order to reach some compromise which would enable Great Britain to participate with the other Powers in a general settlement of the Bulgarian problem, but, like Herbert Bismarck in Berlin, he took care to stress that German desires in the matter should 'be kept dark'.[1] Similarly, Malet noticed that when Herbert Bismarck had looked through the proofs of the dispatches to be published in the forthcoming Blue Book on affairs in Eastern Roumelia, he had been particularly averse to passages which indicated that his father had taken the lead in giving advice upon that subject.[2] Throughout the crisis Nelidov's most eager supporter had been the German ambassador, Radowitz, but Salisbury was convinced that Bismarck had used him simply to distract Russian attention from his own secret approval of British policy: Bismarck obviously wanted to see Russia checkmated in the Balkans, but he was equally anxious that someone else should 'pick the chestnuts out'.[3] Hatzfeldt's behaviour in London strengthened this belief. 'His assignment is to construct resolutions or formulas for the Powers which are to put an end to the Eastern Roumelian difficulty', Salisbury informed Malet early in 1886. 'Having done so, he comes to me,—and with infinite expenditure of ingenuity he persuades me, or thinks he persuades me, that they are my idea....For whose benefit is all this comedy? Is it for the Emperor's?'[4] In fact, it was for the benefit of the Russian rather than the German emperor. Throughout the crisis Bismarck's main object had been to avoid an Austro-Russian conflict and to keep the Three Emperors' Alliance intact, and in order to achieve this result he had had to convince the Russians that Great Britain, not Austria-Hungary, was their main rival in the Balkans.[5] At the end of November, when the Austro-Hungarian government intervened to rescue its Serbian protégé from the victorious Bulgarian army,

---

[1] Salisbury to White, Tel. No. 245 Secret, 12 Dec., F.O. 78/3757; Scott (chargé d'affaires at Berlin) to Salisbury, No. 626 Very Confidential, 11 Dec. 1885, F.O. 64/1080.
[2] Malet to Salisbury, Private, 2 Jan. 1886, F.O. 343/7.
[3] Salisbury to White, Private, 2 Dec. 1885 (printed in Cecil, iii. 253).
[4] Salisbury to Malet, Private, 13 Jan. 1886, F.O. 343/2.
[5] G.P. v, No. 959 (Prince Bismarck to the Emperor William, 9 Oct. 1885); iv, No. 787 (Memorandum by Count Rantzau, 13 Nov. 1885).

Austro-Russian relations had temporarily become strained,[1] but Giers' repeated denunciations of Salisbury proved how firmly the idea had taken root in the Russian mind that Great Britain, not Austria-Hungary, was the real opponent of Russia's policy in the Balkans.[2]

Each member of the Three Emperors' Alliance came out of the Eastern Roumelian crisis with some credit. Bismarck had been able 'to play the part of the silent guide'[3] and turn Russia's ill feeling away from his Austro-Hungarian ally, while the obstinate stand taken by Salisbury had made it easy for him to deflect her hostility towards Great Britain. Kalnoky had likewise been able to restrain the Serbians for a period sufficiently long to allow the anger of the Russians to become concentrated upon the British government. And, in spite of several humiliating setbacks, even Russia had finally achieved some success: after a hard struggle, Giers had been able to check the extreme ambitions of Nelidov and the pan-Slavs, and to prevail upon the Tsar to pursue a more moderate policy with regard to Bulgaria. Thus, although badly shaken, the Three Emperors' Alliance had managed to recover and survive the storms of the Eastern Roumelian crisis.[4]

But Salisbury had scored the most noteworthy triumph. His successful defiance of the rest of Europe enhanced his reputation both at home and abroad: at home, Rosebery saw fit to adopt Salisbury's policy as his own when he succeeded him at the Foreign Office in February 1886, and so closed the breach between the two political parties about Near Eastern policy which Gladstone's 'Bulgarian Atrocities' campaign had opened almost ten years before;[5] abroad, Salisbury's feat had suddenly raised Great Britain 'from contemned singularity to applauded leadership', and had firmly established her Prime Minister as one of the most important figures in European diplomacy.[6]

---

[1] *G.P.* v, Nos. 967–70; B. Nolde, *L'Alliance franco-russe*, p. 333.
[2] A. Meyendorff, *Correspondance diplomatique de M. de Staal*, i. 266–84; W. N. Medlicott, 'The Powers and the Unification of the Two Bulgarias', *E.H.R.* liv. 283.
[3] Malet to Salisbury, Tel. No. 109, 18 Nov. 1885, F.O. 64/1081.
[4] Medlicott, pp. 283–4; Nolde, p. 337.
[5] G. E. Buckle, *The Letters of Queen Victoria*, 3rd ser., i. 55–56; Marquis of Crewe, *Lord Rosebery*, i. 259–67.   [6] Cecil, iii. 256–7.

However, Salisbury owed much of his success to the skilful manner in which White had conducted Great Britain's affairs in the conference room at Pera. 'I think you deserve, and have no doubt gained, great credit for the stand which you made against the doughty three [i.e. the German, Russian, and Austro-Hungarian ambassadors]', a close friend wrote to him from Teheran. 'It is quite a pleasant feeling to think that we have got some legs left to stand upon.'[1] And although both White's private and official correspondence considerably modifies the view that he forced his colleagues into submission by continual bullying, such new evidence does not detract from the value of his ambassadorial *tour de force*. On the contrary, it enhances his reputation as a first-class diplomat. It shows that White favoured a compromise in view of all the difficulties which beset him; that he did not flinch in the face of great odds; and that he nicely sensed the time when circumstances allowed him to transform defence into attack at the conference. The carrying out of Salisbury's instructions called for a pliant and adaptable representative at the Porte, not just a fanatical filibusterer whose only concern was to dominate over the proceedings of every sitting of the conference.

At the time, only Salisbury fully appreciated the part which White had played at the Ambassadors' Conference. 'They none of them appear to like Sir William White which is very unjust', he complained to Malet early in 1886.[2] Perhaps he felt guilty that White, who had once begged him to come to a compromise with the other Powers, had ultimately become one of the main targets for their attacks. Frustrated in the conference room at Pera, and deceived by the contrast between the loud voice and bluff manner of the representative on the spot and the elusive reserve of the Prime Minister in London, the opposition jumped to the conclusion that White, even more than Salisbury, was responsible for the British government's stern defence of the union of the two Bulgarias. 'Perhaps one of the best proofs of the value and effect of your efforts', Salisbury confided to him at the beginning of February, 'has been that you have excited the keenest

---

[1] Arthur Nicolson to White, Private, 19 Jan. 1886, F.O. 364/1.
[2] Salisbury to Malet, Private, 13 Jan. 1886, F.O. 343/2.

antipathy in the Russian heart. I have not told you all the marks of it that have come to my notice, knowing that it was the best proof that you were doing well.'[1] There were also hostile comments about White at Vienna and Berlin: Kalnoky was most upset at the attitude which he had adopted at the Ambassadors' Conference,[2] and Herbert Bismarck kept hinting to Malet that his removal from Constantinople might clear the political atmosphere there. 'White has become a red rag to the Ambassadors at Constantinople simply because he has won the day', Rosebery was informed at the end of March. 'I have no doubt that Radowitz and Nelidoff would be very glad to be rid of him.'[3] 'My position here is a very difficult one', White himself observed to Salisbury. 'The Russians throw suspicion on me and take advantage of my inferior Diplomatic rank and of the temporary character of my mission here to counteract and depreciate me in the mind of the Orientals.'[4]

White was still in charge at Constantinople on 6 February 1886 when Rosebery took over from Salisbury at the Foreign Office. Even later that month, when Thornton arrived at the Porte to occupy the post which had officially been his since the end of 1884, White was ordered not to leave until the new ambassador had become acquainted with the complexities of the situation.[5] On 5 April 1886 the Turkish and Bulgarian governments reached an agreement by which 'the Prince of Bulgaria' was to be named Governor-General of Eastern Roumelia for a period of five years,[6] and in recognition of his services at the Ambassadors' Conference, White was allowed to remain in Constantinople and sign on behalf of his government the protocol by which the Powers gave their assent to that arrangement.[7] Once he had signed the agreement, he was immediately instructed to return to the more humdrum duties which awaited him at Bucharest.[8]

[1] Salisbury to White, Private, 5 Feb. 1886, Additional White Papers.
[2] Phipps (chargé d'affaires at Vienna) to Salisbury, No. 459 Confidential, 7 Dec. 1885, F.O. 7/1081.   [3] Malet to Rosebery, Private, 27 Mar. 1886, F.O. 343/7.
[4] White to Salisbury, Private and Confidential, 28 Nov. 1885, Bound Volume No. 43, Salisbury Papers.
[5] Rosebery to White, Tel. No. 75, 12 Feb. 1886, F.O. 78/3878.
[6] W. L. Langer, *European Alliances and Alignments, 1871–1890*, p. 357.
[7] Rosebery to White, Tel. Private, 9 Mar. 1886, F.O. 78/3878.
[8] Rosebery to Thornton, Tel. No. 147, 6 Apr. 1886, F.O. 78/3878.

The forceful tactics which White employed during the last few sittings of the Ambassadors' Conference attracted European attention and earned him the reputation of being a second Stratford de Redcliffe. But it is the caution which he preached during the earlier phase of the proceedings—less widely known and more easily forgotten—that provides the main clue to the policy which he was to pursue when he returned to Constantinople as a full ambassador. Because he had flouted the wishes of the majority at the conference table in 1885, he might have been expected to carry out a conspicuously independent policy when he returned to the Porte about six months later. In fact, his policy was to attempt to save what remained of Great Britain's influence by going into partnership with Powers who shared common interests with her in the Near East. He realized that his success in the conference room had largely been due to the unexpected victory of Bulgarian arms at Slivnitza, and was not prepared to tempt Providence for a second time. The freakish events of the autumn and winter of 1885 were not likely to be repeated, and, but for Slivnitza, the Eastern Roumelian crisis might have been a second Pendjeh. Whenever White looked back to the Ambassadors' Conference, it was to remember how isolated Great Britain had been at Constantinople throughout 1885, not how easily he had been able to overcome a hesitant opposition during the last few meetings of that assembly.[1]

[1] Cf. White to Salisbury, Private and Confidential, 31 May 1887, F.O. 364/1.

II

ROSEBERY AND THORNTON

Early in 1886, when Salisbury left the Foreign Office and White returned from Constantinople to the relative obscurity of the British legation at Bucharest, the series of Near Eastern questions raised by the events of the previous autumn were reaching a temporary solution. The Bulgarian government, newly united under Prince Alexander, made peace with Serbia on 3 March, and came to terms with its Turkish suzerain a month later. The Greeks, whose demands for territorial compensation had been most vociferous, were silenced before the summer by an international blockade of their coast. Meanwhile Great Britain wielded far more power on the Bosphorus than she had done in the spring of 1885. Her firm stand in defence of the union of the two Bulgarias stood out in sharp contrast to her helplessness during the Pendjeh crisis, and the French chargé d'affaires at Constantinople quickly sensed that the diplomatic scene at that capital had undergone a striking transformation: Russia, supported by Germany, had formerly led a diplomatic campaign against Great Britain, but now, he informed Freycinet, Germany and Great Britain took the initiative while Russia stood alone.[1] But, improved though it was, Great Britain's position at Constantinople remained precarious since so much had depended upon the skill of Salisbury and White in concealing material weaknesses which defied any permanent remedy: an untried foreign secretary and an incompetent ambassador were soon to prove how rapidly British influence could decline when less capable hands were in control.

Rosebery was only in his fortieth year when Gladstone offered him the foreign secretaryship early in February 1886. By his own admission he lacked the qualifications usually required for such a post: 'I have absolutely no experience of the Foreign Office, which I have never entered except to attend a dinner', he confessed to Gladstone. 'My French I fear is rusty.... I have no knowledge of diplomatic practice

[1] *D.D.F.*, 1st ser. vi, No. 191 (Hanotaux to Freycinet, 17 Feb. 1886).

or forms, and little of diplomatic men. And I am sensible of many deficiencies of temper and manner.'[1] However, both the Queen and the newly formed Liberal government were of the opinion that foreign affairs should be conducted by someone younger and more forceful than Granville, and Rosebery accepted Gladstone's offer in spite of his initial display of reluctance.[2]

During the first few weeks of his short stay at the Foreign Office, Rosebery repeatedly stressed the need for continuity in the conduct of foreign affairs, and attempted to carry the 'prudent' Near Eastern policy of his predecessor to its logical conclusion: in regard to Greece, he fulfilled Salisbury's intentions by enforcing the naval blockade of her coast; and in regard to Bulgaria, although Salisbury might possibly have upheld Prince Alexander's position with greater vigour, his policy was essentially a development of Salisbury's.[3] Indeed, his 'deficiencies of temper and manner' did not become widely apparent until the beginning of July, when the Russian government announced its decision to alter the status of the port of Batum on the Black Sea. Following closely upon the Pendjeh and Bulgarian crises, the Russian declaration increased British suspicions of Russia and excited particular nervousness about the Straits. But in spite of this, Rosebery's sharp response was both clumsy and ineffective: clumsy in that it needlessly rankled Giers, and ineffective in that it failed to find support either at Berlin or Vienna. By sending a 'most wounding' note to the Russian government at a time when he was unprepared to translate words into action, he had provided Europe with a gratuitous display of his own government's isolation.[4] Thus, before the expiry of his first short term at the Foreign Office, Rosebery had clearly shown that in spite of his praiseworthy efforts to acknowledge and develop the successful foreign policy of Salisbury, he possessed neither the experience nor the judgement of his predecessor.

[1] Rosebery to Gladstone, Private, 2 Feb. 1886, Add. MS. 44289; cf. also Lord Crewe, *Lord Rosebery*, i. 258–60.

[2] Ibid.; G. E. Buckle, *The Letters of Queen Victoria*, 3rd ser., i. 25–29; Sir Sidney Lee, *King Edward VII*, i. 526.

[3] H. W. V. Temperley and L. M. Penson, *Foundations of British Foreign Policy, 1792–1902*, p. 434; Crewe, i. 263–4.

[4] Temperley and Penson, pp. 436–41.

The contrast between White and Sir Edward Thornton was even more marked. Thornton had been officially appointed as British ambassador at Constantinople in December 1884, but the complexities of the Afghan boundary dispute, and the ability with which White conducted the negotiations at the Ambassadors' Conference, had delayed his arrival at that capital until February 1886.[1] At the conclusion of his embassy at Constantinople, Dufferin had chosen Thornton as a likely successor and recommended him to Granville as being 'careful, conscientious, and conciliatory'.[2] The Queen had also spoken in his favour: she praised him for his knowledge of Russian intrigue, and thought him sufficiently 'wicked' to be useful at the Porte.[3] But except for a brief spell as ambassador at St. Petersburg between 1881 and 1884, Thornton's diplomatic experience had been confined to the American continent.[4] Twenty years at the capitals of numerous South American states, and fourteen more spent as minister at Washington, had not provided him with the ideal training for Near Eastern politics. Accustomed to the quiet orderliness of the legation at Washington, he devoted much of his time at Constantinople to supervising the compilation of an index for the voluminous archives of the embassy at Pera,[5] and to taking measures to define and limit the rights of British protected subjects in the Ottoman Empire.[6] Such activities revealed his talent for dealing with the routine work of a chancery, but they also betrayed the fact that he had completely failed to grasp the nature of his duties at Constantinople. 'Sir Edward Thornton is certainly not the right man to have here,' one of his subordinates confided to Layard, 'he is far too quiet and cautious, and neither sees through intrigues nor conceives it to be his duty to counteract them. In the meantime the Russians rule the roost, and we are entirely out in the cold.'[7]

Nor were Thornton's errors confined to sins of omission.

---

[1] *The Foreign Office List*, 1887, pp. 193–4; cf. White to Salisbury, Private and Confidential, 16 Jan. 1886, F.O. 364/1.
[2] Dufferin to Granville, Personal, 15 Sept. 1884, P.R.O. 30/29/191.
[3] Buckle, 3rd ser., i. 51.   [4] *The Foreign Office List*, 1887, loc. cit.
[5] Thornton to Rosebery, No. 342, 5 July 1886, F.O. 78/3873.
[6] Thornton to Rosebery, No. 250, 21 May 1886, F.O. 78/3871.
[7] Kennedy to Layard, Private, 26 Sept. 1886, Add. MS. 39040.

His well-meant but ill-timed presentation of a memorandum to the Porte on the subject of Asiatic reforms provided his superiors with positive proof of his unfitness for his new post.

By the summer of 1886 a series of questions in Parliament had made it necessary for Rosebery to indicate that the Foreign Office was making every effort to call the Porte's attention to the need for reforms in Asiatic Turkey, and Thornton was therefore asked, on 6 July, to remind the Sultan of his duty to fulfil the engagements laid down in Article LXI of the Treaty of Berlin. All the customary care was observed in rendering these instructions nugatory: Thornton was only to approach the Sultan 'when the opportunity arose', and was left with full discretion to postpone taking any action should he think it inadvisable.[1] It could hardly be imagined that Thornton would fail to recognize that these instructions bore all the marks of a 'Blue Book' dispatch.

Thornton maintained a tactful silence about the subject of Asiatic reforms until 16 August, when, without consulting Iddesleigh who had by then taken charge at the Foreign Office, he prepared a memorandum from Rosebery's dispatch and presented it to the Porte.[2] Eleven days later, Iddesleigh first learnt of his action through the German ambassador at London. On 27 August, when Hatzfeldt asked him if it was true that the British ambassador at Constantinople had presented a dispatch to the Turkish government containing a number of suggestions for the improvement of Ottoman rule in Asia Minor, Iddesleigh firmly denied that any such communication had been made.[3] But a report from the Reuter news agency on the following day bore out Hatzfeldt's information, and prompted Iddesleigh to question Thornton.[4] Thornton did not provide his new chief with a complete account of his actions until 30 August,[5] and by then *The Times* was already commenting upon the possible

[1] Rosebery to Thornton, No. 218, 6 July 1886, F.O. 78/3866.
[2] Thornton to Iddesleigh, No. 428, 24 Aug. F.O. 78/3874 (received at the Foreign Office on 1 Sept. 1886).
[3] Iddesleigh to Malet, No. 409A Confidential, 27 Aug. 1886, F.O. 64/1112.
[4] Iddesleigh to Thornton, Recorder of Tel. No. 211, 28 Aug. 1886, F.O. 195/1539.
[5] Thornton to Iddesleigh, Extender No. 449, 30 Aug. 1886, F.O. 78/3874.

effects at the Porte of what was erroneously described as 'the Armenian Note . . . prepared by Lord Rosebery and Mr. Bryce and forwarded by Lord Iddesleigh'.[1] Worse still, Iddesleigh was obliged to apologize to Hatzfeldt and confess that his ambassador at Constantinople had presented a memorandum to the Turkish government without thinking it necessary to inform him 'either before doing so, or by telegram afterwards'.[2]

Thornton explained to Iddesleigh that particularly severe injustices at Aleppo had persuaded him to act upon the instructions which Rosebery had given him discretion to use, and to remind the Turkish government of its treaty obligations in regard to Asia Minor. He was surprised to find that Iddesleigh took exception to the fact that he was not consulted about this matter, and was even more bewildered to discover that the Sultan had not received the memorandum favourably.[3] Both these reactions revealed his shortcomings as an ambassador: the first indicated his failure to appreciate the elementary fact that it was necessary to acquaint his government with every important move which he made on the Bosphorus, and the second betrayed his complete ignorance of the potentialities of the question of reforms in Asiatic Turkey as an irritant to the Sultan. Indeed, Thornton was never able to grasp the fact that humanitarian interests sometimes had to take second place at Constantinople. Hatzfeldt, who had represented the German government at the Porte in the early 'eighties, was far more realistic. Perhaps it was because he could not conceive it to be possible that the presentation of the 'Armenian Note' was purely the work of Thornton that he warned Iddesleigh that the Sultan feared and suspected Great Britain even more than Russia. He pointed out that Great Britain worried Turkey with reforms, while Russia only took her territory, a remark which Iddesleigh thought sufficiently pertinent to be passed on privately to White at Bucharest.[4]

[1] *The Times*, 30 Aug. 1886.
[2] Iddesleigh to Malet, No. 426, 30 Aug. 1886, F.O. 64/1112.
[3] Thornton to Iddesleigh, Extender No. 449, 30 Aug. F.O. 78/3874; No. 428, 24 Aug. F.O. 78/3874 (received at the Foreign Office on 1 Sept. 1886).
[4] Iddesleigh to White, Private, 27 Aug. 1886 (printed in H. S. Edwards, *Sir William White*, pp. 242–3).

Thornton's days at Constantinople were already numbered: even before his blunder over the 'Armenian Note' became known at the Foreign Office, events in Bulgaria had made the Queen press for his dismissal, and had strengthened the resolve of Salisbury and Iddesleigh to face the 'disagreeable necessity' of recalling him.[1] In some respects, therefore, Thornton's *faux pas* was most fortunate: it provided his superiors with a heaven-sent excuse for forcing him to accept an early retirement on full pension, and it gave Sir William White the opportunity to return to the scene of his greatest diplomatic triumphs.

[1] Buckle, 3rd ser., i. 189.

III

THE FIRST MEDITERRANEAN AGREEMENT
(*February–March* 1887)

IN the summer of 1886 the Near Eastern question was reopened in an acute form by yet another Bulgarian crisis. On the night of 20–21 August, a number of discontented Bulgarian officers seized Prince Alexander and forced him to abdicate. The Prince was escorted to Reni in Russian territory, and from there to Lemburg in Galicia where he arrived on 28 August. The conspirators were convinced—and the local Russian agents in Bulgaria shared and encouraged their belief—that the survival of Bulgaria depended upon the friendship of Russia, and that by deposing their Prince they were removing the sole obstacle to a reconciliation. A provisional government composed of Russophils was set up at Sofia under the Metropolitan Clement and the Liberal leader, Zankov. However, the new government was quickly overthrown by a nationalist counter-revolution headed by Stambulov, and Prince Alexander was summoned to return to Bulgaria. But when he came back to Sofia it was only to make a more dignified exit from the Bulgarian political scene: physically exhausted, and convinced that he would find little support in Bulgaria and even less in Europe, he decided not to continue his rule, and, after a final and unsuccessful appeal to the Tsar's mercy, he formally abdicated on 7 September. Momentarily the Russian victory appeared complete: the stubborn strength of Bulgarian nationalism had yet to be fully tested, and those Powers which were opposed to a Russian domination of Bulgaria had yet to recover from the disarming suddenness of the events of August 1886.[1]

---

[1] For accounts of the kidnapping of Prince Alexander and his subsequent abdication see A. von Huhn, *The Kidnapping of Prince Alexander of Battenberg, his return to Bulgaria and subsequent Abdication*, passim; G. E. Buckle, *The Letters of Queen Victoria*, 3rd ser., i. 179–83, 186–93, 198–214; W. L. Langer, *European Alliances and Alignments, 1871–1890*, pp. 358–61.

St. Petersburg rejoiced at the news of the kidnapping of Prince Alexander. The Tsar proposed to send his friend, Prince Dolgoruki, to Sofia immediately, but Prince Alexander's return to that capital forced him to change his plans. However, once the Prince had formally abdicated, the Tsar became obsessed with the idea of proving that the Bulgarians were Russophils who had been led astray by the treacherous Battenberg, and he therefore sent General Kaulbars to Sofia in order to advise the regents and inquire into the wishes of the Bulgarian population. The fact that Kaulbars was the brother of the notorious Bulgarian war minister of 1883 should have been a sufficient warning of the likely results of his mission: his methods were those of a bullying soldier, not a tactful diplomat; he refused to recognize the legality of the Bulgarian national assembly or any of its decisions; he toured the country clumsily attempting to hector the population into submission to Russia; and he finally summoned two Russian gunboats to Varna on the ground that those who favoured Russia needed protection. In fact, his high-handed proceedings made the Bulgarian regents more uncompromising in their hostility to Russian influence than Prince Alexander had ever been.

In defiance of Kaulbars, the national assembly met at Trnovo on 27 October and elected Prince Waldemar of Denmark, a relative of the Tsar, to the throne. By this time the Tsar's patience was exhausted, and on 17 November Kaulbars and all the Russian consuls left Bulgaria and diplomatic relations between the two governments were broken off. In two months Kaulbars had helped to turn an apparent Russian triumph into a complete disaster. He had heightened anti-Russian feeling in Bulgaria and broadened the basis of European sympathy for the Bulgarian national cause. Thus in a speech delivered to the Austro-Hungarian delegations three days before Kaulbars' departure from Bulgaria, Kalnoky confidently declared: 'He has raised European sympathies for the Bulgarians, sympathies at first vouchsafed only to Prince Alexander, to quite an unprecedented degree.'[1]

---

[1] *The Times*, 15 Nov. 1886; for details of Kaulbars' mission see J. V. Fuller, *Bismarck's Diplomacy at its Zenith*, pp. 165–7; Langer, pp. 365–6.

White was holidaying in Bad Gastein when the kidnapping of Prince Alexander took place. Within a few months of his departure from Constantinople nearly all his diplomatic achievements there had been nullified: Rosebery's mishandling of the Batum affair had given the Powers a gratuitous demonstration of Great Britain's isolation; Thornton's incompetence had almost destroyed the influence which White had so industriously built up at the Porte; and Prince Alexander of Bulgaria, who had recently weathered one Bulgarian crisis, was soon to be swept away by the storms of another.

The struggle which was necessary to secure White's appointment as ambassador to the Porte gives a good idea of the extent to which British influence at Constantinople had declined during the period of Rosebery's foreign secretaryship and Thornton's embassy. For six weeks White's appointment remained uncertain. At the beginning of September, when Thornton was called home for 'consultation',[1] the Sultan expressed surprise and regret at his leaving,[2] and in London, Rustem Pasha spoke of him in glowing terms to Iddesleigh, and pressed in vain for a pledge that the British government had no intention of sending White to Constantinople.[3] After making such obvious hints, Rustem Pasha finally announced, on 23 September, that the Sultan refused to accept White as British ambassador at the Porte owing to the objections of some of the other ambassadors. Iddesleigh retaliated by instructing Thornton, who had temporarily returned to Constantinople, to inform the Sultan that he was about to go home on leave, and that his government intended to appoint White 'ambassador *ad interim*'.[4]

Inquiries made at Berlin and Vienna were answered by assurances that neither the German nor the Austro-Hungarian ambassadors at Constantinople objected to White as a colleague.[5] It seems to have been Nelidov who was the

---

[1] Iddesleigh to Thornton, Tel. No. 215, 2 Sept. 1886, F.O. 78/3878.
[2] Thornton to Iddesleigh, Tel. No. 164, 4 Sept. 1886, F.O. 78/3879.
[3] Iddesleigh to Fane (chargé d'affaires at Constantinople) Confidential, 3 Sept. 1886, F.O. 78/3867.
[4] Iddesleigh to Thornton, Tel. No. 222 Very Secret, 23 Sept. 1886, F.O. 78/3878.
[5] Scott (chargé d'affaires at Berlin) to Iddesleigh, Tel. No. 127 Confidential,

main instigator of the intrigue against White's return, but it should be added that his task was made all the easier because the Sultan approved of his designs.¹ 'In reality, the Sultan's objection appears to be that White is too *remuant*, and too energetic', one of the secretaries at the British embassy suggested. 'He will of course, when he arrives, begin a game of "French and English" with Nelidow, in which the poor Sultan will play the part of the rope.'² But continual pressure from the Foreign Office forced the Sultan to give way, and on 11 October White was confirmed as 'special ambassador-extraordinary and plenipotentiary *ad interim*'. The fact that his appointment did not become permanent until 1 January 1887 is explained partly by the Sultan's vigorous opposition, and partly by Iddesleigh's desire to avoid making Thornton's recall 'unpalatable'.³ Thornton had been sent on leave of absence on 10 October, and his pension was to date from 31 December 1886.⁴ White finally arrived at Constantinople on 26 October.⁵ The struggle for his appointment, so keenly contested on both sides, left no doubt as to the weight of his reputation as a diplomat.

The second Bulgarian crisis confronted the new ambassador with three main difficulties: a split in the Cabinet at London, Turkish apathy at Constantinople, and uncertainty as to the attitude likely to be adopted at Vienna and, above all, at Berlin. All three problems were closely connected: with its counsels divided, the British government was not likely to come to an understanding with Austria-Hungary and Germany, and until some such understanding had been arrived at, the Turks could hardly be expected to stiffen their opposition to Russian demands. Each of these questions requires separate treatment, but it is essential to stress the dependence of each upon the other two.

24 Sept. F.O. 64/1120; Paget to Iddesleigh, Tel. No. 111 Most Confidential, 2 Oct. 1886, F.O. 7/1099.
 ¹ Fane to Iddesleigh, No. 474 Very Confidential, 14 Sept. 1886, F.O. 78/3874.
 ² Kennedy to Layard, Private, Constantinople, 26 Sept. 1886, Add. MS. 39040.
 ³ Buckle, 3rd ser. i. 189; W. N. Medlicott, 'Corrections to the Dictionary of National Biography on Sir William White', *Bulletin of the Institute of Historical Research*, v. 58–59.
 ⁴ Iddesleigh to Thornton, No. 328B, 28 Oct. 1886, F.O. 78/3867.
 ⁵ White to Iddesleigh, No. 528, 26 Oct. 1886, F.O. 78/3875.

First, then, the split in the British Cabinet. As in 1885, the British government was caught unawares by events in Bulgaria. When Salisbury had formed his second administration, late in July 1886, he had not been prepared to repeat the experiment of the previous summer by uniting the foreign secretaryship with the premiership, and he had therefore entrusted the conduct of foreign affairs to his friend Iddesleigh. Iddesleigh was a new-comer to the Foreign Office: plagued with a heart-disease and noticeably hard of hearing, he had only accepted the post after it had been refused first by Lyons and then by Cranbrook, and he was confronted with a serious crisis in Bulgaria before he had had time to settle down to his unfamiliar duties.[1] Moreover, he was badly served by his subordinates in the Near East: Thornton had failed to keep abreast of the situation in Bulgaria,[2] and Lascelles was on leave of absence from Sofia when Prince Alexander was kidnapped.[3]

In the midst of all the confusion, Salisbury was suddenly called upon to defend his colleague at the Foreign Office from a double attack. The Queen, who was personally concerned at the fate of 'poor Sandro', immediately attributed the 'monstrous' revolution to the Russian government; she had made up her mind that 'Russia *must* be unmasked', and therefore urged her government to give the Bulgarians greater support.[4] But Salisbury's chancellor of the exchequer thought otherwise. Churchill argued against giving any support to Prince Alexander which was 'outside a most Platonic range', and sharply attacked Iddesleigh for 'drifting into strong and marked action in the East of Europe'.[5] 'Iddesleigh', he later complained, 'keeps rushing in where Bismarck fears to tread.'[6] His friend Wolff was even harsher in his condemnation of the Foreign Secretary: 'Lord Iddesleigh is both foolish and incompetent. I think the very worst Minister for Foreign Affairs I ever recollected. He is old and

---

[1] Lady G. Cecil, *Life of Robert, Marquis of Salisbury*, iii. 312; Lord Newton, *Lord Lyons*, ii. 371–5; A. E. Gathorne-Hardy, *Gathorne Hardy, First Earl of Cranbrook*, ii. 255–6. [2] *Supra*, p. 46.
[3] Sir R. Graves, *Storm Centres of the Near East*, p. 78.
[4] Buckle, 3rd ser., i. 186–205; Cecil, iv. 5–6.
[5] W. S. Churchill, *Lord Randolph Churchill*, pp. 515–16.
[6] Ibid., p. 519.

almost an imbecile.'[1] 'Poor dear old man!', Lansdowne commented. 'He ought to be sunning himself outside an almshouse.'[2] But much more important than these personal attacks against Iddesleigh was the fact that at least two members of the Cabinet leaned towards Churchill's views about Great Britain and the Near East: neither W. H. Smith nor Lord George Hamilton was inclined to accept the general Eastern policy laid down by Salisbury and Iddesleigh.[3] Salisbury found it difficult, but not impossible, to convince the Queen that Great Britain had not sufficient power in the Near East to pursue a more active policy in regard to Bulgaria.[4] However, he was unable to persuade Churchill that too cautious and negative a policy might be equally dangerous, and Churchill's criticisms of Iddesleigh soon developed into a fundamental disagreement with Salisbury about the principles which were to guide British policy in the Near East.

The conflict which split the Cabinet in the autumn of 1886 had been enacted a year previously on a smaller stage—with Morier playing the role of Churchill and White taking the part of Salisbury. Morier and Churchill, who used almost identical arguments, possessed similar qualities and shortcomings: both were able to throw themselves wholeheartedly into a particular task and become completely absorbed by it; both tended to over-estimate the importance of the problems with which they were well acquainted when they measured them against the general political background; in fact, both could be accused of 'provincialism' in their diplomatic views. Morier was appointed ambassador at St. Petersburg, and Churchill served as Secretary for India in Salisbury's 'caretaker' government, at a time when the Afghan boundary dispute attracted considerable attention in Europe, and it seems possible that this, more than anything else, accounted for their common obsession with Asiatic rather than Near Eastern problems.[5] Thus when White upheld the union of the two Bulgarias at the Ambassadors' Conference in 1885, Morier reminded him that whereas Great

---

[1] Churchill, p. 805. [2] Ibid.
[3] Buckle, 3rd ser., i. 201–2. [4] Cecil, iv. 5–6.
[5] Churchill, pp. 365–73; H. S. Edwards, *Sir William White*, pp. 230–1, 234–8.

Britain's Asiatic interests were *en première ligne*, her rivalry with Russia in Europe was '*en seconde ligne*, and very far behind'.[1] A year later Churchill used similar arguments when he kept impressing upon Salisbury that Great Britain would do better to look to her true interests in Egypt and India instead of attempting to counteract any Russian moves in the Balkans.[2] The replies of White and Salisbury to their respective critics were strikingly similar. White admitted to Morier that Great Britain's 'great interests' were in Asia, but he refused to accept his contention that her policy should therefore be shaped by purely Asiatic considerations —'we still have European duties and a European position, and even European interests'.[3] Salisbury was equally unmoved by the arguments used by Churchill in the following autumn. Although sceptical about the possibilities of defending it successfully, he was firmly resolved to 'draw the line at Constantinople'—'I consider the loss of Constantinople would be the ruin of our party and a heavy blow to the country: and therefore I am anxious to delay by all means Russia's advance towards that goal.'[4]

On 2 October Churchill made a speech at Dartford which seemed to indicate that the split in the Cabinet might be repaired. He announced that there was to be no violent departure from the traditional principles of Great Britain's Near Eastern policy, but that the time had come for the Power most directly interested in the Balkans to take the lead: Austria-Hungary should shoulder the responsibilities which had been British in Palmerston's day.[5] These ideas were completely orthodox; these were the views held both by Salisbury and by White. But Churchill's public pronouncements did not tally with his private opinions. Two days after the Dartford speech, Dilke, an experienced and well-informed observer, hastened to warn White that Churchill's influence in the Cabinet might add to his difficulties at Constantinople: 'You may like a private hint that Randolph is determined to have that which (I know) he has always

[1] Morier to White, 19 Nov. 1885 (printed in Edwards, pp. 230–1).
[2] Churchill, pp. 515–17.
[3] White to Morier, 9 Dec. 1885 (printed in Edwards, pp. 231–4).
[4] Salisbury to Churchill, 1 Oct. 1886 (printed in Churchill, p. 520).
[5] Churchill, pp. 521–5.

favoured—whatever he has sometimes said—viz:—a Peace policy and retrenchment.'¹ He later confided to him: 'The best thing I can do here to help you would be to state as a fact that Randolph is for letting Russia go to Constantinople, which would make him at once declare that he holds the opposite view!'² Dilke's general concern for the widening chasm between Salisbury and Churchill was soon to be justified, for on 23 December Churchill suddenly resigned from the Cabinet.³ Nor were his fears for White's position wholly illusory: Churchill had, in fact, complained to Salisbury that White was likely to act in a high-handed manner at Constantinople.⁴

It had been impossible to conceal the split in the Cabinet from the rest of Europe: potential friends had therefore hesitated to come to understandings, however vague, with a government divided against itself; and traditional enemies, although often puzzled, had taken heart at the embarrassments of the British government. As early as December 1885, Hatzfeldt had detected that Churchill was not in favour of the steps which Salisbury had taken to uphold the union of the two Bulgarias,⁵ and with the advent of the second Bulgarian crisis this divergence in their views became all the more obvious to the German, Austro-Hungarian, French, and Russian governments.⁶ Churchill's informal talks with foreign ambassadors added to the difficulties of Salisbury and his foreign secretary. In September 1886, for instance, Churchill informed Hatzfeldt in a 'chance conversation' that Great Britain was not a European but an Asiatic Power whose main concern was to remain in possession of India, and that as she had no real interests to protect in the Balkan Peninsula, she could allow Russia a free hand there without any anxiety.⁷ He also assured Hatzfeldt's Russian colleague in London that India and Egypt were far more important to Great

---

1 Dilke to White, Private, 4 Oct. 1886, Additional White Papers.
2 Dilke to White, Private, 9 Dec. 1886, Additional White Papers.
3 Churchill, pp. 557–85; Cecil, iii. 329–38.
4 Churchill to Salisbury, 3 Oct. 1886 (printed in Churchill, p. 521).
5 G.P. iv, No. 788 (Hatzfeldt to Herbert Bismarck, 5 Dec. 1885).
6 G.P. iv, Nos. 807, 866–7; A. Meyendorff, *Correspondance diplomatique de M. de Staal*, i. 309; D.D.F., 1st ser., vi, No. 316.
7 G.P. iv, No. 866 (Hatzfeldt to Herbert Bismarck, 24 Sept. 1886).

Britain than Constantinople.¹ But neither of these statements could be identified with the views held by Salisbury and Iddesleigh. The event of Churchill's resignation was the Cabinet's rejection of the proposed economies at the Admiralty and the War Office contained in his draft budget, but this specific issue was only a manifestation of one of its main underlying causes—his fundamental disagreement with Salisbury and Iddesleigh about the conduct of foreign affairs.² Perhaps it is significant that a week after Churchill had left the government, Salisbury had a lengthy interview with Morier in which he 'warned him strongly to keep his unorthodox opinions to himself'.³

Iddesleigh died suddenly on 12 January 1887—a few days after reading about his resignation from the Foreign Office in the *Standard*. Illness and inexperience made him unequal to the performance of his duties, and there had been minor differences with Salisbury.⁴ His dismissal and death, together with Churchill's resignation, marked the end of a period in which disagreements within the Cabinet had seriously hindered the execution of Great Britain's foreign policy. Salisbury was once more free to be both Prime Minister and Foreign Secretary, and as from 1 January White was permanently appointed British ambassador at Constantinople. After almost a year of interruptions, the successful partnership of the winter of 1885-6 was to be resumed: Salisbury was to plan and White was to execute British policy in the Near East.

The split in the Cabinet at London was a temporary embarrassment over which White had no control, but Turkish apathy towards Russian incursions into the Balkans was a permanent and persistent problem which was of immediate concern to the new ambassador. It presented him with a double task: the Sultan had to be convinced, on the one hand, that Great Britain was his natural ally, and, on the other, that Russia was his inevitable enemy. 'Make him understand', Iddesleigh wrote, 'that, whatever he may hear to the contrary,

---
¹ Meyendorff, i. 290; Churchill, pp. 516–17.
² Cf. Churchill to Salisbury, 22 Dec. 1886 (printed in Churchill, pp. 576–7).
³ Salisbury to Queen Victoria, 30 Dec. 1886 (printed in Buckle, 3rd ser., i. 239–40).
⁴ Cecil, iii. 341–4.

England maintains her old traditional policy towards Turkey, desires to see it strong and independent, with Constantinople safe. But much as we value a safe and independent Constantinople, equally should we fear and dislike one which was virtually under Russian control; and that is the sort of contingency which might indeed drive us to consider our position and to ask how we are to safeguard our Eastern communications.'[1] White's first task was made all the more difficult by the recent delivery of the 'Armenian Note', for Thornton's blunder had angered the Sultan and increased his hostility towards Great Britain.[2] His second task had become all the more urgent because of the rumours about the conclusion of a Russo-Turkish alliance which had begun to circulate around Constantinople a few weeks after the Russian declaration concerning Batum.[3] Whether such rumours were true or false was a relatively unimportant question, for as Iddesleigh pointed out to White, 'rumours of mischief' could be 'almost as bad as the mischief itself' at Constantinople: 'The Sultan may be scared by the rumour and driven into foolish courses when there is no more foundation in fact than there is for England's taking possession of the Island of Thasos!'[4]

White had to gain sufficient influence over the Sultan to be able to dissuade him from taking any unwise action. But his first reports from his new post were not encouraging: throughout November 1886 he kept commenting on the apathy which prevailed at the Porte and the Palace; he contrasted 'the present culpable inaction' of the Turks with the objections which they had raised in the past whenever they considered that the slightest encroachment had been made upon their suzerain rights, and he became convinced that there would be no Turkish opposition to any action which the Russians might take in Bulgaria.[5] Criticism of the

[1] Iddesleigh to White, Private, 22 Sept. 1886, F.O. 364/1.
[2] *Supra*, Chapter II.
[3] Thornton to Rosebery, Tel. No. 130 Most Secret, 28 July, F.O. 78/3879; No. 386 Most Secret, 3 Aug. F.O. 78/3873; Thornton to Iddesleigh, Tel. No. 153 Confidential, 27 Aug. F.O. 78/3879; *D.D.F.*, 1st ser., vi, No. 282 (Montebello to Freycinet, 11 Aug. 1886).
[4] Iddesleigh to White, Private, 22 Sept. 1886, F.O. 364/1.
[5] White to Iddesleigh, No. 542 Secret, 1 Nov.; No. 551 Confidential, 6 Nov.; No. 570 Secret, 16 Nov. 1886, F.O. 78/3876.

THE FIRST MEDITERRANEAN AGREEMENT 57

attitude of the German and Austro-Hungarian governments accompanied these reports.[1] Soon after his arrival at Constantinople, White was able to confirm the view which both he and Iddesleigh had already reached. in theory: Turkish lethargy, and consequently the imminent danger of Russian domination of the Ottoman Empire, would continue until the two Central Powers displayed more interest in Near Eastern affairs.

The attitude adopted by Germany and Austria-Hungary in regard to the Near East was the third great difficulty which confronted White during the autumn and winter of 1886. This, more than any other problem, determined the course of White's policy throughout the period of his embassy at Constantinople. 'In a crisis like the present one', he informed Iddesleigh, 'it is much more difficult to ascertain with some precision what friendly Powers aim at than what Russia seeks. The tactics of Germany and Austria are far more obscure than the designs of the Emperor of Russia.'[2] The Pendjeh crisis had taught White the dangers of isolation at Constantinople, and he realized that, but for the unexpected Bulgarian victory at Slivnitza, the lessons of the spring of 1885 might well have been repeated at the Ambassadors' Conference.[3] Moreover, there were other factors which helped to drive home these lessons: the friendship between Radowitz and Nelidov—far more intimate than the relations between their two governments[4]—and White's consciousness of being shunned as an ex-consul must have lent a personal emphasis to his political isolation.[5] Taking stock of his position in November 1886, he declared that he was 'surrounded by apathy, treachery and stubbornness on all sides', and that his only assets were 'the Queen's approbation, your [Iddesleigh's] kind guidance, and the feeling of a *mens conscia recti*'.[6]

Even before the outbreak of the second Bulgarian crisis

[1] White to Iddlesleigh, No. 570 Secret, 16 Nov. 1886, F.O. 78/3876.
[2] White to Iddesleigh, Private and Very Secret, 27 Sept. 1886, F.O. 364/3.
[3] *Supra*, Chapter I.
[4] White to Iddesleigh, Private, 20 Nov. 1886, F.O. 364/1.
[5] Cf. Lord Hardinge of Penshurst, *Old Diplomacy*, pp. 40–41.
[6] White to Iddesleigh, Confidential, 2 Nov. 1886, F.O. 364/1.

and his appointment to Constantinople, and at a time when conferences between the leading statesmen of the two Central Empires at Kissingen (22–24 July) and Bad Gastein (9–10 August) appeared to demonstrate the solidarity of the Bismarckian system, White made active endeavours to ensure that Great Britain should not face Russia alone in the Near East. From the late summer of 1886 until the spring of the following year he looked both to Germany and to Austria-Hungary for support; at first, his hopes were founded upon the enlistment of German aid, but when these were disappointed he turned to Austria-Hungary for assistance. But indecision at Vienna, the marked decline in Austro-Hungarian influence at the Porte, and guarded hints of increased German interest in the Ottoman Empire finally convinced White that Germany, not Austria-Hungary, was the most desirable partner for Great Britain at Constantinople.

White's customary holiday at Bad Gastein coincided with the imperial meeting held there in the summer of 1886.[1] On 12 and 22 August he met Bismarck for the only time during the whole of his career, and had lengthy but informal talks with him. Contrary to rumours in the Viennese press, these conversations were completely unofficial.[2] However, White thought it worth while to report them both in a private letter to Salisbury and in an official dispatch. Giving an account of his interview with Bismarck on 12 August, White commented:

> Numerous topics were touched upon, but His Highness laid even more than his habitual stress on his pet view that Germany had no interests in the East and could even view with equanimity Constantinople falling to Russia which, he added, the latter says she requires as the *Key of her House*.... In expatiating on this subject, the Great Chancellor hinted that Austria might have interests in that part of the world which might bring her into collision with Russia.[3]

Bismarck then went on to speak of France as the permanent danger to Germany. He stressed his need for Russian friend-

---
[1] The *Standard*, 10 Aug. 1886; the *Morning Post*, 18 Aug. 1886; the *Daily Telegraph*, 10 Aug. 1886.
[2] Ibid.
[3] White to Salisbury, Confidential, 18 Aug. 1886, Salisbury Papers (unbound).

ship, and outlined the strategic and climatic difficulties involved in a German invasion of Russia. White attempted to turn these arguments to his own account by pointing out to him that for these very reasons it would be much easier to attack Russia, if necessary, from the south with the combined forces of Austria-Hungary and Turkey, than from the north where Napoleon Bonaparte had failed. But Bismarck remained unmoved, and on 22 August, when White saw him for the second and last time, their conversation was limited to conjectures about the meaning of the unexpected news of Prince Alexander's kidnapping.[1]

Three days later, while waiting for the train back to Bucharest, White had an interview with Kalnoky at Vienna. He deplored the apathy of the Turks in the face of the attempted deposition of Prince Alexander, and the imminent danger that Bulgaria might become a Russian province extending from Widdin on the Danube to the very gates of Adrianople. But he added that their attitude was at least understandable, for they were naturally puzzled and disheartened when they saw that Nelidov was supported by 'two of his colleagues' [i.e. Radowitz and Calice] at Constantinople. Kalnoky replied to these criticisms by pointing to the strong reaction against the conspirators at Sofia, and stating that Bulgaria was not likely to become a Russian province. He went on to inform White that Bismarck was on his way to Franzenbad to see Giers and try to persuade the Russians not to send an armed force to occupy Bulgaria. In answer to this piece of information White assured Kalnoky that if he and Bismarck were to join hands to prevent a Russian occupation of Bulgaria they were sure to succeed.[2]

From his meetings with Bismarck and Kalnoky, White derived a general impression that Bismarck would remain indifferent to the fate of Constantinople 'until such a time as the Powers more directly interested come forward with overtures as to the sacrifices they are prepared to make to avert such a calamity'.[3] But this did not prevent him from being

[1] White to Iddesleigh, No. 102 Very Secret, 27 Aug. F.O. 104/52; to Salisbury, Confidential, 15 Aug. 1886, Salisbury Papers (unbound).
[2] White to Iddesleigh, No. 102 Very Secret, 27 Aug. F.O. 104/52; cf. Paget to Iddesleigh, No. 282 Strictly Confidential, 25 Aug. 1886, F.O. 7/1095.
[3] Ibid., F.O. 104/52.

optimistic about Bismarck's proposed intercession with Giers. When it was rumoured that the Tsar was to send Prince Dolgoruki to Bulgaria as special commissioner for Russia, Iddesleigh toyed with the idea of sending White to Sofia as a counterpoise,[1] But White persuaded him that such a measure might ruin Bismarck's efforts to pacify the Russian government.[2] Yet a few days later, when it became obvious that Prince Alexander's return to Bulgaria had not been welcomed by Bismarck and that his abdication was imminent, White's attitude changed completely. Bismarck's conduct made White both puzzled and indignant: 'What is difficult to account for', he explained to Iddesleigh on 2 September, 'is the manner in which Bismarck goes out of his way in his condescension to the Czar, for Russian supremacy in Bulgaria implies serious injury to Austria as well as permanent danger to her, to Servia, Roumania and Turkey.'[3] 'Two principal causes operate to discourage Prince Alexander,' he telegraphed on the following day, 'the acts of treachery which are being revealed to His Highness since his return on the part of many of his supposed adherents, and the hostility of Prince Bismarck, the cause of which cannot yet be sufficiently accounted for.'[4]

After the abdication of Prince Alexander on 7 September, White had second thoughts about his conversations with the German chancellor. But in spite of the light manner in which the Prince had been sacrificed, he remained convinced that Bismarck's policy in regard to Bulgaria was to seize any pretext to procrastinate, but to ensure at the same time that the Tsar was not provided with an excuse for a military occupation.[5] These conclusions were confirmed by Malet's reports from Berlin. Malet suggested that Bismarck's opposition to Prince Alexander, which was not in keeping with the general sympathies of his countrymen, might be attributed to his fear

---

[1] Iddesleigh to White, Confidential, 27 Aug. Additional White Papers; to Kennedy (chargé d'affaires at Bucharest), 27 Aug. 1886, F.O. 104/53.
[2] White to Iddesleigh, Tel. No. 49, 28 Aug. 1886, F.O. 104/53.
[3] White to Iddesleigh, Tel. Private and Very Secret, 2 Sept. 1886, F.O. 364/3.
[4] White to Iddesleigh, Tel. Private, 3 Sept. 1886, F.O. 364/3.
[5] Undated memorandum by White entitled 'Recent events in Bulgaria seen in the light of private conversations with Prince Bismarck at Gastein on 12th and 22nd of August'. F.O. 364/3.

of difficulties with the Russian government which would be 'the signal for an attack on the part of France'.[1] The diplomatic manœuvres of the German Foreign Office seemed complicated and contradictory. On 7 September Herbert Bismarck impressed upon Malet that Giers had assured his father that Russia would not occupy Bulgaria, but when the British ambassador asked point blank what Germany would do if civil war broke out in Bulgaria and Russia occupied it in spite of all her assurances, he replied with equal bluntness —'We should fold our arms.'[2] But, two days later, he hastened to inform Scott, the British chargé d'affaires at Berlin, that the Russian pledge not to intervene in Bulgaria with armed force was 'unconditional, holding good under all circumstances'.[3]

Malet's summing up of German policy was similar to White's: 'Notwithstanding an apparent parade of frankness, Prince Bismarck's policy is decidedly dual, an open and an outspoken one, which maintains the alliance with Russia at all hazards, and a hidden and silent one, which derives satisfaction from every rebuff which Russia receives.'[4] Bismarck repeatedly urged the British government to take the lead in opposing Russia in the Balkans. But whereas he was loud and ostentatious in the assurances which he gave Russia, he was only prepared to give Great Britain private and noncommittal hints of his goodwill. In such circumstances, all immediate ideas of German co-operation had to be abandoned.

With his hopes of German support temporarily shattered, White turned his attention towards Austria-Hungary. Throughout the September of 1886 his main theme was that Austria-Hungary was Great Britain's obvious partner in the Near East: Germany, only indirectly threatened by Russian advances in the Balkans, could wait until others took the initiative, but Austria-Hungary, more directly menaced by such moves, could not afford to hesitate. 'As regards Austria', he confided to Iddesleigh, 'the occasion appears unique for

---

[1] Malet to Iddesleigh, Private, 1 Sept. 1886, F.O. 343/8.
[2] Malet to Iddesleigh, Tel. No. 117 Confidential, 7 Sept. 1886, F.O. 64/1120.
[3] Scott to Iddesleigh, Tel. No. 121 Confidential, 9 Sept. 1886, F.O. 64/1120.
[4] Malet to Iddesleigh, Private, 4 Sept. 1886, F.O. 343/8.

drawing her out and testing her security and no time ought to be lost in doing this, the opportunity may never occur again. Our two Empires have no rival interests anywhere and our common ones are in imminent peril.' He went on to point out that Great Britain might offer Austria-Hungary a friendly exchange of views without entering into any further commitments: the two governments might agree 'as to a common line of action for the purpose of preserving the actual territorial and Treaty arrangements of Eastern Europe and counteracting Russia's growing interest at Constantinople', and a 'free and friendly confidential intercourse' between the British and Austro-Hungarian ambassadors at the Porte might prove a useful step towards that object and would undoubtedly impress the Sultan.[1]

White's suggestions were cautious. In fact, they were close in spirit to the ideas which were later embodied in the notes exchanged between Great Britain and Austria-Hungary when the latter adhered to the First Mediterranean Agreement on 24 March 1887. But their more immediate significance was that they were in keeping with the advice which Iddesleigh received from Paget at Vienna. From a conversation which he had with Kalnoky soon after the imperial meeting at Kissingen, Paget gathered that although the two Central Powers were anxious to maintain friendly relations with Russia, they were equally eager for a cordial understanding and intimate friendship with Great Britain.[2] Moreover, he later became convinced that the main purpose of the conferences at Kissingen and Bad Gastein was not to discuss Near Eastern problems, but to demonstrate the solidarity of the Austro-German alliance and discourage the formation of a Franco-Russian grouping.[3] Paget, like his ambassadorial counterparts at Berlin and Constantinople, considered one of the main keys to the diplomatic problem raised by the second Bulgarian crisis to be Bismarck's determination not to be involved in a war against France and Russia combined.[4]

On 24 August Paget found Kalnoky indignant about the

---

[1] White to Iddesleigh, Private and Very Secret, 27 Sept. 1886, F.O. 364/3; cf. G. E. Buckle, *The Letters of Queen Victoria*, 3rd ser., i. 206–7.
[2] Paget to Rosebery, No. 246 Very Confidential, 28 July 1886, F.O. 7/1095.
[3] Paget to Iddesleigh, No. 263 Very Confidential, 12 Aug. 1886, F.O. 7/1095.
[4] Paget to Iddesleigh, No. 305 Very Confidential, 4 Sept. 1886, F.O. 7/1096.

kidnapping of Prince Alexander of Bulgaria. Without waiting for any instructions from the Foreign Office, he seized the opportunity to ask him whether or not those Powers interested in the maintenance of the Ottoman Empire should attempt to reach an understanding to prevent further encroachments and curb Russia's aggressiveness. However, Kalnoky refused to express his views on this subject until he had become more fully informed about the recent events in Bulgaria.[1] But, ten days later, he admitted to Paget that he was greatly disturbed by the Tsar's 'brutal' telegram dismissing Prince Alexander's appeal for mercy, and the ambassador again warned him that Bulgaria would become a Russian province unless Austria-Hungary, Great Britain, Germany, and Italy agreed to support the Prince and the Bulgarian people. Once more Kalnoky was evasive: his refusal to take any step in support of the Prince without the concurrence of the German and Russian governments was tantamount to a rebuff.[2]

These early overtures by Paget foreshadowed the unsuccessful negotiations for an Anglo-Austrian accord which continued throughout the autumn and winter of 1886. On 4 September Hengelmüller, the Austro-Hungarian chargé d'affaires in London, assured Iddesleigh that any proposal he might make for a secret understanding with Austria-Hungary would be favourably received in Vienna, but he insisted upon Great Britain taking the initiative since she was in a much freer position.[3] Kalnoky spoke to Paget in similar terms almost three weeks later. He confessed that Austria-Hungary could not allow herself to be encircled by an 'iron band of Pan Slavism', and admitted that her interests were identical with those of Great Britain. But he went on to explain that since 'a school of politicians in England professed the fate of the Balkans, even Constantinople, to be of little account to England', he thought it essential, if the two governments were ever to work together, that he should have some knowledge of the general principles of British policy

[1] Paget to Iddesleigh, No. 277 Confidential, 24 Aug. 1886, F.O. 7/1095.
[2] Paget to Iddesleigh, Tel. No. 93 Very Confidential, 3 Sept. F.O. 7/1099; No. 305 Very Confidential, 4 Sept. 1886, F.O. 7/1096.
[3] W. N. Medlicott, 'The Mediterranean Agreements of 1887', *Slavonic Review*, v. 68; cf. Iddesleigh to Paget, Nos. 165A–B, 5–6 Sept. 1886, F.O. 7/1092.

and of the views of the British government.[1] Iddesleigh responded to these overtures by making two attempts to define British policy and reach an understanding with Austria-Hungary: in his confidential memorandum of 30 September—'intended to convince the Austrians that they might under certain circumstances count on aid from this country'[2] —he pointed out that Great Britain would fight Russia provided that she was assured of the support of the other interested Powers;[3] and in a second memorandum to the Austro-Hungarian government, written on 13 November when Kaulbars's activities in Bulgaria were at their height, he again urged the need for joint European action.[4] Neither of these approaches was successful. On 2 October Kalnoky answered the first memorandum by drawing a sharp distinction between Constantinople and the Balkans, and implying that Anglo-Austrian co-operation would therefore be difficult: whereas the gate of Constantinople was a matter of primary concern to Great Britain, it was only of minor interest to Austria-Hungary; and with regard to the Balkans the reverse was true.[5] In replying to the second, on 23 November, he admitted that the two governments 'had been proceeding on parallel lines and that the two lines would ultimately meet when the occasion arose', but he also observed that the departure of Kaulbars had modified the situation in Bulgaria and removed the immediate necessity for their joint action.[6]

Bismarck tried hard to convince Kalnoky that he should remain on good terms with Russia,[7] and Giers gave Wolkenstein, the Austro-Hungarian representative at St. Petersburg, confidential assurances that the Russian government had no intention of occupying Bulgaria, but thought it un-

[1] Paget to Iddesleigh, No. 345 Most Confidential, 23 Sept. 1886, F.O. 7/1096; cf. Medlicott, p. 68.
[2] Iddesleigh to White, Confidential, 12 Oct. 1886, F.O. 364/1.
[3] Iddesleigh to Paget, No. 188A, 29 Sept. 1886, F.O. 7/1092; cf. Medlicott, pp. 68–69.
[4] Iddesleigh to Phipps (chargé d'affaires at Vienna), No. 231, 13 Nov. 1886, F.O. 7/1092; cf. Medlicott, p. 70.
[5] Paget to Iddesleigh, No. 358A Most Confidential, 2 Oct. 1886, F.O. 7/1096; cf. Medlicott, p. 69.
[6] Phipps (chargé d'affaires at Vienna) to Iddesleigh, No. 459 Secret, 23 Nov. 1886, F.O. 7/1097.   [7] *G.P.* v, No. 1008.

THE FIRST MEDITERRANEAN AGREEMENT 65

wise to advertise the fact, especially in Bulgaria.[1] In these circumstances Kalnoky had no desire to rush into a policy of active opposition to Russia, and the Anglo-Austrian negotiations reached a deadlock. 'Austria waits on England and England upon Austria', Dilke commented. 'Austria declares that she would be delighted to take the first step, if Lord Salisbury will begin by taking the second.'[2] 'We seem to be in the position of the uncles and nieces in the "Critic", and how we are to be got out of it I don't see', Iddesleigh complained to White. 'We are keeping quiet; Russia is apparently keeping quiet also; Austria has one solution ... Italy has another ... Germany does not seem disposed to do anything; and France still less so.'[3]

White's views about Austria-Hungary were in keeping with the conclusions reached by Iddesleigh and Salisbury. Both his private and official correspondence shows that he was a warm advocate of an Anglo-Austrian understanding; that he was kept fully informed of the progress of the negotiations; and that he was constantly consulted by his superiors. Moreover, the exasperation of the Foreign Office at the Austro-Hungarian government's continued adherence to an 'attitude of observation' was paralleled by White's growing conviction that Austro-Hungarian influence on the Bosphorus was negligible: 'It is surprising to hear the low opinion the Turks in office have of Austria', he observed to Iddesleigh towards the end of November.[4] And, a month later, he remarked to the same correspondent:

> Nothing can be more striking in the diplomacy carried on at Stamboul than the entire disappearance of Austrian influence with the Turks. Twelve months ago, it was an important factor of the Alliance of the Three Emperors, and its voice was heard and listened to on the Bosphorus—but this is no longer the case. The Turks quickly observed that the Austrian Ambassador had no longer the support of

---

[1] Medlicott, pp. 69–70.
[2] Sir C. Dilke, *The Present Position of European Politics*, p. 23.
[3] Iddesleigh to White, Private, 2 Dec. 1886, F.O. 364/1; cf. R. B. Sheridan, *The Critic; or a Tragedy Rehearsed*, Act III, Scene i: 'There's a situation for you! there's a heroic group! You see the ladies can't stab Whiskerandos—he durst not strike them for fear of their uncles—the uncles durst not kill him because of their nieces. I have them all at a dead lock!—for every one of them is afraid to let go first.'
[4] White to Iddesleigh, Private, 20 Nov. 1886, F.O. 364/1.

his German colleague whenever he happened to be at variance with his Russian one. . . . Austria is, in fact, mistrusted even more than we are at the Palace of Yildiz and she is less feared.¹

Even before it became obvious that the Anglo-Austrian negotiations were bound to end in a deadlock, increasing concern in London about the Egyptian question had turned the British government's attention from Austria-Hungary to Italy. Italy, being a naval rather than a territorial Power, might prove to be more useful to Great Britain in the Near East than Austria-Hungary, and she might also be more amenable to British approaches for an understanding. In 1882 Gladstone had failed to persuade the Italians to co-operate with Great Britain in a joint Egyptian policy, but in the same year they had given her tangible proof of their goodwill by entering the Triple Alliance only on condition that none of the provisions of the treaty should be directed against Great Britain.²

The First Mediterranean Agreement sprang from the negotiations opened in November 1886 between Salisbury and Corti, the Italian ambassador in London, and these in turn were the outcome of the failure of the British government to come to an understanding with Austria-Hungary, and the increase of French hostility to the position of Great Britain in Egypt. The British and Italian governments finally reached an understanding on 12 February 1887; on 24 March it was extended to include the Austro-Hungarian government, and on 2 May the Italian and Spanish governments came to a separate agreement. The fundamental principle involved in these arrangements was the preservation of the *status quo* in the Mediterranean, Adriatic, and Black seas, while more specifically, in the Anglo-Italian agreement, Italy offered to support British policy in Egypt in return for a British promise to support Italian policy in North Africa.³

Like his superiors, White became increasingly perturbed as the Egyptian problem underwent one of its sporadic trans-

[1] White to Iddesleigh, No. 654 Secret, 27 Dec. 1886, F.O. 78/3877.
[2] Cf. Medlicott, pp. 70–71; H. W. V. Temperley and L. M. Penson, *Foundations of British Foreign Policy (1792–1902)*, p. 446; A. F. Pribram, *The Secret Treaties of Austria-Hungary*, pp. 35–38.
[3] Medlicott, pp. 71–72; Temperley and Penson, pp. 446–8; G. P. Gooch and H. Temperley, *British Documents on the Origins of the War, 1898–1914*, viii. 3–4, 6–7.

THE FIRST MEDITERRANEAN AGREEMENT 67

formations from being an African into being a European question; he soon became aware that Montebello, the new French ambassador at the Porte, was Nelidov's most active supporter, and that the Egyptian question was the most useful instrument at hand for the exertion of their joint pressure upon Great Britain at Constantinople.[1] Yet he does not appear to have taken any great interest in his government's overtures to Italy—overtures which were the direct result of Great Britain's failure to reach an understanding with Austria-Hungary, and of her growing embarrassments in Egypt. In fact, White was only on the fringe of the negotiations which led to the conclusion of the First Mediterranean Agreement: the official correspondence of the Foreign Office shows that none of the important documents dealing with those negotiations was forwarded to Constantinople, and Salisbury's private letters reveal that White was first informed of the existence of the agreement late in April 1887.[2] Instead of looking to Italy for support, White seems to have returned to the views which he had held immediately after his interviews with Bismarck at Bad Gastein, and to have based his main hopes upon ultimately securing the assistance of Germany at Constantinople. However, his attitude differed from that of the Foreign Office in emphasis rather than aim, for their common object was to ensure that Great Britain was not forced to shoulder the burdens of the Near East while the other interested Powers looked on.

Bismarck had always been anxious to prevent his Austro-Hungarian ally from being drawn into groupings which were hostile to Russia, but at the beginning of 1887 he found it necessary to encourage Great Britain to co-operate with Austria-Hungary and Italy in order to secure the renewal of the Triple Alliance between the two Central Empires and Italy. The British approaches to Austria-Hungary and Italy in the autumn and winter of 1886 prove that Bismarck was not the creator of the original desire for a new Mediterranean

[1] Iddesleigh to White, Confidential, 21 Oct. 1886, F.O. 364/1.
[2] Salisbury to White, Private and Secret, 20 Apr. 1887, Additional White Papers; cf. Salisbury to Lumley, No. 99 Secret, 29 Mar. 1887, F.O. 45/572 (the Foreign Office minutes on the copy of this dispatch reveal that copies of the notes exchanged between Salisbury and Karolyi, the Austro-Hungarian ambassador at London, were sent to Vienna, Rome, Berlin, and Paris, but not to Constantinople).

alignment. Nevertheless, he was mainly responsible for the impetus given to the later negotiations and for the devising of the final grouping.[1] Indeed, he pressed for the conclusion of the First Mediterranean Agreement far more eagerly than Salisbury. Before the exchange of notes between the governments concerned, Salisbury kept insisting that a parliamentary government such as Great Britain could not enter into engagements which were binding in the Bismarckian sense, and, after the agreement had been concluded, he took care to stress that the question of material co-operation had been carefully avoided.[2] Bismarck, on the other hand, was anxious to extend the agreement, and during April he even suggested that Turkey should be admitted into it. But Salisbury refused to entertain this proposal: he knew that the Turks found it difficult to keep a secret, and was puzzled by the enthusiasm of the German government for the new grouping.[3] 'These agreements', he confided to White, 'have been adopted to a great extent by the advice of Germany which has evidently attached a very great—and to my eyes inexplicable—importance to them.'[4]

Towards the end of 1886 Bismarck's position in Europe became increasingly uncomfortable. The Three Emperors' Alliance was crumbling under the pressure of crises both in the East and West: the second Bulgarian crisis made Russia a difficult friend at a time when a revived desire for *revanche* turned France into an imminent foe. 'The only object of Prince Bismarck's friendliness towards Russia', Malet commented to Iddesleigh, early in November, 'is to prevent her from becoming an enemy; but if he has to choose between Austria and Russia there can be no doubt where his choice would lie.'[5] A week later he suggested that the Three Emperors' Alliance had become 'a mere fiction',[6] and by the end of the month he was convinced that 'Germany had somewhat

[1] Cf. Medlicott, pp. 75–76.
[2] *G.P.* iv, Nos. 880–1, 894; Lady G. Cecil, *Life of Robert, Marquis of Salisbury*, iv. 20–24.
[3] Salisbury to White, Tel. No. 67 Most Secret, 19 Apr. F.O. 78/4002; Private and Secret, 20 Apr. 1887, Additional White Papers; H. Trützschler von Falkenstein, *Bismarck und die Kriegsgefahr des Jahres 1887*, p. 88.
[4] Salisbury to White, Private and Secret, 20 Apr. 1887, Additional White Papers.
[5] Malet to Iddesleigh, Private, 6 Nov. 1886, F.O. 343/8.
[6] Malet to Iddesleigh, Private, 13 Nov. 1886, F.O. 343/8.

lost its position at the helm'.¹ In France the rise of Boulanger was a spectacular symptom of the resurgence of a desire to settle old scores with Germany. There could be no return even to the limited Franco-German *entente* of the early eighties, and the change in Franco-German relations which had begun with the fall of Ferry in March 1885 threatened to run its full course and end in a war between the two countries.² Meanwhile in Russia Giers found it difficult to pursue a pro-German policy in the face of stiff opposition from Katkov and the Russian nationalists. Although Katkov himself simply urged that Russian foreign policy should be emancipated from subservience to German wishes, other Russian publicists eagerly borrowed from his arguments and extended them to include pleas for a definite understanding between Russia and France.³ Indeed, the Tsar's reception of Laboulaye at St. Petersburg, in November 1886, after a period of over nine months during which there had been no French ambassador at the Russian Court,⁴ and the failure of the negotiations between Herbert Bismarck and Paul Shuvalov for a Russo-German Alliance, in the following January,⁵ seemed to indicate that Russia might abandon her connexion with Germany in favour of some agreement with France.

Austro-Russian relations had also deteriorated under the continued strain of the Bulgarian crisis. Kalnoky, although far less Russophobe in his utterances than Andrassy and the Hungarian opposition, announced to the delegations on 13 November that even a temporary single-handed occupation of Bulgaria by foreign troops, or any attempt to interfere with Bulgarian self-government, would not be tolerated by his government.⁶ But until as late as December 1886, Great Britain still seems to have been the main enemy as far as Russia was concerned.⁷ Yet as early as October 1886 Paul Shuvalov, the Russian ambassador at Berlin, had vehemently

---
[1] Malet to Iddesleigh, Private, 27 Nov. 1886, F.O. 343/8.
[2] W. L. Langer, *European Alliances and Alignments, 1871–1890*, pp. 378–85.
[3] B. Nolde, *L'Alliance franco-russe*, pp. 380–8; I. Grüning, *Die russische öffentliche Meinung und ihre Stellung zu den Grossmächten, 1878–1894*, p. 44.
[4] *D.D.F.*, 1st ser., vi, No. 362; Nolde, pp. 388–96.
[5] Langer, pp. 386–7.
[6] J. V. Fuller, *Bismarck's Diplomacy at its Zenith*, pp. 108–9; Langer, p. 369.
[7] A. Meyendorff, *Correspondance diplomatique de M. de Staal*, i. 325–7 (Giers to Boutenev (Russian chargé d'affaires at London), 19/28 Nov.; 19/31 Dec. 1886).

attacked the Austro-Hungarian government, and when his tongue had been loosened by alcohol, he had even suggested that Russia and Germany should combine and make Austria-Hungary vanish from the map of Europe.[1] It is not surprising, therefore, that Bismarck summed up his position in regard to his Austro-Hungarian and Russian allies by comparing himself to a man standing between two vicious dogs which were ready to fly at each other directly they were unleashed.[2]

Nor were Bismarck's difficulties confined to external affairs. His fears of French military preparations—partly genuine and partly manufactured—caused him to bring a new Army Bill before the Reichstag on 25 November. But that Bill, which raised the numbers in the German army from 427,000 to 468,000 men, was not passed until 11 March 1887, and then only as a result of dissolving the Reichstag and making dangerous use of a 'war in sight' scare in order to drum up support in the ensuing election campaign.[3]

Moreover, there were divided counsels about the conduct of foreign affairs both at the Court and at the Wilhelmstrasse. In contrast to Bismarck, who did not intend to be hurried into abandoning his position as mediator between his two great neighbours in the East, Radolinsky, the Court Marshal, and Holstein, who was growing more and more influential as an adviser at the German Foreign Office, were scheming to implement a policy which would encourage Austria-Hungary to resist Russia and take a more active and decisive part in the Bulgarian question. Explaining this *nebenzimmerpolitik* to the Austro-Hungarians towards the end of 1886, Radolinsky wrote:

It is true that topsy-turvydom prevails completely in our ambassadorial palace in Constantinople, but they are not satisfied here with Radowitz and he has received repeated reprimands. They ought to seize the initiative, work with White and bring the Sultan round to their side. Should that happen we shall not leave you in the lurch. Yet we wish you to seek and find allies. Your most natural and most necessary ally would be Turkey, and then would come Italy.... As far as England is concerned, it is conceivable that with its changes of government one

---

[1] *G.P.* v, No. 989 (Memorandum by Count Herbert Bismarck, Berlin, 17 Oct. 1886).
[2] L. von Ballhausen, *Bismarck-Erinnerungen*, p. 359; cf. Langer, pp. 369–70.
[3] Ibid., pp. 379–83.

does not believe the same can be relied upon, nevertheless you can be assured that at the first shot fired on your part in the Balkan peninsula the British fleet will enter the Bosphorus.[1]

Meanwhile, at a conference held at the Wilhelmstrasse in the early autumn of 1886, Holstein had suggested that the press might 'arouse' Great Britain: it should be pointed out to her that she could not afford to let Russia become master on the Bosphorus, and that even if she were to annex Egypt —as had been proposed in certain quarters—it would not be a sufficient compensation for the loss of Constantinople.[2] Holstein's ideas were soon put into practice. At the end of October Malet reported that Mr. Bashford, the Berlin correspondent of the *Daily Telegraph*, was frequently being supplied with 'information' from the German Foreign Office: he had recently been told that 'any step which the British Government might take in the Mediterranean would encounter no opposition from the German Government'; he had been assured that this meant 'not only Egypt, which was of course included, but anything else'; and when he had inquired if he was to be allowed to publish this news, he had been informed that he could do so 'provided it did not appear in the "Telegraph" as emanating from Berlin'.[3] Commenting to Salisbury upon this connexion between Bashford and the German Foreign Office, Malet wrote:

It should be mentioned that Mr. Bashford, when he receives confidentially information is specially cautioned never to allow it to appear in the 'Daily Telegraph' as coming from Berlin. It is generally therefore to be found in the guise of a letter from an outside correspondent not on the staff of the paper, or else as emanating from any other capital in Europe than Berlin.[4]

These remarks were made on 14 January 1887. On the following day the *Daily Telegraph* published a letter to its editor signed 'Diplomatist' and dated 'Constantinople, 8 January'. The writer claimed that Russia had no intention of occupying Bulgaria for the time being, but that she was aiming to make for the Straits instead; he therefore urged that Turkey

[1] H. Krausnick, *Holsteins Geheimpolitik in der Ära Bismarck, 1886–1890*, pp. 105–6.
[2] Ibid., p. 56.
[3] Malet to Iddesleigh, Private, 30 Oct. 1886, F.O. 343/8.
[4] Malet to Salisbury, No. 10 Secret, 14 Jan. 1887, F.O. 64/1155.

—and presumably Great Britain—should make haste and see that the northern approaches to the Bosphorus were strengthened. These arguments bore a striking resemblance to those used by Count Waldersee, the Quarter-Master General of the German army, in a conversation which he had with Colonel Swaine, the British military attaché at Berlin, on 28 December 1886. After making vague hints that Russia's peaceful intentions were not to be relied upon, Waldersee suddenly became more specific and asked Swaine to remind the British military attaché at Constantinople of the fact that the Turks needed to fortify the northern end of the Bosphorus where a landing of troops could easily be effected.[1]

White derived great satisfaction from all these signs of German willingness to support his government in the Near East. He agreed with Malet that there was 'strong internal evidence' that the 'Diplomatist' letter had been written by 'a person inspired in some high quarters in Berlin',[2] and after reading a confidential account of Waldersee's conversation with Swaine, he was struck by the sudden and encouraging change in the attitude of Germany and her Austro-Hungarian ally towards the Straits problem: in the spring of 1885 those two Powers had urged the Sultan to arm himself with Krupp guns of the heaviest calibre and guard the defences of the Dardanelles against the British fleet; but within less than two years they were secretly exhorting him to strengthen the fortifications of the Bosphorus so as to make an invasion by a Russian army impossible.[3] In March 1887 Austria-Hungary made her position clear by adhering to the Mediterranean Agreement between Great Britain and Italy, but White still felt the need of some more tangible proof of the goodwill of her more powerful German partner.

Meanwhile, in spite of the fact that the Bulgarian throne was still vacant, Anglo-Russian relations about the Bulgarian question had markedly improved by the beginning of 1887. On 18 January Salisbury assured Boutenev, the Russian

[1] Malet to Iddesleigh, No. 523 Confidential, 31 Dec. 1886, F.O. 64/1119 (encloses Memorandum by Swaine giving an account of his conversation with Waldersee on 28 Dec.).

[2] White to Salisbury, No. 49 Secret, 5 Feb. 1887, F.O. 78/3996.

[3] Memorandum by White dated 5 Feb. 1887 and marked 'Very Secret', F.O. 78/3996.

chargé d'affaires at London, that the British government no longer looked upon the Bulgarian question as being 'en première ligne de compte'.[1] Four days later he informed White that he was 'very anxious for the adjustment of the controversy in the Balkan Peninsula', and laid down three points as the basis of his policy towards Bulgaria: the British government was to act in accordance with the Berlin Treaty, to take the wishes of the Bulgarian people into consideration, and to respect the legitimate desires of Russia.[2] No mention was made of how each of these three principles was to be reconciled with the other two. Indeed, the very vagueness of Salisbury's formula gave it an air of conciliation, and once it had been laid down the Bulgarian problem temporarily receded into the background of European politics.[3]

But this did not leave White idle, for during the spring and summer of 1887 the problem of Egypt came to the fore. Since August 1885, when Sir Henry Drummond Wolff had been appointed 'Envoy Extraordinary and Minister Plenipotentiary to the Sultan of Turkey, on a Special Mission with reference to the affairs of Egypt', the British government had been trying to reduce the heavy burden of its commitments in the Near East by coming to an agreement with the Turks about the evacuation of Egypt. The advantages of such a policy were obvious: relations with both Turkey and France would be improved, and at the same time both Russia and the Central Powers would be deprived of a diplomatic stick most ready to their hands. But there could be no question of withdrawing British troops until Egypt's finances had become solvent, her administration efficient, and her frontiers undisturbed. Moreover, Great Britain would have to be assured that her own strategic and imperial interests would be safeguarded after the evacuation. But none of these conditions could be fulfilled unless she were free from international interference while her control lasted, and at liberty to determine the date and the terms of her eventual withdrawal.[4]

[1] A. Meyendorff, *Correspondance diplomatique de M. de Staal*, i. 336–7 (Boutenev to Giers, 6/18 Jan. 1887).
[2] Salisbury to White, Tel. No. 11, 22 Jan. 1887, F.O. 364/4.
[3] Temperley and Penson, p. 445.
[4] For full and recent accounts of the Wolff Mission see M. P. Hornik, 'The

As a result of patient bargaining both at Cairo and at Constantinople, Sir Henry Drummond Wolff finally concluded a convention with the Porte on 22 May 1887. The convention upheld the Imperial Ottoman firmans which governed the relationship between the Egyptian government and its Turkish suzerain, and confirmed those which defined the territory of Egypt. It also declared that the Great Powers should recognize the neutrality of the Suez Canal, and the right of free passage in war and peace. But the articles which dealt with Great Britain's position in Egypt were the most significant. Article IV conferred a *droit de surveillance* upon Great Britain, and stipulated that she should maintain in Egypt sufficient military strength to keep order. Article V was even more important. The first clause stated that British troops would be withdrawn from Egypt 'at the expiration of three years from the date of the present Convention', but it was followed by another clause which laid down that such a withdrawal would not take place at the end of the agreed period if there were any 'appearance of danger in the interior or from without'. There was no mention of who was to decide whether the internal or external danger was sufficient to justify the retention of the British garrison in Egypt, but the very absence of any specific provision implied that the British government would be the judge in such circumstances. In addition, Article V gave both the British and the Turkish governments the right to re-occupy Egypt if, at any time after the evacuation, 'order and security in the interior were disturbed, or if the Khedivate of Egypt refused to execute its duties towards the Sovereign Court, or its international obligations'. It also provided that if, 'by reason of hindrances', the Sultan did not avail himself of the right to reoccupy, the British government would be entitled to take independent military action, and the Sultan would be allowed to send a commissioner to remain in Egypt 'during the period of the sojourn of the British troops with their commander'. After the withdrawal of the British garrison, Egypt was to be neutralized, and the Great Powers were to be invited to guaran-

---

Special Mission of Sir Henry Drummond Wolff to Constantinople 1885–1887', E.H.R. v. 598–623; D. C. Weeks, *The Egyptian Question in British Foreign Policy with special reference to 1885–1887*, typescript thesis (Ph.D. (London), 1952).

tee her territorial integrity. An annexe was enclosed containing minor instructions, and Article VI stipulated that, after ratification by Great Britain and Turkey, both documents should be submitted to the Mediterranean Powers for their consent.[1]

Ever since the autumn of 1886, when he had returned to Constantinople as a full ambassador, White's main aim had been the achievement of closer co-operation between Great Britain and the Triple Alliance Powers throughout the Near East. Although these Powers seemed willing to give the British government their secret support at that capital, he considered that a more obvious display of their readiness to co-operate was needed. The deadlock in the Balkans convinced him that Germany and Austria-Hungary were too closely tied to Russia to take the initiative in giving any anti-Russian advice concerning Bulgaria, and he therefore suggested to Iddesleigh that they should be asked to prove the sincerity of their expressions of goodwill by supporting British policy in Egypt.[2] If a start could be made in Egypt, co-operation in other areas of the Near East might follow, and his 'grand design' would then be accomplished.

The support which Wolff had received from the German and Austro-Hungarian ambassadors at Constantinople during the spring of 1887 made White believe that Bismarck's attitude towards his government had undergone a radical change,[3] and the successful signing of the Anglo-Turkish Convention in the early summer convinced him that in future Great Britain, not Russia, was to enjoy the favour of German support on the Bosphorus:

On this point the policy of the Courts of Berlin and Vienna has undergone a complete *vice-versa* at Constantinople from what it was in the spring of 1885 when I was sent here by Lord Granville. At that time their Ambassadors went out of their way to support M. de Nelidov against us. It was quite amusing now to observe M. de Radowitz under stringent injunctions from his Chief working against his bosom friend

---

[1] *A. & P.*, Egypt No. 7 (1887), xcii [C-5050], 534-45; cf. also Hornik, pp. 615-16; the Earl of Cromer, *Modern Egypt*, ii. 374-7.

[2] White to Iddesleigh, Private, 2 Nov. 1886, F.O. 364/1.

[3] White to Salisbury, Tel. Private and Very Secret, 16 Mar. 1887, F.O. 78/4002 (minuted by Salisbury): 'Circulate but do not print. Care must be taken to keep this Secret.'

on the Egyptian question, and dreading all the time lest the discomfiture of his friend and colleague might lead to his recall from here. . . .[1]

White felt that at last the 'Cinderella days' of his isolation at the Porte were over.

However, Bismarck's support of British policy in Egypt had caused some uneasiness at the Foreign Office. During the course of the negotiations for the First Mediterranean Agreement, Malet confided to Salisbury: 'I do not think that Prince Bismarck has the least intention of backing out of his engagements towards us with regard to Egypt. . . . All his civilities to us . . . are designed to effect combinations in which France is left out.'[2] Salisbury replied that he had similar fears, but he was determined neither to allow the French to force him out of Egypt, nor to let Bismarck drag him into a quarrel with France.[3] His assistant under-secretary shared these suspicions, and Wolff's announcement that Radowitz had eagerly offered to support him at Constantinople prompted Sanderson to comment: 'The Germans have scented the possibility of too good an understanding between us and the French.'[4]

The 'Holmwood Incident' added to this general distrust of German intentions. On 28 April Radowitz suddenly announced that he had been instructed to maintain 'the greatest reserve' regarding Egypt since Bismarck had noticed that the British government was creating difficulties for Germany in Zanzibar.[5] The conduct of Consul Holmwood had irritated Bismarck, and without any warning he made his continued support in Egypt dependent upon the settlement of this petty grievance. Salisbury had always understood that the help which he received from Germany in Egyptian affairs was largely governed by the willingness of the British government to be accommodating in colonial disputes. Yet he was shocked at the 'monstrousness' of this particular demand,

---

[1] White to Salisbury, Private and Confidential, 31 May 1887, F.O. 364/1.
[2] Malet to Salisbury, Private, 19 Feb. 1887, F.O. 343/8.
[3] Salisbury to Malet, 23 Feb. 1887 (printed in Lady G. Cecil, *Life of Robert, Marquis of Salisbury*, iv. 40–41).
[4] Wolff to Salisbury, Tel. No. 26 Confidential, 4 Mar. 1887, F.O. 78/4060 (with minute in T. H. Sanderson's handwriting).
[5] Wolff to Salisbury, No. 77 Secret and Confidential, 29 Apr. 1887, F.O. 78/4059; cf. *G.P.* iv, Nos. 809–16.

THE FIRST MEDITERRANEAN AGREEMENT 77

and annoyed at his own helplessness to resist Bismarck's personal whims.[1] Once Holmwood had been removed from his post at Zanzibar, German support was restored as rapidly as it had been withdrawn. The whole incident was over in a week, but it had conjured up fears and suspicions which could not be so hastily dispelled.[2]

Salisbury had been forced to pay a high price for German assistance, but its value was not fully tested until Nelidov and Montebello opened their attack upon the Wolff Convention. In spite of assurances from Berlin that Germany would continue to aid Great Britain in her Egyptian policy,[3] there was a growing suspicion at Constantinople that the measures taken by Radowitz to induce the Sultan to ratify the convention were less forceful than those adopted by his Austro-Hungarian and Italian colleagues.[4]

The sudden and unexpected violence of the Russian onslaught against the convention had seriously compromised Bismarck's position. To put an end to Salisbury's hesitation about entering into a Mediterranean *entente*, he had held out the inducement of German support for British policy in Egypt, but at the same time he had been conducting negotiations with Shuvalov at Berlin which demanded that Germany should not take up a stand which was opposed to Russia.[5] The secret Re-insurance Treaty between Germany and Russia was signed on 18 June 1887. In an 'additional and very secret protocol' to the treaty, Germany gave Russia two promises: first, she would assist her 'to establish a regular and legal Government in Bulgaria'—the restoration of Prince Alexander of Battenberg being expressly excluded—and, secondly, she would give her 'benevolent neutrality' and

[1] Salisbury to Scott (chargé d'affaires at Berlin), 4 May 1887 (printed in Cecil, iv. 43).
[2] Ibid., pp. 42–44; Wolff to Salisbury, No. 83 Secret and Confidential, 5 May, F.O. 78/4059; Malet to Salisbury, Private, 7 May 1887, F.O. 343/8; *G.P.* iv, Nos. 811–16.
[3] Malet to Salisbury, No. 207 Confidential, 7 June; No. 216 Confidential, 11 June, F.O. 64/1157; Tel. No. 31 Confidential, 14 June, F.O. 64/1161; Private, 25 June 1887, F.O. 343/8.
[4] Wolff to Salisbury, No. 103, 11 June, F.O. 78/4059; Tel. No. 139 Urgent, Secret and Confidential, 15 June; Tel. No. 147 Most Secret and Confidential, 23 June; Salisbury to Wolff, Tel. No. 93 Secret, 25 June 1887, F.O. 78/4060.
[5] S. Gorianov, 'The End of the Alliance of the Emperors', *American Historical Review*, xxiii. 324–50; J. V. Fuller, *Bismarck's Diplomacy at its Zenith*, pp. 185–204.

'moral and diplomatic support' to Russia should the Tsar 'find himself under the necessity of assuming the task of defending the entrance of the Black Sea in order to safeguard the interests of Russia'.[1] It was this second undertaking which complicated the German position in regard to Egypt. Although the discussions between the German and Russian governments had been in progress since January 1887, there had been no signs that Russia would take any serious action in the Egyptian question until the signature of the Anglo-Turkish Convention on 22 May. Nelidov suddenly launched his attack upon the Convention at a time when the Russo-German negotiations were reaching their close at Berlin, and Bismarck was therefore unwilling to oppose Russian wishes too strongly. Thus when she most urgently needed German assistance at Constantinople, Great Britain found it half-hearted. Indeed, that lack of German support played as important a part as the Franco-Russian opposition in wrecking the Wolff Convention.

The failure of the Wolff Convention is an important landmark in the history of the Near Eastern question. The Franco-Russian opposition to its terms has been regarded as a significant step towards the formation of the Franco-Russian Alliance of 1891–4,[2] and it has also been claimed that Salisbury's project for a Turkish partition in 1895 can be traced from the disappointments of these negotiations with Turkey between 1885 and 1887.[3] But there is no need to look so far ahead in order to discover its most direct and most important result. Its immediate effect was neither a Franco-Russian *rapprochement*, nor a Salisburian partition scheme, but the beginning of those attempts to bind Germany closer to the Mediterranean *entente* which resulted in the Second Mediterranean Agreement of December 1887.

The empty but spectacular success of the French and Russian ambassadors at the Porte had made the Italian government keenly suspicious of French designs in the

---

[1] A. F. Pribram, *The Secret Treaties of Austria-Hungary*, i. 278–81.
[2] Cf. W. L. Langer, *The Franco-Russian Alliance, 1890–1894*, pp. 92–94; *European Alliances and Alignments*, pp. 428–9; M. P. Hornik, 'The Special Mission of Sir Henry Drummond Wolff to Constantinople, 1886–1887', *E.H.R.* lv (Oct. 1940), 599.
[3] Hornik, pp. 622–3.

Mediterranean.¹ Baron Blanc, the Italian ambassador at Constantinople, noticed that since the signing of the Convention, the Egyptian question had retired into the background, and that much wider issues, which involved the balance of power throughout the Mediterranean, had come to dominate the scene. As long as the discussion with the Porte had been purely Egyptian, Bismarck had actively supported the negotiations in the hope that the Anglo-Turkish Convention would become the pivot of a Mediterranean combination on which Germany might count in case of need. But when the Convention had been signed and the Sultan refused to ratify, the pivot had failed, and the struggle became no longer one of Egyptian organization but of the respective strength of the Powers in the Mediterranean. Until Bismarck felt that he could rely upon the co-operation of a powerful Mediterranean grouping, it would be impossible for him to place any further strain upon his relations with Russia and France by challenging their opposition to the Convention. Blanc therefore suggested that Great Britain should make the Convention the basis of an immediate arrangement between herself and the Mediterranean Powers. Austria-Hungary, Italy, and Spain should be invited to give their formal adhesion to the arrangement, and once this had been accomplished, he felt sure that Germany would also join. A combined invitation would then be extended to Turkey, but her refusal to accept the offer should not be allowed to prevent the interested Powers from preparing a general scheme for the future administration of Egypt. Either during the preparation of this scheme, or after it had been drawn up, France would also be asked to co-operate. The Italian ambassador was convinced that such a previous understanding between the Mediterranean Powers, less France, would inspire German confidence and guarantee German co-operation long after the completion of the new arrangements for Egypt.² Blanc's proposals for the solution of the Egyptian question were ignored

---

[1] White to Salisbury, Private and Confidential, 16 July 1887, F.O. 364/1; D.D.F., 1st ser., vi bis, No. 49 (Moüy to Flourens, Rome, 9 July 1887).

[2] Wolff to Salisbury, No. 113 Most Secret and Confidential, 12 July, F.O. 78/4059 (seen by the Queen, printed for the Cabinet, and copies sent to embassies at Berlin, Rome, and Vienna); White to Salisbury, Private and Confidential, 16 July 1887, F.O. 364/1.

at the Foreign Office: for the past two years the British government had been struggling to free Egypt from international fetters, and it had no wish to extend an eleventh-hour welcome to a scheme which envisaged further interference by the Powers. But the rejection of this specific project did not detract from the wider importance of Blanc's 'July Memorandum'—here in embryo were suggestions which were to serve as the basis for the Second Mediterranean Agreement. Thus the 'December Agreements' were born in Egypt, not Bulgaria: the crisis which resulted from Prince Ferdinand of Saxe-Coburg's acceptance of the Bulgarian throne merely crystallized ideas that owed their origin to the failure of the Wolff Mission.[1]

White's reaction to the defeat of the Wolff Convention provides the main clue for the understanding of his general attitude towards the problem of Egypt. According to one anecdote, he was so elated by the failure of the negotiations that he playfully informed Nelidov and Montebello that he had asked his government to reward them both for their services with the Grand Cross of the Bath.[2] But an examination of his correspondence with the Foreign Office reveals that he had fears which were not in keeping with this outward expression of joy. 'It must be borne in mind that it is not this Convention alone, but our future relations with Turkey and our influence in the East that are at stake', he impressed upon Salisbury soon after Nelidov and Montebello had launched their joint attack. 'The ratification of the Convention previous to its reference to the Powers will it is hoped be insisted upon', he concluded.[3] Yet as it became evident that the struggle was hopeless, he consoled himself—as Blanc had done—with the thought that the violent opposition to the Convention might benefit British interests in the long run—'we shall continue to have German and Italian support as long as French opposition takes this form'.[4] But unlike his

---

[1] But cf. W. N. Medlicott, 'The Mediterranean Agreements of 1887', *Slavonic Review*, v. 76; H. W. V. Temperley and L. M. Penson, *Foundations of British Foreign Policy (1792–1902)*, p. 455. Both these authorities state that these ideas first arose in August, and that they were inspired by the need to meet the new situation in Bulgaria. [2] Sir V. Chirol, *Fifty Years in a Changing World*, p. 37.
[3] White to Salisbury, Tel. No. 50 Very Secret, 3 June 1887, F.O. 78/4002.
[4] White to Salisbury, No. 232 Secret, 12 July 1887, F.O. 78/3999.

Italian colleague, he was against the employment of any more forceful measures to impose an Egyptian settlement upon the Sultan. Once it became obvious that a friendly understanding between Great Britain and Turkey was impossible, he urged that there should be no attempt to renew the negotiations at the Porte and the Palace.[1]

White had no interest in the Egyptian question *per se*. He always thought of it in terms of its likely effect upon his influence at Constantinople. The success of the Anglo-Turkish Convention would have greatly enhanced his position at the Porte, and he therefore gave it his loyal support as long as there was the faintest chance of it being ratified. But once it became apparent that it was certain to fail, he hastily reverted to his former policy of cutting himself adrift from the Egyptian negotiations and attempting to avoid the humiliation which would result from too close a connexion with their failure. His approach to the Egyptian problem may have been parochial, but it becomes easy to understand when it is remembered that he, more than anyone else, had to bear the brunt of the Sultan's long rancour.

On 16 July Wolff left Constantinople in a 'sadly dejected mood', but this fit of depression had deserted him by the time he reached Paris—'where Lord Lyons had warmed him up with a good dinner'.[2] At the Foreign Office his success in persuading the Sultan even to sign the convention was regarded as a 'tour de force diplomatique'.[3] He could at least congratulate himself for a brave attempt to reconcile the irreconcilable. At Cairo Baring soon realized that the year 1887 was an important turning-point in the history of Great Britain in Egypt. 'The Wolff negotiations had one great advantage', he reflected some time after their failure, 'that they gave us a fair case for declining to negotiate again—for the time being at all events.' The removal of this main cause of uncertainty as regards Egypt's future, combined with the improvement of her finances and the consolidation of her Sudan frontier, enabled him to broaden the scope of his

[1] White to Salisbury, No. 240 Very Secret, 19 July 1887, F.O. 78/3999.
[2] Fane (First Secretary at Constantinople) to Bunsen, Private, 29 July 1887 (printed in E. T. S. Dugdale, *Maurice de Bunsen. Diplomat and Friend*, p. 73).
[3] Salisbury to Wolff, No. 64, 22 July 1887, F.O. 78/4057 (draft copy minuted by Salisbury and Pauncefote).

reforms.[1] Meanwhile, Great Britain as a whole was yielding to the dictates of the acquisitional feeling: in 1885 few had opposed the idea of an early evacuation from Egypt, but by 1887 the clamour for the withdrawal of British troops was beginning to die down. In the eyes of the British public, Egypt was fast becoming a second India; to British officials it offered the attractive challenge of a complicated administrative problem; and to Salisbury, who was losing faith in Great Britain's ability to close the Straits in the event of a war with Russia, Egypt was beginning to assume a new strategical importance.[2]

[1] The Marquess of Zetland, *Lord Cromer*, pp. 155, 179.
[2] Salisbury to White, 10 Aug. 1887 (printed in Cecil, iv. 50–51); Sir A. Milner, *England in Egypt*, pp. 429–44; Zetland, pp. 145–57.

IV

THE SECOND MEDITERRANEAN AGREEMENT
(*December* 1887)

BY August 1887 Egypt had ceased to be a European problem, and White suddenly found himself free from the burden of continuing the negotiations for an Anglo-Turkish Convention. But this temporary respite from Egyptian complications did not leave him idle, for there were other questions which were causing increasing concern at Constantinople: in the West, the growing strength of the Boulangist movement in France was accompanied by a corresponding increase in Franco-German hostility; in the Balkans, the latest turn of events in Bulgaria was an equal menace to the peace of Europe; and farther east, there remained the perennial threat that Turkish misrule in Asia Minor might provide an excuse for a Russian *coup de main* against Constantinople by way of Asiatic Turkey. During the first half of 1887 White had been preoccupied with the Egyptian question and the struggle to ratify the Drummond Wolff Convention, but during the second half of that year he was to focus his attention upon the Bulgarian question, the danger of a Russian invasion of Asia Minor, and the negotiations for the Second Mediterranean Agreement.

The final phase of the Drummond Wolff negotiations coincided with the outbreak of yet another Bulgarian crisis. On 7 July the Bulgarian assembly, weary of Russian intrigues to set up a new regency under General Errnroth, asserted its independence by formally electing Prince Ferdinand of Saxe-Coburg-Kohary to the throne which had stood vacant since the abdication of Prince Alexander nine months earlier. In spite of the disapproval of both Bismarck and the Tsar, Prince Ferdinand accepted the throne, and on 22 August he was on Bulgarian soil.[1]

Although these new developments in Bulgaria soon

---

[1] J. V. Fuller, *Bismarck's Diplomacy at its Zenith*, pp. 205–24; W. L. Langer, *European Alliances and Alignments*, pp. 426–8.

overshadowed the Egyptian conflict, they did not lessen the effects of that earlier struggle upon White's influence at Constantinople. Indeed, they accentuated those very weaknesses which had been exposed during the Egyptian negotiations, and emphasized the need for their quick repair. Yet White's greatest and most immediate fear was not realized. The violent impact of the opposition to the Wolff Convention had convinced him that a Franco-Russian alliance was in the offing; like many of his contemporaries, he had mistaken the personal co-operation between Montebello and Nelidov for a close understanding between Paris and St. Petersburg.[1] But there was no further evidence of the two governments drawing closer together: the informal partnership between the two ambassadors at Constantinople did not give rise to a Franco-Russian *rapprochement*, but to separate attempts on the part of France and Russia to establish more cordial relations with Great Britain.

At the Quai d'Orsay, exultation at Montebello's triumph had quickly turned to alarm as Flourens realized that his reckless sacrifice of British goodwill had not brought him any closer to a definite understanding with Russia, and that any sudden change of whim on the part of the Tsar would leave France isolated in the face of a hostile Europe. The French government therefore hastened to substitute an *esprit conciliant* for the defiant attitude which it had previously adopted towards Great Britain.[2] Meanwhile Salisbury, who had recently experienced the humiliation of being completely at Bismarck's mercy, had become equally anxious to improve Anglo-French relations.[3] In the autumn of 1887 the renewal of discussions between the two governments about the Suez Canal helped to achieve this object, and Salisbury therefore brushed aside German and Italian protests that these separate negotiations threatened to weaken the Mediterranean *entente*.[4] But this improvement in Anglo-French relations did

---

[1] White to Salisbury, Private and Confidential, 16 July 1887, F.O. 364/1; W. Köhler, *Zur Europäischen Politik*, v. 200.

[2] *D.D.F.*, 1st ser., vi *bis*, Nos. 51–52.

[3] Cecil, iv. 47–49, 71; Lord Newton, *Lord Lyons*, ii. 409.

[4] White to Salisbury, Tel. Private and Confidential, 2 Oct.; Tel. Private, 4 Oct.; Salisbury to White, Tel. Private, 3 Oct. F.O. 364/4; Private, 4 Oct. 1887, F.O. 364/1; Cecil, iv. 71.

not outlive the conclusion of the Suez Canal Agreement on 24 October. The French government, which had remained consistently anti-British as far as Bulgaria was concerned,[1] chose to look upon the new agreement as a step towards ousting the British from Egypt, and Salisbury, exasperated by its extravagant claims, once more directed the whole of his attention towards working for a better understanding with the Triple Alliance Powers.[2]

The Russian government had also attempted to come to terms with Great Britain. The successful conclusion of the Afghan boundary dispute on 22 July encouraged Giers to sound out the possibility of a wider understanding with the British government. In a long conversation with Morier on 26 July, he expressed alarm at the prospect of a Franco-German war, and went on to argue that a *rapprochement* between Great Britain and Russia might yet preserve peace in Europe. He pointed out that the Bulgarian problem was the only obstacle to such a *rapprochement*, and that for Russia this question was one of national dignity more than anything else—'a question of *amour propre*, but of a legitimate *amour propre*'. He saw no reason why the amicable settlement of Anglo-Russian differences in Central Asia should not be followed by a solution of the Bulgarian problem: a solution which would give the Russian government the *amende honorable* to which it was entitled, and the autonomy for Bulgaria which the British government required.[3]

During August Giers again raised the subject with Morier, and repeated all his earlier arguments. Yet he took care to impress upon him that nothing which he had said should be regarded as a formal overture or proposal: all he desired was 'an exchange of views between two Powers who had no real cause of antagonism, and whose closer approach to each other would be a benefit to all concerned'. He explained that he was not suggesting an agreement in opposition to or apart from the other Powers, but an understanding between the two governments which would help to bring about a general

[1] Lyons to Salisbury, No. 380A Confidential, 7 Oct.; No. 387, 12 Oct. 1887, F.O. 27/2857; *D.D.F.*, 1st ser., vi, No. 593.
[2] Fuller, pp. 244–5, 249.
[3] Morier to Salisbury, No. 260 Confidential; No. 261 Most Confidential, 26 July 1887, F.O. 65/1297.

understanding among the Powers.¹ Late in September Giers made a final attempt to draw closer to the British government. This time he laid even greater stress upon the danger of a Franco-German war: however high the popular tide in Russia might rise against Germany in the event of such a conflict, the Tsar could hardly be expected to ally himself with 'Revolutionary France' against the 'great Conservative bulwark of Central Europe', but on the other hand, Russia could not afford to stand aside while France suffered a defeat which would end her existence as a Great Power; Great Britain and Russia would have to co-operate, if only as neutral spectators, to avoid the destruction of one belligerent by the other, and to decide upon a final settlement.²

News of these soundings quickly reached Constantinople. Nelidov, eager to seize any opportunity to sow discord among his colleagues, immediately hailed these manœuvres at St. Petersburg as a serious step towards an Anglo-Russian *rapprochement*, but White, distrustful of every new Russian move, was less enthusiastic.³ Russia, like France, had soon discovered that she had only gained a Pyrrhic victory by wrecking the Drummond Wolff Convention, for her rash flirtation with France had annoyed Bismarck and driven him to retaliate by declaring a tariff war against her. During July the officially inspired German newspapers issued a series of warnings to investors against the insecurity of Russian stock which caused considerable panic on the Berlin Exchange.⁴ White therefore suspected that Giers's overtures were directed towards restoring more cordial relations with Berlin, not London, and that his apparent eagerness to bring about a diplomatic revolution was explained by the success of Bismarck's tariff war rather than by a desire for friendship with Great Britain. 'No doubt the "echo" of this rumour will have reached Berlin and Rome', he suggested to Salisbury at

¹ Morier to Salisbury, No. 287 Secret, 17 Aug. 1887, F.O. 65/1298.
² Morier to Salisbury, No. 325, 21 Sept. 1887, F.O. 65/1298.
³ White to Salisbury, Tel. No. 60, 30 July; Tel. No. 61, 4 Aug. F.O. 78/4002; No. 260 Confidential, 5 Aug. F.O. 78/3999; Tel. Private and Confidential, 3 Aug. 1887, F.O. 364/4.
⁴ Scott (chargé d'affaires at Berlin) to Salisbury, No. 274 Confidential, 16 July 1887, F.O. 64/1158; *D.D.F.*, 1st ser., vi *bis*, No. 52 (Herbette to Waddington, 26 July 1887); W. Köhler, *Zur Europäischen Politik*, v. 201–2; Fuller, pp. 201–4; B. Nolde, *L'Alliance franco-russe*, pp. 501–13.

THE SECOND MEDITERRANEAN AGREEMENT

the beginning of August, 'and is likewise calculated to influence the financial market favourably for a new loan.'[1]

White's suspicions were well founded, but his warnings were unnecessary. Although Salisbury cautiously asked Bismarck for advice about an understanding between Great Britain and Russia, there was never any question of his entertaining Giers's suggestions. On 3 August, when he first discussed the subject with Hatzfeldt,[2] he had already confided to his own ambassador at St. Petersburg:[3]

> ... As long as Russia moves, however slowly, towards Constantinople her actions will be watched jealously here. But I do *not* think there is any natural antagonism. Many years ago the wrongs of Poland made a strong party against her on the Liberal side: but since that time the Manchester School for a period sent the pendulum the other way. Now both movements are almost forgotten. The real cause of friction, which may be durable, is the Stamboul sentiment in Russia. I doubt if the Englishman will for a long time reconcile himself to seeing the Black Sea a Russian lake: and I therefore look upon any cordial friendship as problematical.

Thus when Bismarck called his bluff and suggested that the proposed agreement might be extended to include Austria-Hungary, and even Italy, Salisbury confessed his doubts of Russia's sincerity, and quickly let the matter drop.[4] Like his Russian rival, he had made an unsuccessful attempt to use the threat of an Anglo-Russian *rapprochement* as a means of securing closer co-operation from Bismarck.[5]

Increased German support was the only possible remedy for Great Britain's two major weaknesses in the Near East— for her inability to rely upon assistance from either the Turkish government, or those Powers which had entered into the

[1] White to Salisbury, Tel. Private and Confidential, 3 Aug. 1887, F.O. 364/4. Kalnoky's views upon this subject were identical with White's: cf. Paget to Salisbury, No. 287 Confidential, 9 Aug. 1887, F.O. 7/1117.

[2] G.P. iv, No. 907 (Hatzfeldt to Bismarck, 3 Aug. 1887); cf. W. L. Langer, *European Alliances and Alignments*, pp. 430–1. Professor Langer, relying solely upon German documents, assumes that the proposed Anglo-Russian *rapprochement* was British, not Russian, in origin.

[3] Salisbury to Morier, Private, 2 Aug. Morier Papers; cf. also: Salisbury to Morier, Tel. No. 112, 19 Aug. 1887, F.O. 65/1300.

[4] G.P. iv, No. 913 (Memorandum by Count Herbert Bismarck, London, 24 Aug. 1887).

[5] H. Trützschler von Falkenstein, *Bismarck und die Kriegsgefahr des Jahres 1887*, pp. 110–12; W. L. Langer, pp. 431–2.

First Mediterranean Agreement with her. The sudden Turkish refusal to ratify the Wolff Convention was a sharp reminder for Salisbury that no trust could be placed in the 'sickly, sensual, terrified, fickle Sultan';[1] and in answer to a War Office recommendation that it would be essential for Great Britain to have the command of the Turkish army in the event of an Anglo-Russian war, he made the significant comment: 'It is as certain as any diplomatic forecast can be that Britain will never have that command.'[2] But the second weakness was even more serious than the first, for had the Mediterranean grouping been able to take a firmer stand against Montebello and Nelidov, the Sultan might have been encouraged to ignore the threats of that headstrong pair. But, at the eleventh hour, the grouping had been denied unstinted German support, and had therefore been easily defeated by the two ambassadors. Once the battle for the Wolff Convention had died down, Salisbury expressed little regret at the adjournment of the Egyptian negotiations *sine die*, but he was disturbed, nevertheless, by the half-heartedness of the support which he had received from both the German Powers during the course of that struggle. 'The Convention was not sufficiently popular in England', he wrote to White, 'to make it possible for us to have enforced the ratification with ironclads: even if that had been in itself a wise policy. But it would have ended with our taking the settlement of the Eastern question by a war with Russia, France and Turkey, while Germany and Austria looked on.'[3]

Bismarck's reaction to the renewed crisis in Bulgaria confirmed these suspicions. For Bismarck, everything turned upon the secret Re-insurance Treaty with Russia: in order to secure its signature he had become lukewarm in his support of British policy in Egypt; and in order to fulfil its terms he had to assist Russian policy in Bulgaria.[4] During August White became increasingly anxious about Bismarck's refusal to accept Prince Ferdinand's election to the Bulgarian throne,

[1] Salisbury to White, 10 Aug. 1887 (printed in Cecil, iv. 50–51).
[2] Foreign Office to War Office, 26 Aug. 1887, F.O. 195/1564.
[3] Salisbury to White, Private, 10 Aug. 1887, Additional White Papers (this part of the letter is not printed in Cecil, iv. 50–51).
[4] S. Gorianov, 'The End of the Alliance of the Emperors', *American Historical Review*, xxiii. 324–50; Fuller, pp. 185–204.

and his insistance that General Errnroth should be appointed as Regent. He informed Salisbury on 19 August: 'It is clear that Germany for some unaccountable reason is doing her best at Constantinople to paralyse the advice given by her Austrian ally, and to obtain a triumph for Russia in opposition to the wishes and supposed interests of Austria-Hungary in Bulgaria.'[1]

Reports from Vienna indicated that the Austro-Hungarian government did not object to Bismarck's Bulgarian policy. The meeting between the Austro-Hungarian and German emperors at Gastein, on 6 August, had served to strengthen the ties between the two allies: Prince Reuss, the German ambassador at Vienna, assured his British colleague that the two emperors had expressed their determination 'de se soutenir contre vent et marée',[2] and Kalnoky's account of their interview was equally optimistic.[3] When Paget pointed out that Bismarck's attitude towards Bulgaria implied that Germany was deserting the Mediterranean grouping, Kalnoky hinted that his government could still rely upon German assistance in the last resort.[4]

The liveliness of the Italian response to Bismarck's latest moves was as disconcerting as the apparent unconcern of Austria-Hungary. The failure of the Wolff Convention had already prompted Blanc, the Italian ambassador at Constantinople, to seek stronger commitments from the British government; in his 'July Memorandum' he had suggested that Great Britain, Italy, Austria-Hungary, and Turkey should form a 'Mediterranean League' to maintain the *status quo* in the Near East.[5] Crispi, who succeeded Depretis as Prime Minister early in August, almost immediately offered

---

[1] White to Salisbury, Tel. No. 67 Secret, 19 Aug. F.O. 78/4002; cf. also: Tel. No. 66 Confidential, 15 Aug. F.O. 78/4002; Confidential, 30 Aug. 1887, F.O. 364/1.

[2] Paget to Salisbury, No. 297 Very Confidential, 11 Aug. 1887, F.O. 7/1117.

[3] Paget to Salisbury, No. 302 Very Confidential, 12 Aug. 1887, F.O. 7/1117; cf. O. Mitis, *Das Leben des Kronprinzen Rudolf*, pp. 374–5; J. M. von Radowitz, *Aufzeichnungen und Erinnerungen*, ii. 274.

[4] Paget to Salisbury, No. 315 Secret, 25 Aug. 1887, F.O. 7/1117; cf. Kalnoky to Calice, 18 Aug. 1887, Austrian Archives (cited in W. N. Medlicott, 'Austria-Hungary and the War Danger of 1887', *Slavonic Review*, vi. 438–9).

[5] Wolff to Salisbury, No. 113 Most Secret and Confidential, 12 July 1887, F.O. 78/4059; cf. *supra*, pp. 78–80.

Salisbury an Anglo-Italian understanding with military co-operation in Egypt and Africa.[1] But neither of these ambitious projects met with Salisbury's approval: both were unhesitatingly dismissed with the familiar argument that it was impossible for Great Britain, with her parliamentary government, to enter into any specific engagements with respect to her future action.[2] At the same time Salisbury disagreed with Crispi's attitude towards the Bulgarian problem; whereas Crispi insisted that the election of Prince Ferdinand should be regarded as the expression of the wish of the Bulgarian people, Salisbury argued that it would be better to wait upon events and attempt to discover if the Prince would be generally acceptable to the Bulgarians.[3] 'Under Crispi's hand', he warned White, 'Italy is running a little wild and treating the support of the Bulgarians as a democratic question. You need not meddle with that.'[4]

Salisbury was not prepared to commit himself to a more active policy in the Near East until he was sure of German support. In Egypt the equivocal nature of that support had been largely responsible for the failure of the Wolff Convention; and now in Bulgaria its open transference to Russia guaranteed that any interference by the other Powers would be ineffective. 'Quant à l'Angleterre', a Belgian diplomat observed, 'depuis l'échec de la convention avec la Turquie concernant l'Egypte, elle boude et s'abstient de toutes choses.'[5] But there were also other reasons for Salisbury's reluctance to pursue an adventurous Bulgarian policy. The Russian ambassador at London equated the change in his attitude with the disappearance of Prince Alexander of Battenberg from the Bulgarian political scene: once he had departed, the Bulgarian problem gradually ceased to attract the attention of the British public, and the Queen, who had devoted herself with such energy to 'dear Sandro's' cause,

---

[1] Salisbury to Kennedy (chargé d'affaires at Rome), Tel. No. 71 Confidential, 19 Aug. F.O. 45/577; No. 254 Secret, 25 Aug. 1887, F.O. 45/573; Francesco Crispi, *Memoirs*, ii. 186–7.
[2] Ibid., and Salisbury to Kennedy, No. 220 Secret, 20 July 1887, F.O. 45/573.
[3] Salisbury to Kennedy, No. 264A, 1 Sept.; No. 264B, 2 Sept. 1887, F.O. 45/573; Crispi, ii. 176–84.
[4] Salisbury to White, Tel. No. 109 Secret, 19 Aug. 1887, F.O. 78/4002.
[5] W. Köhler, *Zur Europäischen Politik*, v. 205.

took little interest in the fate of 'foxy Ferdinand'.¹ In 1885 popular opinion and royal demands had played an important part in persuading Salisbury to gamble upon a European acceptance of Prince Alexander's *fait accompli*; but two years later, the absence of such pressures and his personal conviction that Prince Ferdinand's election would not lead to any permanent settlement, made him anxious to avoid any undue interference in Bulgarian affairs.² Writing privately to White on 23 August, he pointed out that one of three things must soon happen in Bulgaria: if Prince Ferdinand remained on the throne, a long diplomatic struggle with Russia would follow, and Great Britain, Austria-Hungary, Italy, and, in secret, Germany, would take the Bulgarian side: if, as seemed more probable, he were expelled, the result would be either the appointment of some Regent or a popular rising. Of these last two possibilities, the second was more likely but less desirable, for should such a movement spread into Macedonia, either Turkey, Austria-Hungary, or Russia—or all three—would intervene with armed force, and that was bound to result in 'some advanced step being made towards the further settlement of the Eastern question, to the disadvantage of Turkey'. In such circumstances the British government could not afford to stand aside, but it was doubtful if its intervention would save Turkey. 'The upshot of all this', he concluded, 'is that there is no prospect sufficiently promising of advantage resulting from an active policy to make us abandon the dilatory and negative line we have hitherto pursued. Whatever happens will be for the worse, and therefore it is our interest that as little should happen as possible.'³

White, who had pleaded with his chief for a compromise during the Eastern Roumelian crisis of 1885, had always recognized the need for caution in dealing with the Bulgarian problem, and the 'dilatory and negative' policy which Salisbury now advocated met with his entire approval. He seized every opportunity to warn the Sultan that any rash move on

---

¹ A. Meyendorff, *Le Correspondance diplomatique de M. de Staal*, i. 357–8 (Staal to Giers, 8/20 Aug. 1887); G. E. Buckle, *The Letters of Queen Victoria*, 3rd ser., i. 337, 351.
² Salisbury to White, Tel. No. 92, 11 July 1887, F.O. 78/4002; to Paget, Tel. No. 67, 11 July 1887, F.O. 7/1120; Meyendorff, i. 357–8.
³ Salisbury to White, Private, 23 Aug. 1887, F.O. 364/1.

his part might provoke a serious conflict in Bulgaria, and at the same time he impressed upon the Bulgarians that the stirring up of any trouble in Macedonia would be tantamount to an act of political suicide: a revolutionary movement there would arouse the hostility of Austria-Hungary, Serbia, and Greece, and so ruin any chance of Bulgaria gaining her autonomy.[1] But in answer to Salisbury's pessimistic observations upon Great Britain's position in the Near East, White could only reply: 'We must do our best, our very best, but the prospect is a gloomy one.'[2]

Throughout the autumn of 1887 Salisbury and White played a waiting game: it was not so spectacular as their sudden seizure of the initiative during the Eastern Roumelian crisis, but it forced Bismarck to reveal most of his hand, and soon put the British government in a far stronger position than that which it had occupied at the end of 1885. In spite of his ostentatious support of Russia's Bulgarian policy, Bismarck was unable to hide his fear and distrust of his eastern ally. By the end of August Malet had already begun to suspect that he was only keeping up the appearance of acting in concert with Russia, and that he would be delighted if the other Powers thwarted her plans, and if Bulgaria, even with Prince Ferdinand at its head, remained independent.[3] Bismarck's continued insistence that the Powers should consent to the nomination of General Ernroth as Bulgarian Regent did not shake Malet's belief. Writing to Salisbury on 17 September he explained that Bismarck's plan was to persuade the Powers to consent to the Ernroth scheme in principle, and to rely upon their raising difficulties later when the details were discussed. 'By this means', he added, 'the Chancellor imagines that some satisfaction will have been given to Russia, but that her scheme will break down through the inability of the Powers to come to an understanding in detail.'[4] After conversations with Bismarck at Friedrichsruh

---

[1] White to Salisbury, No. 282 Secret, 19 Aug. F.O. 78/3999; Tel. No. 70, 22 Aug. F.O. 78/4002; Paget to Salisbury, No. 309 Confidential, 23 Aug. 1887, F.O. 7/1117.

[2] White to Salisbury, Confidential, 30 Aug. 1887, F.O. 364/1.

[3] Malet to Salisbury, No. 311 Confidential, 20 Aug.; No. 326 Confidential, 26 Aug. 1887, F.O. 64/1158.

[4] Malet to Salisbury, Private, 17 Sept. 1887, F.O. 343/8.

THE SECOND MEDITERRANEAN AGREEMENT

during the middle of the same month, Kalnoky's impressions closely resembled those of the British ambassador at Berlin: although Bismarck was anxious to keep on good terms with Russia, and was therefore giving his 'theoretical' support to the Ernroth scheme, he could nevertheless be relied upon to join those Powers opposed to Russia should it be found impossible to keep her ambitions within reasonable bounds.[1]

Russo-German relations became increasingly strained during the autumn and winter of 1887. Confident that the financial acumen of the French would be a sufficient guarantee against an extensive purchase of Russian securities in Paris, and oblivious of the fact that economic considerations might effect the political relationship between Russia and Germany, Bismarck intensified his financial war against Russia, and revealed that his mastery of politics was not matched by a corresponding skill in handling economic problems. On 10 November the Imperial Bank of Germany was instructed to announce that deposits of Russian stock could no longer be used as securities for loans. This measure, it was assumed at Berlin, was simply a 'retort courteous' to an increase in Russia's military activities on the frontier—a means of putting pressure upon the Russian government without endangering the diplomatic relations of the two Empires.[2] The Tsar's brief and embarrassing visit to Berlin, eight days later, did little to ease the tension. In a conversation with the Tsar which lasted over an hour, Bismarck hastily dismissed his recent measures against Russian credit as a matter of general financial policy; turning to Bulgaria, he denied harbouring any designs against Russia, and reaffirmed his desire to support Russian policy there. The Tsar, for his part, declared that he had no intention of allying himself with the French Republic, but when he began to speak bitterly against

[1] Paget to Salisbury, Recorder Tel. No. 65 Strictly Confidential, 22 Sept. F.O. 120/654; No. 340 Strictly Confidential, 22 Sept.; No. 345A Strictly Confidential, 1 Oct. 1887, F.O. 7/1118; cf. W. N. Medlicott, 'Austria-Hungary and the War Danger of 1887', *Slavonic Review*, vi. 438–9.

[2] Morier to Salisbury, No. 372 Most Confidential, 12 Nov. F.O. 65/1299; Malet to Salisbury, No. 432, 12 Nov. F.O. 64/1160; Phipps (chargé d'affaires at Vienna) to Salisbury, No. 412 Very Confidential, 22 Nov. 1887, F.O. 120/654; cf. *D.D.F.*, 1st ser., vi *bis*, No. 60; B. Nolde, *L'Alliance franco-russe*, pp. 508–9; J. V. Fuller, *Bismarck's Diplomacy at its Zenith*, pp. 290–1; A. Dorpalen, 'Tsar Alexander III and the Boulanger Crisis in France', *Journal of Modern History*, xxiii, No. 2, 131.

Austria-Hungary, Bismarck promptly reminded him of the terms of the Austro-German Alliance of 1879.[1]

The Tsar and Bismarck parted with mutual assurances of goodwill, but their meeting did not lead to any immediate improvement in Russo-German relations: although the Russian press was ordered to cease its attacks upon the German government, hostile criticisms continued to appear in its columns, and in spite of a decline in Russian military activity on the German frontier, Russian troop concentrations on the borders of Austria-Hungary caused increasing anxiety at Berlin. Meanwhile Bismarck hastened to arm himself against the dreaded threat of a war on two fronts: the passing of the German Army Bill late in November increased the number of men liable for military service by six hundred thousand, and provided him with an effective answer to the French Bill of August 1887, and the signing of the German-Italian Military Convention at the end of the year further strengthened his hand against France; in the East, he made use of the strained relations between Vienna and St. Petersburg to persuade the Austro-Hungarian government to increase its armaments, and by publishing the terms of the Austro-German Alliance of 1879, on 3 February 1888, he ensured that his old ally would not wage an offensive war against Russia, and at the same time convinced the Russians that a war with Austria-Hungary would not solve their Balkan difficulties.[2] Most important of all, he abandoned his traditional approach to the Near Eastern problem, defined less than six months previously in the Re-insurance Treaty with Russia, and adhered to the second Mediterranean Agreement of December 1887—an agreement between Great Britain and his Triple Alliance allies to keep Russia in check and preserve the *status quo* in the Near East.[3]

Only in a negative sense was Bismarck the promoter of the negotiations for the Second Mediterranean Agreement. To a

[1] For a full account of this conversation see Fuller, pp. 258–65; cf. also *G.P.* v, Nos. 1127–36; Lucius von Ballhausen, *Bismarck-Erinnerungen*, pp. 404–5; *D.D.F.*, 1st ser., vi *bis*, No. 64; W. L. Langer, *European Alliances and Alignments*, p. 441; Nolde, pp. 515–16.

[2] Fuller, pp. 266–302; Langer, pp. 444–51.

[3] H. W. V. Temperley and L. M. Penson, *Foundations of British Foreign Policy (1792–1902)*, pp. 454–5; cf., however, Langer, pp. 423–4.

great extent those negotiations owed their origin to his hostile actions at Constantinople: they had been set in motion by Blanc's 'July Memorandum'—a document which advocated the formation of a 'Mediterranean League' to remedy such half-heartedness as Bismarck had displayed during the struggle for the Wolff Convention;[1] and they had gathered momentum during August when Bismarck insisted upon the adoption of the Ernroth scheme, and even his Austro-Hungarian ally became secretly alarmed at the possible effects of such strong German encouragement of Russia's policy in Bulgaria.[2] But as it became obvious that all his efforts to conciliate Russia had failed, Bismarck drew closer to the Mediterranean grouping and automatically assumed his accustomed role of European 'factotum' in the pending negotiations between Austria-Hungary, Italy, and Great Britain. During interviews with Crispi at Friedrichsruh on 2 and 3 October he gave the Italian prime minister the cryptic assurance that: 'Should a breach of peace occur in the East, Germany would join her allies, but would remain in the background',[3] and before the end of the month he had committed himself to the task of persuading Salisbury to enter into negotiations with the Austro-Hungarian and Italian governments.[4]

Meanwhile the bases of an *accord à trois* had taken shape at Constantinople. On 17 September Calice forwarded draft proposals for such an *accord* to Vienna, and on 25 October, after Kalnoky had persuaded Bismarck to take the lead, they were communicated to Salisbury simultaneously by the German, Austro-Hungarian, and Italian governments.[5] These draft proposals contained eight 'points'. The first two articles insisted upon the maintenance of peace and of the *status quo*

[1] *Supra*, pp. 78–80.
[2] W. N. Medlicott, 'Austria-Hungary and the War Danger of 1887', *Slavonic Review*, vi. 438–9; W. N. Medlicott, 'The Mediterranean Agreements of 1887', ibid. v. 76.
[3] Francesco Crispi, *Memoirs*, ii. 216; Medlicott, 'The Mediterranean Agreements', p. 80.
[4] Ibid., p. 81.
[5] Malet to Salisbury, Private and Secret (with enclosure), 25 Oct. 1887, F.O. 343/9 (printed in G. P. Gooch and H. W. V. Temperley, *British Documents on the Origins of the War, 1898–1914*, viii. 14–15; Medlicott, p. 82; Temperley and Penson, p. 457.

in the Near East, based on existing treaties, to the exclusion of all policy of compensation; and the third and fourth articles upheld the principles of the maintenance of local autonomies and the independence of Turkey from all foreign preponderating influence. The fifth article stated that, as a corollary to the preceding articles, Turkey should neither cede nor delegate her suzerain rights over Bulgaria to any other Power, nor intervene to establish a foreign administration there, nor tolerate acts of coercion undertaken with this latter object, under the form either of a military occupation or of the dispatch of volunteers; such actions would not only constitute an infraction of the *status quo*, but would be prejudicial to the interests of the three Powers. In the sixth and seventh articles the three Powers announced their willingness to join with Turkey in the common defence of these principles, and their preparedness, in the case of Turkish resistance to illegal enterprises, to come immediately to an agreement concerning the assistance to be given to the Porte. Finally, the eighth article laid down that should the Porte be in connivance with an illegal enterprise of the character indicated, or should the Porte not oppose to it a serious resistance, the three would agree to occupy provisionally, by military or naval forces, certain points of Ottoman territory in order to re-establish the political and military equilibrium necessary for safeguarding the principles already mentioned.[1]

Salisbury assumed that White had closely co-operated with his Austro-Hungarian and Italian colleagues in the formulation of these draft proposals. He congratulated him upon the success of his labours, and intimated that he was prepared to accept the eight points as the basis for an agreement with the Triple Alliance Powers. On 2 November he wrote to White:[2]

> The result of your meditations and consultations at Constantinople with your two colleagues has come to birth. Germany, Austria and Italy have each communicated to me your eight bases with an earnest recommendation that we should accept them.... My own impression

---

[1] For the text of these proposals see Gooch and Temperley, viii. 14–15; *G.P.* iv, No. 918 (enclosure); Medlicott, pp. 77–78.
[2] Salisbury to White, Private, 2 Nov. 1887, F.O. 364/1 (printed in Cecil, iv. 70–71).

THE SECOND MEDITERRANEAN AGREEMENT 97

is that we must join: but I say it with regret. I think the time inopportune and that we are merely rescuing Bismarck's somewhat endangered chestnuts. If he can establish a South Eastern raw, the Russian bear must perforce forget the Western raw on his huge carcase. If he can get up a nice little fight between her and the three Powers, he will have leisure to make France a harmless neighbour for some time to come. It goes against me to be one of the pawns in that unscrupulous game. But a thorough understanding with Austria and Italy is so important to us, that I do not like the idea of breaking it up on account of risks which *may* turn out to be imaginary.

White telegraphed in reply that he was in complete agreement with Salisbury's views, but hastened to add that he had taken 'no part whatever' in drawing up the proposals: Calice had read the eight points out to him, but he had refused to accept a copy of their text, and had even declined the offer of a second reading, because he was unwilling to discuss such matters without instructions, and reluctant to share the responsibility for what he considered to be an imperfect draft.[1] But these were technical excuses for his conduct, not fundamental explanations of his policy. Throughout the autumn of 1887 the events of the two previous years remained fresh in White's memory. He had never forgotten the precariousness of his position during the Pendjeh and Eastern Roumelian crises when he had struggled alone at Constantinople against the influence of the Three Emperors' Alliance.[2] And, far more recently, the failure of the Wolff Convention had demonstrated to him how easily and how suddenly Great Britain's position on the Bosphorus might revert to the isolation of 1885. Thus at the end of September, when Calice and Blanc asked him to join them in recommending their three respective governments to take active measures against Russian influence at the Porte, he cited the Drummond Wolff fiasco as an example of the futility of such co-operation. Never again would he allow himself to be lured into taking the lead against Russia only to find himself deserted when serious difficulties arose; he would make no move until his Austro-Hungarian and Italian colleagues had

---
[1] White to Salisbury, Tel. Private and Secret, 7 Nov. 1887, F.O. 364/1.
[2] White to Salisbury, No. 329 Very Secret, 3 Oct. F.O. 78/4000; Private and Confidential, 18 Oct. 1887, F.O. 364/1.

proved their loyalty by taking the initiative.[1] Moreover, he shrewdly sensed that Bismarck must soon commit himself to an anti-Russian policy in the Near East, and that this would entail a radical change in his attitude towards the Ottoman Empire. 'Germany is now watching with quite as keen an interest as I have done all along the movements of Russia here', he confided to Salisbury. '... With the possibility of having Russia sooner or later as an open enemy, Prince Bismarck cannot allow the Sultan to become a sort of Khan of Bokhara or even a Shah of Persia. The Ottoman Empire may still be one of his trump cards.'[2]

The correspondence which passed between Berlin and London during November bore out White's suspicions and justified the patient, cautious, and unspectacular policy which he had modestly pursued throughout the autumn. On 13 November Herbert Bismarck informed Malet that the German Emperor would give his 'moral approbation' to any agreement which might be reached between Great Britain, Austria-Hungary, and Italy based upon the eight points, and at the same time he communicated to him the terms of the Austro-German Treaty of 1879.[3] He also stated that should Salisbury wish to adhere to this treaty in any form, it would be very agreeable to Prince Bismarck, but he added that it was thought that the Prime Minister would prefer simply to make use of its terms—without, of course, revealing its text—to explain the general situation more easily to the Cabinet.[4] Nine days later Prince Bismarck followed the precedent of 1885[5] and made a direct approach to Salisbury by means of

[1] White to Salisbury, Tel. Private and Confidential, 28 Sept. 1887, F.O. 364/4.
[2] White to Salisbury, Private and Confidential, 18 Oct. 1887, F.O. 364/1; cf. P. Kluke, 'Bismarck und Salisbury', *Historische Zeitschrift*, Apr. 1953, p. 300.
[3] Malet to Salisbury, Private and Secret, 14 Nov. 1887, F.O. 343/9; *G.P.* iv, No. 928; Medlicott, 'The Mediterranean Agreements', p. 83. For the text of the Austro-German Treaty see A. F. Pribram, *The Secret Treaties of Austria-Hungary*, i. 18–31. Article III, which determined the time limit, was not submitted to Salisbury.
[4] Malet to Salisbury, Private and Secret, 14 Nov. 1887, F.O. 343/9; cf., however W. L. Langer, *European Alliances and Alignments*, p. 438; Medlicott, p. 83. Professor Langer dismisses the idea that Bismarck offered Salisbury an alliance as 'quite untenable', but Professor Medlicott is nearer the mark when he suggests that if such an offer was ever made, its purpose was simply to strengthen Bismarck's assurances of his goodwill towards the proposed agreement between Great Britain, Austria-Hungary, and Italy.
[5] *G.P.* iv, No. 783.

THE SECOND MEDITERRANEAN AGREEMENT 99

a private letter. He assured him that Germany acknowledged interests beyond the defence of her own frontiers, and that the most immediate of these was the protection of Austria-Hungary's integrity and her continued existence as a Great Power.[1] In order to calm Salisbury's fear that the advent of a new emperor might result in drastic changes in Germany's foreign policy, he stated in a covering letter that he had obtained Prince William's approval of these views by reading the whole letter to him.[2]

Within a month of receiving this assurance of the ultimate support of Germany, Salisbury concluded an agreement with the Austro-Hungarian and Italian governments. On 12 December he exchanged correspondence embodying its terms with the Austro-Hungarian ambassador in London, and four days later Kalnoky and Crispi affirmed their adhesion by an exchange of notes in Vienna. The final draft contained nine points: added to the fifth article of the original proposals were the words: 'likewise Turkey, constituted by the treaties guardian of the Straits, can neither cede any portion of her sovereign rights, nor delegate her authority to any other Power in Asia Minor'; the seventh and eighth articles were revised to recognize specifically the maintenance of 'the independence of the Ottoman Empire and the integrity of its territory'; and a ninth article was included which laid down that 'the existence and contents of the present Agreement between the three Powers shall not be revealed, either to Turkey or to any other Powers who have not yet been informed of it, without the previous consent of all and each of the three Powers aforesaid'.[3]

Salisbury belittled the importance of the Second Mediterranean Agreement: 'It is like putting a coarse sieve under a fine one', he complained to White immediately after its conclusion, and he went on to argue that it guaranteed nothing which had not been secured already by more formal treaties.[4] But with Salisbury such scepticism was almost habitual. In spite of this typical expression of his doubts, the new

---

[1] *G.P.* iv, No. 930.
[2] Ibid., No. 931; Cecil, iv. 72–73; Medlicott, pp. 85–86.
[3] Pribram, i. 124–33; Medlicott, pp. 85–86.
[4] Salisbury to White, 14 Dec. 1887 (printed in Cecil, iv. 78–79).

agreement offered him many advantages. At the end of 1887 Great Britain's position at Constantinople was far stronger than it had been when Salisbury and White first combined their respective skills in shaping and executing British policy in the Near East. In the event of further Russian incursions into Ottoman territory, the British government was assured of close support from both Austria-Hungary and Italy: no longer was Austria-Hungary to be intimidated into a policy of *rapprochement* with Russia, a policy which had seriously threatened the stand taken up by Salisbury and White during the Eastern Roumelian crisis, and at the same time Italy, whose colonial ventures on the Red Sea coast had frequently embarrassed the Foreign Office, was to be kept within prescribed limits by the terms of the agreement. Most important of all, Bismarck had undertaken to support the agreement, an act which meant that the Three Emperors' Alliance had received its *coup de grâce*.[1]

White could at last feel free from any immediate danger of a return to the isolation of 1885. In December 1887 it seemed that all his plans for working in close partnership with the Triple Alliance Powers at Constantinople would be realized since Austria-Hungary, Italy, and even Germany had agreed to co-operate with Great Britain in the Near East and to share the burden of guarding the Straits against Russia. 'You are rather more interested than Radowitz, but not quite so interested as Calice and Blanc . . .', Salisbury impressed upon him, and he went on to explain: 'Of course it may be said that this plan sacrifices the ideal we have pursued since Lord Stratford's days of a leading influence at Constantinople. But is not that idea a chimera? Can anyone have that leading influence for more than a month together?'[2] But Salisbury's reminder was superfluous because White, who had served his apprenticeship at Constantinople during the Pendjeh and Eastern Roumelian crises, had long since realized that the concept of a 'leading influence' on the Bosphorus was an anachronism.

[1] L. M. Penson, 'The Principles and Methods of Lord Salisbury's Foreign Policy', *Cambridge Historical Journal*, v. 98–99; H. W. V. Temperley and L. M. Penson, *Foundations of British Foreign Policy (1792–1902)*, pp. 455, 458; G. P. Gooch and H. W. V. Temperley, *British Documents*, viii. 8–18; Cecil, iv. 77–79.
[2] Salisbury to White, 14 Dec. 1887 (printed in Cecil, iv. 78–79).

If any fault could have been found with White's conduct of affairs during the winter of 1887–8, it would have been his slowness to appreciate that the Bulgarian question was dying a natural death. By a strange paradox, the question which had dominated the negotiations for the Second Mediterranean Agreement was ceasing to be an important problem in European politics by the time that arrangement was finally concluded. As far back as July, when St. Petersburg had been startled by the first news of Prince Ferdinand's formal election to the Bulgarian throne, Giers confessed to Morier that his government was disgusted both at the ingratitude of the Bulgarians and at its own folly in shedding so much blood and wasting so much treasure for such a people. 'Let them make an *amende honorable*', he exclaimed, 'and we shall be only too happy to leave them alone.'¹ By the end of the year Giers had become even more emphatic in his protests that Russia was indifferent to the fate of the Bulgarians: 'They may do anything and everything they please', he declared to the British ambassador during December, 'from cutting each other's throats to declaring themselves an Empire. We shall not move a finger to prevent them. We wash our hands of the whole concern.'² There is no evidence that such expressions of disgust were simulated. Indeed, Russia's next move in regard to Bulgaria seems to have been prompted not by any aggressive designs on her part, but by a desire to ascertain the existence and extent of any anti-Russian coalitions.³ Early in February 1888 the Russian government proposed that the Powers should declare the presence of Prince Ferdinand at the head of the Bulgarian government to be illegal, and that this declaration should be communicated to the Porte together with the request that Turkey, as the suzerain Power, should notify the usurping prince of the declaration.⁴ Great Britain, Austria-Hungary, and Italy used strikingly

¹ Morier to Salisbury, No. 260 Confidential; No. 261 Most Confidential, 26 July 1887, F.O. 65/1297.

² *A. & P.*, Turkey No. 1 (1888), cix [C–5370], 566 (Morier to Salisbury, 17 Dec. 1887); cf. No. 404 Most Secret, 7 Dec.; No. 411, 17 Dec. 1887, F.O. 65/1299; J. V. Fuller, *Bismarck's Diplomacy at its Zenith*, p. 285.

³ Medlicott, 'The Mediterranean Agreements', p. 87; *D.D.F.*, 1st ser., vii, No. 25; A. Meyendorff, *Le Correspondance diplomatique de M. de Staal*, i. 368–72; Malet to Salisbury, Private, 18 Feb. 1887, F.O. 343/9.

⁴ Medlicott, loc. cit.; *D.D.F.*, 1st ser., vii, No. 47.

similar language in rejecting these proposals, whereas France and Germany gave them their support.[1] 'Germany ostensibly supports, while France ostensibly opposes the Russian proposals', Kennedy telegraphed from Rome on 21 February.[2] Bismarck, torn between the conflicting obligations of the Re-insurance Treaty and the Second Mediterranean Agreement, chose to back the Russian government in a move which was bound to result in a check by the Mediterranean grouping, and his ambassador at Constantinople played a prominent part in persuading the Porte to brave the outcries of the other Powers and issue the declaration of illegality at the simple request of Russia.[3] Meanwhile Flourens, who had described the Russian proposals to Lytton as 'ill advised and dangerous',[4] secretly supported them.[5] On 6 March the Porte officially informed Prince Ferdinand that his presence in Bulgaria was illegal, but the announcement caused little concern either in Sofia or any of the major European capitals. Far from heralding the approach of a more acute phase in the Near Eastern problem, the Turkish declaration was destined to mark the end of the series of Bulgarian crises which had annually disturbed Europe since 1885. Under Stambulov's guidance, the Bulgarian government turned its attention towards domestic politics, and the Russian government, encouraged by renewed evidence of Bismarck's diplomatic support, rested content with the Porte's ineffective protest against Prince Ferdinand's rule.[6]

None of these manœuvres had shaken Morier's belief that Russia's policy towards Bulgaria was dictated by wounded pride rather than by any pan-Slavic feelings towards the Bulgarian people, or by a desire to use their country as a military base against Turkey.[7] But White was not so easily converted to the view that Russia was prepared to cut her losses in Bulgaria. Whereas Morier insisted that the Russian government

[1] Medlicott, p. 88.
[2] Kennedy (chargé d'affaires at Rome) to Salisbury, Tel. No. 4, 21 Feb. 1888, F.O. 45/604.
[3] Medlicott, p. 88; Malet to Salisbury, Private, 18 Feb. 1888, F.O. 343/9.
[4] Lytton to Salisbury, Tel. No. 7, 13 Feb. 1888, F.O. 27/2909.
[5] *D.D.F.*, 1st ser., vii, Nos. 53, 55.
[6] Medlicott, p. 88; *D.D.F.*, 1st ser., vii, Nos. 68, 77; Cecil, iv. 83; J. M. von Radowitz, *Aufzeichnungen und Erinnerungen*, ii. 280.
[7] Morier to Salisbury, No. 90, 8 Mar. 1888, F.O. 65/1330.

was only seeking to beat a peaceful retreat,[1] White suspected that it had ulterior motives in insisting upon an official declaration of the illegality of Prince Ferdinand's rule. He pointed out to Salisbury that a protest against the Prince's position in Bulgaria, even if it remained purely nominal, might have serious consequences: first, it would shut the door upon any hopes the Bulgarians might have of their Prince being recognized at some future date, and might therefore make them look upon him as a barrier to their achievement of political and economic stability; secondly, it would loosen the bonds of mutual understanding which had recently been formed between the Bulgarian government and its Turkish suzerain, and make the Bulgarians regard their vassalage as both irksome and unprofitable; and finally, such a protest by all the Great Powers might be sufficient to reduce the Bulgarians to despair, and to make them seek a reconciliation with Russia. All these considerations, and the fact that the Russian government was again receiving strong German support at Constantinople, kept alive White's interest in the Bulgarian question.[2] But on 9 March, three days after the issue of the Porte's declaration against Prince Ferdinand, the death of the German Emperor William I made all other questions dwindle into insignificance, and even White was ready to admit to Salisbury: 'Bulgaria will probably leave us alone for a while.'[3]

White may have been slow to appreciate the decreasing importance of the Bulgarian problem in European politics, but he was not guilty of thinking of the Near Eastern question solely in Balkan terms. During the final stage of the negotiations for the Second Mediterranean Agreement, Salisbury had insisted that the 'eight points' of the original draft should be modified in two important respects: the guarantee to protect Turkey's sovereign rights in Bulgaria should be extended to include Asia Minor, and a ninth clause should be added stipulating that the agreement should be kept secret.[4] No doubt his bitter experiences at the end of the

[1] Ibid.; to Currie, Private and Confidential, 2 Mar. 1888, F.O. 65/1330.
[2] White to Salisbury, Private and Confidential, 23 Feb.; Confidential, 28 Feb.; Private and Confidential, 7 Mar. F.O. 364/1; No. 93 Secret, 6 Mar. 1888, F.O. 78/4099.   [3] White to Salisbury, Private, 10 Mar. 1888, F.O. 364/1.
[4] Pribram, i. 124–33; Medlicott, pp. 85–86.

previous decade, when he had unsuccessfully attempted to reform and strengthen the administration of Asia Minor,[1] were largely responsible for these suggestions, but it is possible that they were also inspired by the advice which he received from his ambassador at Constantinople. On 18 October, a week before Salisbury was in possession of the actual text of the draft proposals, White had explained to him the important connexion between the need to include Asia Minor in any arrangement for the protection of Turkey, and the necessity of insisting upon secrecy: as long as his Armenian flank remained unprotected, the Sultan would do little to resist Russia, but if Great Britain displayed any willingness to support him there, he would be reminded of the Cyprus Convention of 1878, and this alone might be sufficient to throw him into the arms of Russia.[2]

The spectacular events taking place in the Balkans had never blinded White to the danger of a sudden Russian attack upon Turkey by way of Asia Minor. In September 1885, when Prince Alexander's *coup d'état* at Philippopolis re-opened the Bulgarian question, one of White's greatest fears had been that the Russian government was only waiting for the Turks to exhaust their financial reserves in restoring order in Eastern Roumelia before thrusting at Turkey at its own convenience on the Asiatic side.[3] Major-General Brackenbury, who was sent by the War Office during the following summer to report on the military situation at Constantinople, had similar apprehensions. He endorsed the view of many military experts that since any further Russian advance in the Balkans would lead to Austro-Hungarian, and probably German, intervention, Russia's next move towards Constantinople would be through Asia Minor where neither Austro-Hungarian nor German interests were involved.[4] Such fears became all the more urgent

---

[1] Cf. Lady G. Cecil, *The Life of Robert, Marquis of Salisbury*, ii. 300–26; L. M. Penson, 'The Foreign Policy of Lord Salisbury, 1878–80', in A. Coville and H. Temperley, *Studies in Anglo-French History during the Eighteenth, Nineteenth and Twentieth Centuries*, pp. 125–42.

[2] White to Salisbury, Private and Confidential, 18 Oct. 1887, F.O. 364/1.

[3] White to Salisbury, No. 407 Very Secret, 29 Sept. 1885, F.O. 78/3753.

[4] *General Sketch of the Situation at Home and Abroad*, War Office Print, Secret, 3 Aug. 1886, F.O. 364/3.

THE SECOND MEDITERRANEAN AGREEMENT

as the Bulgarian problem ended in an uneasy stalemate, and in February 1888 Salisbury did not discount the alarm expressed by Rustem Pasha, the Turkish ambassador at London, that by an advance on Erzeroum, Russia would be able to destroy Turkey without disturbing the peace of Europe:[1]

> He [Rustem] does not believe in an attack on Bulgaria, because he thinks that the Russians will endure a great deal rather than widen the breach between themselves and a Slav nation. But no such impediment will restrain them on the Asiatic side; and once Erzeroum [is] taken there is nothing to hold them as far as the Persian Gulf. All this seems to me probable enough: I am very much surprised that we have heard nothing lately of Armenian 'atrocities'. But a disagreeable report comes to us from Vienna, to the effect that the Czar is going this summer to the Caucasus, and may extend his trip as far as Asia Minor.

During the later years of his embassy, White became increasingly concerned with the problem of protecting Asiatic Turkey against Russian incursions. It might be argued that since Bulgarian nationalism had served as an effective bulwark against further Russian advances down the Balkan Peninsula, his most obvious course would be to attempt to make similar use of Armenian nationalism to build up a second bulwark in Asia Minor. But White realized that such a scheme was neither desirable nor possible. In contrast to his wide knowledge of eastern European languages and politics, he was ignorant of Oriental languages and Asiatic history, and therefore had no personal sympathies for the Armenian national cause.[2] Moreover, the efforts of Salisbury, Layard, and Goschen, less than a decade previously, to fulfil the terms of the Cyprus Convention had given him an object lesson in the futility of attempting to interfere with the Turkish administration of Asia Minor.[3] Even more recently, in August 1886, Sir Edward Thornton, then British ambassador at Constantinople, had presented the Sultan with a memorandum on the subject of Asiatic reforms—a blunder which had hastened his dismissal and enabled White to reach

---

[1] Salisbury to White, Private, 8 Feb., Additional White Papers; cf. Paget to Salisbury, No. 34 Very Confidential, 1 Feb. 1888, F.O. 7/1131.

[2] Sir A. Hardinge, *A Diplomatist in the East*, p. 11; cf. G.P. ix, No. 2178.

[3] Cf. L. M. Penson, 'The Foreign Policy of Lord Salisbury 1878–80', pp. 125–42; W. N. Medlicott, 'The Gladstone Government and the Cyprus Convention', *Journal of Modern History*, XII. ii. 186–208.

full ambassadorial rank.¹ The revival of the fanatical spirit of pan-Islam among the Turks, a force more easily conjured up than controlled, had made the Sultan far more sensitive to the preservation of his dignity as Caliph than to the maintenance of Turkey in Europe.² White was among those who realized that 'next to Egypt, the Sultan is most sensitive with regard to England on subjects connected with Arabia and Armenia',³ and was therefore chary of repeating the errors of his predecessors. 'The Turks of the present day', he explained to Salisbury, 'appear more and more to look, not to Imperial, but to Mussulman interests, and to consider the Balkan Peninsula as lost to them.'⁴

White was in an extremely difficult position: if he openly condemned Turkish misrule in Asia Minor, the only results would be an increase in the Sultan's hostility towards him, and the loss of what little influence he still possessed at the Porte and the Palace; but if he ignored it, there would be outcries at home against the Salisbury government, and sharp criticisms of his ability as an ambassador. For instance, the outrages of the notorious Kurdish chieftain, Moussa Bey, attracted considerable attention in Great Britain during the summer of 1889. The eventual arrest of Moussa Bey, his protracted trial, and his subsequent acquittal by a Turkish court gave rise to speeches by Carnarvon and the Archbishop of Canterbury in the Lords,⁵ and by Gladstone and Bryce in the Commons:⁶ members of both political parties asked questions in the House,⁷ and the government was forced to produce a crop of hundred-page Blue Books.⁸ On 30 August 1889 the *Daily News* used its editorial column to congratulate the Salisbury government for having 'broken away from the old conditions and assimilated itself to the policy of Mr.

---

¹ *Supra*, pp. 44–46.
² Sir W. Ramsey, *The Revolution in Constantinople and Turkey*, pp. 260–1; Alma Wittlin, *Abdul Hamid*, pp. 117–24.
³ White to Salisbury, No. 75 Confidential, 22 Feb. 1889, F.O. 78/4201; cf. *G.P.* ix, No. 2175.
⁴ White to Salisbury, No. 4 Confidential, 4 Jan. 1889, F.O. 78/4201.
⁵ *Hansard's Parliamentary Debates*, 3rd ser., cccxxxvii. 979–86.
⁶ Ibid. cccxxxvi. 1309–16, 1320–24.
⁷ Ibid., pp. 1316–17; cccxxxvii. 1252–3, 1581.
⁸ *A. & P.*, Turkey No. 1 (1889), lxxxvii [C–5723], 91 pp.; Turkey No. 1 (1890), lxxxii [C–5912], 130 pp.; Turkey No. 1 (1890–1), xcvi [C–6214], 101 pp.

Gladstone', but it added a warning that in regard to Armenia 'the difficulty of governing Christian races by Moslem methods' threatened to disturb 'the comfortable arrangements of diplomacy'. But White could do no more than make formal protests at the Porte whenever more extreme crimes were perpetrated against the Christian populations of the Asiatic provinces, or whenever the Liberal opposition and the Armenian committees in London put exceptional pressure upon the Salisbury government. In the absence of these two driving forces, he chose to remain inactive; although he did not deny that the situation in Armenia was becoming increasingly acute, he was convinced that the movement for autonomy there existed only in the minds of Gladstone and the Armenian committees in London.[1] Thus in August 1890, news of fresh outrages against the Armenians at Erzeroum only prompted him to remind Salisbury how sensitive the Sultan was about this particular subject, and to ask for instructions giving him 'latitude and greater discretion' to deal with the Armenian problem.[2] 'There has been very little pressure lately in such matters, but the H[ouse] of C[ommons] insists on a certain amount', Currie suggested to his chief at the Foreign Office, but Salisbury had great faith in his ambassador's judgement and therefore decided to grant his request.[3]

White's attitude towards the Armenian problem was also tempered by the knowledge that even the mildest protest would receive no support from his colleagues at Constantinople. The German and Austro-Hungarian ambassadors were particularly reluctant to co-operate: unharassed by indignant outcries at home, they could let well alone and cultivate the friendship of the Sultan.[4] Moreover, the Russian government was making widespread attempts to throw suspicion upon the policy which its British rival was pursuing in Asia Minor. To Gosling, the British chargé d'affaires at St.

[1] *G.P.* ix, Nos. 2175–6, 2178 (Radowitz to Caprivi, 1 Aug., 3 Aug., and 28 Sept. 1890).
[2] White to Salisbury, No. 397 Secret, 9 Aug. 1890, F.O. 78/4277.
[3] Ibid., F.O. 78/4277 (minute by Sir Philip Currie, Parliamentary Under-Secretary); Salisbury to White, No. 257 Secret, 12 Sept. 1890, F.O. 78/4273.
[4] White to Salisbury, No. 397 Secret, 9 Aug. 1890, F.O. 78/4277; *G.P.* ix, Nos. 2175–6, 2178.

Petersburg, Giers insisted that he was not prepared to support the Armenians beyond occasionally calling their sorry condition to the attention of the Turkish ambassador, and receiving in return—'des belles phrases'.[1] To the French and German representatives at that capital, he likewise declared that he had no wish to raise the Armenian question, but went on to explain to them that the British government planned to turn Armenia into a second Bulgaria, a second bulwark against Russia's advance towards the Mediterranean.[2] And, at Constantinople, Nelidov worked hard to retrieve the reputation which he had lost because of his mishandling of the Bulgarian problem, and applied himself to the not too difficult task of persuading the Sultan that the British were about to embark upon a crusade to set up an Armenian national state.[3]

These rumours contained only a fragment of the truth: the British government certainly meant to prevent the Russians reaching Constantinople by way of Asia Minor, but it would not, and could not, create a 'second Bulgaria' in order to do so. Nationalism in Bulgaria had been turned into a strong weapon for the protection of the Ottoman Empire, but nationalism in Armenia was too weak and unnatural a growth to respond to similar treatment; it lingered on as a sporadic embarrassment which threatened to hasten its final collapse. Different conditions demanded different methods: economic penetration, not resurgent nationalism, was to be the means of forming a bulwark against Russia in Asia Minor.

[1] Gosling to Salisbury, No. 225 Secret, 3 Sept. F.O. 65/1383; cf. Phipps to Salisbury, No. 254 Very Confidential, 25 Sept. 1890, F.O. 7/1160.

[2] *D.D.F.*, 1st ser., viii, No. 171 (Laboulaye to Ribot, 21 Sept. 1890); *G.P.* ix, No. 2177 (Pourtales (German chargé d'affaires at St. Petersburg) to Caprivi, 15 Sept. 1890).

[3] Gosling to Salisbury, No. 225 Secret, 3 Sept. 1890, F.O. 65/1383; cf. White to Salisbury, No. 45 Secret, 7 Feb. 1891, F.O. 195/1706; *D.D.F.*, 1st ser., viii, No. 171; *G.P.* ix, No. 2178 (Radowitz to Caprivi, 28 Sept. 1890).

V

THE PROBLEM OF ASIA MINOR

THERE was nothing new about the method by which White attempted to strengthen the resistance of the Turks to a Russian invasion of their Asiatic provinces. Indeed, shortly after the Crimean war Lord Stratford de Redcliffe himself had announced his intention to encourage economic penetration into Asia Minor through the medium of a well-planned railway system. After laying the cornerstone of a railway station at Smyrna in 1858, he had declared that the construction of railways in Asiatic Turkey would involve reform in every sense; railways would lead to 'a progressive diminution of abuses, prejudices, and national animosities', and the property created by them 'would call for securities in matters of police, of finance, and of administrative justice'. 'Western civilization', he had concluded, 'is knocking hard at the gates of the Levant, and if it be not allowed to win its way into regions where it has hitherto been admitted so partially, it is but capable of forcing the passage and asserting its pretensions with little regard to anything but their satisfaction.'[1] This view was still fashionable in the 'eighties, and one of its most famous exponents was Joseph Chamberlain. During his visit to Constantinople in November 1886, he pointed out to the Sultan the strategic and commercial advantages which would accrue from the spreading of a railway network over Asia Minor, and advised him to appoint competent European engineers to work out a practical railway system so that reputable European financial houses might undertake its construction. But although the Sultan thanked him profusely for his suggestions and expressed his desire to make further progress in the matter, he had not allowed the discussion to extend beyond such general terms.[2]

[1] *The Times*, 16 Nov. 1858 (cited in L. H. Jenks, *The Migration of British Capital to 1875*, pp. 298–9).

[2] Memorandum by Sir William White, dated 25 July 1887: 'Remarks applying to different British schemes for the construction of Turkish Railways in Asia.' F.O. 78/3999; J. L. Garvin, *The Life of Joseph Chamberlain*, ii. 269, 448–51; cf. Hobart Pasha, 'A Strategical View of Turkey', *Nineteenth Century*, cvi. 993–1002.

The very elusiveness of the Sultan excited the curiosity of Great Britain's financiers and diplomats, and made them all the more anxious to pursue the matter further. And, as White's first secretary explained in a long memorandum upon the subject, there were many other reasons for their enthusiasm: first, they believed that a centralized and prosperous Turkey would be better equipped to resist the long-awaited Russian thrust into the Asiatic provinces of her empire; secondly, they contended that Turkey would not be without allies in such an eventuality provided that there were vast amounts of foreign capital invested in Asia Minor—'Capital and commerce are in these days more than mere moral forces, and they would be inclined to say *à bas les armes* to any foreign Power that attempted to interfere with a country whose growing prosperity would be so mixed up with their interests'; finally, they claimed that the construction of a railway system in Asiatic Turkey would help to revive Great Britain's respect and friendship for the Turk—'British philanthropists would acknowledge that our policy of upholding the integrity of the Ottoman Empire was no longer a hindrance to the advancement and well-being of the native population.'[1]

It has been assumed—both by White's contemporaries and by modern historians—that Abdul Hamid shared this European enthusiasm for railway enterprises; it has been asserted that his opposition to all forms of Westernization did not include the one Western innovation which might have helped him to impose an oriental absolutism upon the protesting Armenians and lawless Kurds; it has been taken for granted that he saw that the restoration of order in Asia Minor, and the development of its economic resources, would open up a new source of revenue for the sadly depleted imperial coffers. Poor roads made rebellion difficult to put down, slowed and disorganized trade, discouraged extensive cultivation of the fertile soil, and accounted for the vast store of unextracted mineral wealth. Railways, on the other hand, would transform Asia Minor from a distant and mountainous waste peopled by poly-

[1] White to Salisbury, No. 137 Commercial, 1 Nov. 1887 (encloses Fane's 'Report on the Exports and Imports of Turkey', dated Oct. 1887), F.O. 195/1569.

THE PROBLEM OF ASIA MINOR

glot and rebellious subjects, into a wealthy, firmly ruled, and easily accessible province. The Sultan could not miss such an obvious opportunity for a death-bed repentance: even at the eleventh hour, the Ottoman Empire might undertake the construction of a railway network in that area and achieve 'not only financial, but political salvation'.[1]

White had always been conscious of the weakness of Turkey's position in Asia Minor. Even in the autumn of 1885, when Europe's attention was focused upon the Balkans, he had remained alert to the fact that it was his duty to protect Asiatic as well as European Turkey. Indeed, during the opening stages of the Eastern Roumelian crisis, he had suspected that the Russians were encouraging the Porte to exhaust its financial reserves in restoring order in the Balkans so that they could attack Turkey at their own convenience by way of Asia Minor.[2] He had similar fears in March 1887 when he instructed one of his third secretaries, Bax-Ironside, to collect information on the subject of railways in Asia Minor, and Bax-Ironside's report, which stated that their construction would strengthen the Ottoman Empire both economically and politically, aroused considerable interest at the embassy and at the Foreign Office.[3] However, it was the failure of the Drummond Wolff Convention which finally prompted White himself to write at great length about Turkish railways in Asia Minor.[4] And his classic memorandum, dated 25 July 1887, stands apart from all other writings upon this topic, not because of its originality, but because of the cautiousness of its tone.[5] Unlike most of his contemporaries, White remained calm and objective amid the general clamour and enthusiasm for the construction of railways in Asiatic Turkey as a panacea for the economic and political ills which beset the Ottoman Empire.

---

[1] Ibid., F.O. 195/1569; E. M. Earle, *Turkey, the Great Powers, and the Bagdad Railway*, p. 29; H. Feis, *Europe, the World's Banker, 1870–1914*, p. 342.

[2] White to Salisbury, No. 497 Very Secret, 29 Sept. 1885, F.O. 78/3753.

[3] White to Salisbury, No. 48 Commercial, 2 Apr. 1887 (encloses Bax-Ironside's report, dated 29 Mar. upon which Fergusson, Pauncefote, and Sanderson wrote congratulatory minutes), F.O. 78/4008.

[4] White to Salisbury, Private and Confidential, 25 July 1887, Bound Volume No. 43, Salisbury Papers.

[5] 'Remarks applying to different British schemes for the construction of Turkish Railways in Asia', 25 July 1887, F.O. 78/3999. See Appendix IV.

White began by noting that little had been done about the construction of Turkish railways in Asia Minor since the signing of the Peace of Paris. In 1856 the Euphrates Valley Railway Company had been formed by a group of British financiers to construct a railway through the Euphrates valley connecting the Mediterranean with the Persian Gulf, but the company had eventually failed because it had been unable to raise the necessary capital for the financing of such an ambitious scheme. Only the smaller projects had succeeded: a British company had constructed a line from Smyrna to Aidin with branch connexions; other British companies held concessions for the line from Mersina to Adana, and for that from Smyrna via Kassaba to Alashir; and during the early years of White's embassy, the nucleus of the future Berlin–Baghdad railway was represented by the fifty-seven miles of line from the village of Haidar Pasha, opposite Constantinople, to Ismidt. In 1871 the Turkish government had employed a German engineer, von Pressel, to construct this line on its own account, but nine years later it had conceded the line for exploitation to an Anglo-Greek group represented by Messrs. Alt, Seefelder, Hanson, and Zafiropoulo.[1] Thus the broad projects of 1856 had given way to small and scattered lines which hugged the coast and failed to open up the interior of Asia Minor—lines which had little commercial and no strategic value, lines which tended to dismember rather than give cohesion and unity to the Asiatic provinces of the Ottoman Empire.[2] Looking back at the thirty years which had elapsed since the signing of the Treaty of Paris, White commented: 'Future historians will no doubt wonder how so few important results were accomplished after the conclusion of the Crimean War when British interest in the East was still fresh and our influence paramount and shared only with France.'[3] He then laid down four 'propositions' or

[1] (Alwyn Parker), 'The Bagdad Railway Negotiations', *Quarterly Review*, ccxxviii. 489–90; G. Young, *Corps de Droit Ottoman*, iv. 117–18; L. Ragey, *La Question du chemin de fer de Bagdad*, pp. 12–13; W. von Pressel, *Les Chemins de fer en Turquie d'Asie*, p. 55; H. Nicolson, *Lord Carnock*, pp. 92–93.

[2] Fane's 'Report on the Exports and Imports of Turkey', dated Oct. 1887 (enclosed in White to Salisbury, No. 137 Commercial, 1 Nov. 1887, F.O. 195/1569); K. Helfferich, *Die Deutsche Türkenpolitik*, p. 11.

[3] 'Remarks applying to different British schemes for the construction of Turkish Railways in Asia', 25 July 1887, F.O. 78/3999.

THE PROBLEM OF ASIA MINOR 113

principles upon which Great Britain should act in order to arrest the decline of her economic interests in Asia Minor and her political influence throughout the Ottoman Empire:

1. It is an essentially British interest that there should be railway communications established throughout Asiatic Turkey.
2. It is desirable that this should be a British Enterprise and should not fall into French or Franco-Russian hands.
3. It is essential that it should be a sound financial undertaking and should not require or expect any material support whatever from Her Majesty's Government.
4. The great difficulties for obtaining a concession of this kind must not be overlooked, and the alleged propitious disposition of the Sultan, knowing his irresolute and suspicious character, must not be counted for too much in its favour.¹

In spite of his own assertion that no argument was needed to prove that all these propositions were true, White felt that it was necessary to elaborate upon them. Commenting on the first three propositions, he observed: 'Our present system of supporting concessions without any regard to our general interests appears to me objectionable, and would be called by a German "planlos".'² It had long been the general rule of the Foreign Office, as Granville explained to his consuls in March 1881, that the British government should not be committed to the promotion of any specific commercial or industrial enterprise abroad: the impossibility of the Foreign Secretary being able to judge the respective merits of such schemes, and the danger and embarrassment of his showing favouritism, made it essential that letters of introduction to foreign officials should merely ensure their bearers 'such a reception as a traveller of respectability is entitled to'.³ Early in 1886, when a considerable clamour in the press forced the Foreign Office to re-examine its attitude towards such enterprises, the Parliamentary Under-Secretary for Foreign Affairs asked the consuls for their opinions and suggestions as to the proper limits of their action in regard to British trade abroad.⁴ And, as a result of these inquiries and consultations with the Chamber of Commerce and other trade

¹ Ibid.   ² Ibid.
³ Granville's Circular to Consols, Commercial, 8 Mar. 1881, F.O. 83/702.
⁴ Bryce's Circular to Consuls, 9 Apr. 1886, F.O. 83/907; cf. *The Times*, 2 Feb. 1886.

associations, the Foreign Secretary urged his consuls to give greater diplomatic support to such interests. But Rosebery found it impossible to lay down any hard and fast rules, and made his exhortations purely nominal by adding a proviso that such support should be 'manifestly regulated by considerations of time and peace'.[1] Thus the traditional principle enunciated by Granville remained virtually unaltered during the period of White's embassy at Constantinople.

The attitude adopted by the Foreign Office provided British bondholders and concession seekers with a simple explanation for the decline of Great Britain's commerce and finance on the Bosphorus. They glanced back nostalgically at the palmy days when Stratford de Redcliffe had dominated the Turkish scene, and kept asking for increased support from their government in furthering their interests at the Porte and the Palace.[2] Nor did White escape their criticism. For example, he was bitterly attacked by a certain Mr. Kynock, a munitions manufacturer and Conservative Member of Parliament for Aston Manor, who had submitted a tender for cartridges to the Porte in August 1887 only to find that the contract had been given to a German firm which had asked for higher terms. Kynock complained to the Foreign Office that White failed 'personally and domestically' as Great Britain's representative on the Bosphorus, and drew an unfavourable comparison between him and the German ambassador who eagerly fostered his country's financial interests at the Porte and the Palace.[3] He had previously given a public display of his indignation before his electors at a meeting of the Aston Conservative Association, but the *Daily News*, quick to answer the 'aggrieved Conservative', commented ironically that in future White would 'doubtless recognise the imperative duty of considering himself not only Ambassador of her Majesty, but commercial traveller for England, Kynock and Co.'[4]

It was criticisms such as these that White attempted to answer in his memorandum on Turkish railways in Asia

[1] Rosebery's Circular to Consuls, 31 July 1886, F.O. 83/908.
[2] Cf. 'German Methods in Turkey', *Quarterly Review*, ccxxviii. 296–314.
[3] Sanderson to Fergusson, Private, 12 May 1888 (with minute by Fergusson), F.O. 78/4095.
[3] The *Daily News*, 18 Nov. 1887.

Minor. He argued that even the limited support which the Foreign Office allowed its representatives to give to the commercial and industrial enterprises of British subjects should not be bestowed at random: he pointed out that any sound financial undertaking should not require or expect any material support from the British government, and that any support which it might give to speculators who were unable to fulfil their obligations was bound to result in a further loss of Great Britain's political influence at the Porte. But he went on to explain that 'the chief and almost insurmountable impediment' to his coming forward as 'the patron and active supporter' of railway or other concessions was the increasingly extensive use of baksheesh both at the Porte and the Palace.[1] 'I have come to the end of my tether...', he wrote, after hearing that the Sultan had given a contract for rifles to the Mauser Company, 'the public believe it was *solely* through the diplomatic intervention of the German embassy, but I am assured that £200,000 was spent as baksheesh on the parties immediately concerned at the Palace and elsewhere.'[2] Great Britain, with her Parliament jealously guarding against any increase in her Secret Service money, could not hope to compete in the use of large bribes to gain influential supporters for any scheme she might favour.[3] Moreover, as White constantly complained to Radowitz, the really first-rate London financial houses were so disgusted by the corruption and sheer administrative incompetence which prevailed in Turkey that they would have nothing to do with large undertakings there, and they consequently ignored the Asiatic railway scheme—the scheme which was so important to Great Britain politically.[4]

White's reference to the Sultan in the fourth of his 'propositions' is also interesting. For those who assumed that the Sultan's mind worked according to Western logic, it was easy to argue that he was eager to have a large railway network spread over the Asiatic provinces of his empire. But for

---

[1] 'Remarks applying to different British schemes for the construction of Turkish Railways in Asia', 25 July 1887, F.O. 78/3999.
[2] White to Pauncefote, Private and Confidential, 12 Mar. 1887, F.O. 78/4022.
[3] Lady G. Cecil, *The Life of Robert, Marquis of Salisbury*, iv. 2; G. E. Buckle, *The Letters of Queen Victoria*, 3rd ser., i. 193.
[4] H. Holborn, *Deutschland und die Türkei, 1875–1890*, pp. 83–85.

White, who credited the Sultan with a more instinctive and more oriental cunning, it seemed far more likely that his assent to such a project would only be obtained by a financial inducement in the form of a sum advanced to the Imperial Treasury, and that even this would not succeed until he was 'particularly pinched for money'.[1] Events were to prove that White's summing up of the Sultan's attitude was the correct one. It has been stated—without any evidence—that there was 'great rejoicing' at Constantinople when the first through express from Paris and Vienna reached the Golden Horn on 12 August 1888.[2] But what struck White was the absence of any celebration on the part of the Turks. Sending home his report on this important occasion, he confided to Salisbury:

> In any other country but this the opening of an International Railway Line . . . would have been celebrated with great solemnity. This was, however, by no means the case at Constantinople. . . . The Turkish authorities had removed on the previous evening all flags and other signs of rejoicing, and no Ottoman official was allowed to take any part in the celebration of that important occasion.
>
> This strange proceeding, showing the ill-humour of the Ottoman authorities, tends only to confirm the view shared by a great many persons that the Porte does not contemplate with joy the completion of the Railway.[3]

Besides having misgivings about the Sultan's attitude towards such schemes, White received information from London which confirmed him in his belief that great caution was needed in regard to such projects. Late in August 1887, when Prince Ferdinand's arrival on Bulgarian soil made war with Russia seem imminent, Salisbury impressed upon the War Office: 'That struggle will be a war not of battles but of devastation. The security of British India will be not to defeat Russia but to make it impossible for a Russian army to live within reach of the British possessions. And this im-

---

[1] 'Remarks applying to different British schemes for the construction of Turkish Railways in Asia', 25 July 1887, F.O. 78/3999.

[2] Cf. E. M. Earle, *Turkey, the Great Powers, and the Bagdad Railway*, p. 29. Earle cites the *Annual Register* for 1888 (pp. 44, 310) as his authority for this statement, but there is no reference to any Turkish 'rejoicing' at this event in that volume. Other authorities have also assumed that the Sultan was anxious to promote railway schemes throughout his empire. Cf. D. C. Blaisdell, *European Financial Control in the Ottoman Empire*, p. 127; H. Feis, *Europe, the World's Banker, 1870–1914*, p. 343.

[3] White to Salisbury, No. 320, 17 Aug. 1888, F.O. 78/4102.

plies not a frontier line but a frontier region.'[1] This general observation by Salisbury, together with a remark that Great Britain was never likely to have command of the Turkish army in the event of such a conflict, made Major-General Brackenbury of the Intelligence Branch change his opinion about the political and strategic value of Turkish railways in Asia Minor. In a secret memorandum, dated 7 September 1887, Brackenbury admitted that he had formerly agreed with White that these railways were of great strategic importance to the British government, but he went on to explain that this belief had been based on the assumption that, in the event of an Anglo-Russian war, British money could be successfully spent in obtaining the services of the Turkish army in Transcaucasia. In view of Salisbury's statements, however, he had come to the conclusion that a network of railways in Asiatic Turkey would hasten rather than delay the end of the Ottoman Empire: such a network, spreading out towards the Russian frontier, might easily be captured and put to good use by an invading Russian army.[2]

White was ready to accept this view of the situation for the time being. In fact, he used Brackenbury's arguments to strengthen his pleas for extreme caution. He advocated the maintenance of 'a friendly but reserved attitude' towards British enterprises for the construction of Turkish railways in Asia,[3] and perhaps it is significant that he delayed the publication of the embassy report on the economic condition of Turkey in the year 1887—'lest it might prove too much of a *réclame* for the Railways.'[4] However, the military attaché at Constantinople, Major Trotter, still insisted that the construction of a railway system in Asia Minor would strengthen the Ottoman Empire, and that this in itself meant the weakening of Russia: as an ally of Great Britain, Turkey would be stronger; as a neutral, she would be less easily intimidated by Russia; and even in the unlikely event of her

[1] Salisbury to White, No. 265 Very Secret, 10 Nov. 1887 (encloses Salisbury to War Office, Secret, 26 Aug. 1887), F.O. 195/1564.
[2] Secret Memorandum by Major-General Brackenbury, War Office, 7 Sept. 1887 (enclosed in Salisbury to White, No. 265 Very Secret, 10 Nov. 1887, F.O. 195/1564.
[3] White to Salisbury, No. 374 Very Secret, 10 Dec. 1887, F.O. 78/4001.
[4] Fane to Kennedy, Private, 15 Mar. 1888, F.O. 195/1569.

being an enemy, such railways would give Great Britain access to Kurdistan and Mesopotamia where discontent against the Sultan could easily be stirred up among the Arab tribes.[1] In April 1888, perhaps partly as a result of the arguments and information provided by Trotter, the War Office announced to Salisbury that it considered the building of railways in Asiatic Turkey to be of great political and commercial importance to the British government, and advised him to give any enterprises directed towards that purpose 'a very considerable amount of support'.[2] Salisbury's comment upon this recommendation neatly summed up Great Britain's major difficulty: 'What is the use of all this unless we know where the money is coming from?'[3] British businessmen lacked any powerful and serious financial backing, and the British embassy was unable to compete with the embassies of the other Powers in the extensive use of baksheesh. Faced with such difficulties, and with so few resources at their command, neither White nor Salisbury was prepared to commit a British government to the support of ambitious schemes for the construction of a railway system in Asia Minor. Each advocated caution, and waited for someone else to take the lead.

The initiative came from the Italian government. Soon after his famous visit to Friedrichsruh early in October 1887, Crispi spoke to the British ambassador at Rome about Russia's aims in Bulgaria and the need to free Turkey from her fatal influence. He went on to suggest that the formation of an International Commission—'similar to that established in Egypt'—would alleviate the financial difficulties of the Porte and help to end its dependence upon Russia.[4] When sounded about this proposal by Catalani, the Italian chargé d'affaires in London, Salisbury declared that its only result would be to throw the Sultan into the arms of Russia. However, he promised to consult White before giving the Italian

---

[1] White to Salisbury, No. 3 Very Secret, 7 Jan. 1888 (encloses Memorandum by Major Trotter, dated 3 Jan. 1888), F.O. 78/4097.
[2] War Office to Foreign Office, Secret, 9 Apr. 1888, F.O. 78/4126.
[3] Ibid., F.O. 78/4126. Minute by Salisbury.
[4] Lumley to Salisbury, No. 255, 15 Oct. 1887, F.O. 45/576.

government any definite answer.[1] White had no wish to further 'a repetition of all the experiments that have been tried in Egypt'. He dismissed the Italian proposal as 'a mere *ballon d'essai*, too crude, too vague to allow of my discussing it seriously',[2] and there the matter was dropped.

But with the conclusion of the Second Mediterranean Agreement in December 1887, and the signing of the German-Italian Military Agreement in the following January, the Italian government, under the guidance of the assertive and quick-tempered Crispi, became increasingly conscious of the role which it felt was demanded of a great Mediterranean Power. Also, the more closely Italy became connected with Great Britain and the two Central Powers the more strained her relations grew with France, and during 1888 and 1889 a series of political and commercial disputes kept those two countries on the brink of war.[3] Nowhere was this bitter hostility reflected more clearly than at Constantinople where the Italian ambassador, Blanc, was highly sensitive to any indication of a forward movement on the part of France, and eager to sound a loud general alarm.

On 13 December 1887, with the Second Mediterranean Agreement only a day old, Blanc wrote a long memorandum on the financial situation at Constantinople in which he conjured up the spectre of French finance and Russian militarism working hand in hand to gain complete control over Turkey.[4] Crispi sent copies of this memorandum to London, Vienna, and Berlin.[5] And, at Constantinople, Blanc consulted White and Radowitz, who thought him guilty of making 'great exaggerations'.[6]

But the Italian ambassador remained undaunted. While on leave in Paris, in May 1888, Blanc repeated his allegations about France and Russia to the British ambassador at that capital. He added that French money and Russian force

[1] Salisbury to White, Tel. No. 127 Secret, 17 Oct. 1887, F.O. 78/4002.
[2] White to Salisbury, No. 342 Very Confidential, 18 Oct. 1887, F.O. 78/4000.
[3] W. L. Langer, *European Alliances and Alignments, 1871-1890*, pp. 432-48; 479-81.
[4] White to Salisbury, No. 73 Secret, 21 Feb. 1888 (encloses undated copy of Blanc's Memorandum), F.O. 78/4098; H. Holborn, *Deutschland und die Türkei, 1875-1890*, p. 78.
[5] Holborn, loc. cit.
[6] White to Salisbury, No. 73 Secret, 21 Feb. 1888, F.O. 78/4098.

could not be overcome at Constantinople by diplomatic means alone, and suggested to Lytton that the League of Peace should make a bold stroke—'a local demonstration, but no territorial aggrandisement'—in order to convince the Turks of its reality.[1] The effect of this proposal was startling: at Rome, Kennedy expressed his relief that poor Italian and lack of parliamentary debating skill would prevent Blanc from ever becoming Foreign Minister;[2] at St. Petersburg, Morier complained of Blanc's political deficiencies and accused him of wishing to plunge Europe into a war;[3] and at London, Salisbury thought it wiser not to repeat the Italian ambassador's observations to Kalnoky.[4] But the menace of French finance and Russian arms at Constantinople had already become Blanc's parrot-cry: filled with a *saeva indignatio* about the contempt with which Italy, Great Britain, and Austria-Hungary were regarded on the Bosphorus, he continually advocated a naval demonstration to prove to the Turks that the League of Peace was 'no mere phantom'.[5]

On 10 June 1888, soon after his return from leave, Blanc wrote a second memorandum on the Franco-Russian threat to Constantinople in which he stressed all his earlier arguments. But he also pointed specifically to French attempts to obtain a concession for the construction of a railway network in Anatolia, and suggested two remedies: the foundation of an 'Anglo-German-Italian Banking Association' at Constantinople, and a closer understanding between the British, German, and Italian delegates on the Council of the Ottoman Public Debt Administration.[6] These proposals were treated more respectfully by his British and German colleagues than the vague allegations contained in his memorandum of the previous December. In the summer of 1888 White had serious misgivings about Russian naval preparations in the Black Sea, and was convinced that the German embassy

[1] Lytton to Salisbury, No. 304 Confidential, 24 May 1888, F.O. 27/2906.
[2] Kennedy (chargé d'affaires at Rome) to Salisbury, No. 161 Confidential, 12 June 1888, F.O. 45/602.
[3] Morier to Salisbury, No. 212 Most Secret, 13 June 1888, F.O. 65/1331.
[4] Salisbury to Paget, Tel. No. 40, 5 June 1888, F.O. 7/1136.
[5] Cf. Fane (chargé d'affaires at Constantinople) to Salisbury, No. 266 Confidential, 11 July 1888, F.O. 78/4102.
[6] Malet to Salisbury, No. 180 Confidential, 29 June 1888 (Blanc's memorandum, dated 10 June, is enclosed), F.O. 64/1187.

shared his fears.¹ He was also anxious about the strong support which Montebello was giving to a French financial syndicate in its efforts to secure an extensive railway concession in Asiatic Turkey.² Meanwhile, although Busch, the German chargé d'affaires at Constantinople, regarded Blanc's proposed 'Banking Association' as impractical, he thought that greater co-operation between the delegates of the friendly Powers on the Council of the Ottoman Debt Administration was possible, and that provided it did not assume the proportions of an international finance committee and so arouse Turkish suspicion and resentment, such co-operation might put an end to France's financial predominance on the Bosphorus. White was in general agreement with this view.³

Blanc's language had been extravagant, his fears had been exaggerated, and most of his proposals had been wildly impractical. Nevertheless, he had served a most useful purpose during the spring and summer of 1888. In spite of his concern for the fate of Asiatic Turkey, White had remained reluctant to make any move which might arouse the Sultan's suspicions or invite sharp Franco-Russian opposition. But Blanc had rushed in where White feared to tread, and had protected his British colleague from the full force of the Franco-Russian onslaught against the policy pursued by the League of Peace at Constantinople. 'They are now directing all their shafts against Blanc, who was the first [sic] originator of a scheme for counteracting the preponderance of French capitalists by the joint efforts of England, Germany and Italy', White pointed out to Salisbury when the struggle for railway concessions was at its height.⁴ He also explained that it was largely due to 'the spirit of enquiry' which Blanc had awakened that the subject had 'found an echo in the Imperial Chancery at Berlin'.⁵ Once they had set the stage for action, the Italians made their exit as sudden as their entry: in September 1888 it was observed that Crispi had dropped all his

[1] White to Salisbury, No. 230 Secret, 6 June 1888, F.O. 78/4101.
[2] White to Salisbury, No. 291 Confidential, 1 Aug. 1888, F.O. 78/4102.
[3] Malet to Salisbury, No. 180 Confidential, 29 June 1888 (Busch's comments on Blanc's Memorandum are enclosed), F.O. 64/1187.
[4] White to Salisbury, Private, 16 Oct. F.O. 364/1; No. 395, 11 Oct. 1888, F.O. 78/4264.
[5] White to Salisbury, No. 456 Confidential, 15 Nov. 1888, F.O. 78/4105.

plans for the reform of Turkey's administration,[1] and two months later it was even rumoured that Blanc was to be recalled from Constantinople.[2]

The questions raised by the Italians were destined to be solved by the Germans. Germany's policy towards Turkey was founded upon a contradiction—the contradiction between her signature of the secret Re-insurance Treaty with Russia and her adhesion to the Second Mediterranean Agreement. Bismarck wished to retain Russia's friendship by promising her increased diplomatic support in the Near East, but at the same time he sought to lessen the effects of her displeasure by building up a connexion with Turkey and the Mediterranean *entente*: while he let it be known at St. Petersburg that he was not opposed to a Russian entry of Bulgaria or even Constantinople, he intimated in other quarters that he was anxious to strengthen Turkey by quietly fostering Great Britain's influence on the Bosphorus.[3] Thus his statements about his Turkish policy did not always tally with his actions. In May 1889, for example, he noted: 'The more difficult Constantinople is to take directly, the stronger is the temptation for Russia to seize Austria in the first place.' But in spite of this observation, he continued to support British influence at that capital. Indeed, four months earlier he had gone so far as to offer Salisbury an alliance with Germany.[4]

The Kaiser's visit to Constantinople in November 1889 gave rise to similar contradictions and misunderstandings. Bismarck hastened to inform the Tsar that this visit 'was only prompted by a love of travel', and that Germany did not intend to contract an alliance with Turkey.[5] But although the Kaiser did not enter into any political discussions during his stay at Constantinople, White realized that his visit in itself would tend to strengthen the Sultan's will to resist Russia.

[1] Kennedy (chargé d'affaires at Rome) to Salisbury, No. 244 Confidential, 17 Sept. 1888, F.O. 45/603.
[2] Kennedy to Salisbury, Nos. 285, 293, and 297 Confidential, 13, 14, and 15 Nov. 1888, F.O. 45/603.
[3] *Supra*, pp. 92–100; H. Holborn, *Deutschland und die Türkei*, p. 56; O. Hammann, *The World Policy of Germany, 1890–1912*, p. 17; J. B. Wolf, *The Diplomatic History of the Bagdad Railroad*, pp. 10–11.   [4] Holborn, p. 56.
[5] Malet to Salisbury, No. 282 Secret, 13 Oct.; No. 290 Confidential, 19 Oct. F.O. 64/1214; Morier to Salisbury, No. 334 Secret, 30 Oct. 1889, F.O. 65/1363.

Moreover, he was convinced that both the Kaiser and Herbert Bismarck, who accompanied him, had been impressed with what they had seen of Turkey, and that they had come to the conclusion that it was worth defending.[1] Herbert Bismarck had called twice upon White during his stay, but had ignored the ambassadors of the other Powers. He had explained to him that he was fully aware of 'the importance which is attached by the Turks to these external demonstrations', and that the purpose of his visits was to give them proof of the cordial relations which existed between the German and British governments.[2] This small but significant gesture aptly illustrates the policy which the Germans wished to pursue on the Bosphorus: British influence was to be quietly encouraged, Russian fears were not to be unnecessarily aroused, and Germany was to remain in the background as far as possible. But by the time the Kaiser visited Constantinople this policy was already beginning to fail. It was failing because Germany was growing more and more conspicuous at Constantinople, and Germany was growing more and more conspicuous at that capital because her banking and business interests there were becoming too strong to accept the role of silent partner to Great Britain. The Kaiser's visit to Constantinople at the end of 1889 only confirmed the change which was taking place in Germany's attitude towards the Ottoman Empire. It will be seen that that change had already begun with the granting of the Anatolian railway concession to the Kaulla group in the autumn of the previous year.

In June 1888 the German chargé d'affaires at Constantinople pointed out that although the Sultan was distrustful of British and French finance, he might be prepared to welcome German financial undertakings in his empire because Germany had no obvious political axe to grind in the Near East.[3] The Sultan soon acted according to this theory by

[1] White to Salisbury, Nos. 438 and 440 Confidential, 6 and 8 Nov. 1889, F.O. 78/4207.
[2] Ibid., F.O. 78/4207; Paget to Salisbury, No. 321 Very Confidential, 13 Nov. 1889, F.O. 7/1149.
[3] Malet to Salisbury, No. 180 Confidential, 29 June 1888 (encloses Memorandum by Busch, dated 11 June), F.O. 64/1187; Holborn, pp. 84–85.

sending the German engineer, Wilhelm von Pressel, to Berlin as his agent to bring plans for the construction of an Anatolian railway system before leading German bankers.¹ The concession consisted of the right to administer the existing 57 miles of line from Haidar Pasha to Ismidt; to extend that line for 300 miles to Angora; to have preferential rights for eventual extensions beyond there; and to retain the whole undertaking with substantial financial guarantees from the Ottoman government for a period of ninety-nine years.² Alfred Kaulla of the Würtembergische Vereinsbank and Dr. Georg Siemens, Director of the Deutsche Bank, decided to compete for the concession and announced their plans to the German Foreign Office. And, in spite of the fact that his friend Bleichröder had an interest in a French group which was seeking the concession, Bismarck gave Siemens and Kaulla his non-committal blessings.³ Writing to Siemens on 2 September 1888 he assured him that the representative of the Deutsche Bank at Constantinople would receive the full support of the German embassy there; he added, however, that the German government would not assume any responsibility for German money invested in 'speculative' enterprises in Turkey.⁴

Three other serious competitors had already entered the lists for the concession: a French group headed by the Imperial Ottoman Bank; another French group headed by Collas, the contractor for the Ottoman lighthouses; and, as a poor third, an Anglo-Italian group headed by Caillard, the President of the Council of the Ottoman Public Debt. The first French group had the backing of Bleichröder, and the second had the support of Alt and Seefelder who had been in precarious possession of the Haidar Pasha to Ismidt trunk line since 1880. To complicate matters further, Alt was a British subject and had constantly sought his government's support for his claims to rights for the extension.⁵ Until Sep-

---

¹ Wolf, p. 13; *G.P.* xiv, footnote to p. 441; K. Helfferich, *Georg von Siemens*, iii. 33–34. ² G. Young, *Corps de Droit Ottoman*, iv. 117–18.
³ Wolf, p. 13; Helfferich, iii. 33–34; White to Salisbury, Private, 16 Oct. F.O. 364/1; No. 395, 11 Oct. 1888, F.O. 78/4264.
⁴ E. M. Earle, *Turkey, the Great Powers, and the Bagdad Railway*, p. 41 (prints letter from Bismarck to Siemens dated 2 Sept. 1888).
⁵ Wolf, pp. 12–13; Holborn, pp. 83–84.

tember 1888, when Kaulla arrived at Constantinople, it seemed almost certain that the concession would be given to one of these French groups, and that French finance would add yet another victory to its long series of triumphs on the Bosphorus.

At first sight it seems difficult to reconcile White's sudden enthusiasm for the Anatolian railway concession in the autumn of 1888 with the circumspection with which he had hitherto regarded such schemes. But for all his cautious scepticism, White had always maintained that the Sultan might agree to such a project in exceptional circumstances, and in the autumn of 1888 the circumstances were exceptional. In the first place, Blanc's warnings about the threat of French financial predominance at Constantinople had attracted considerable attention at the German Foreign Office: Herbert Bismarck had admitted to Malet that he attached much importance to the subject, but he had also insisted that Great Britain should take the lead because 'its interests were greater and it would be more easy to find the starting point there on account of the vastly superior wealth of its capitalists'.[1] But in August 1888 the completion of the European section of the Oriental Railway system put Germany in direct railway communication with the Bosphorus, and Turkish securities, hitherto almost unknown in Berlin, suddenly found a ready market there.[2] Most important of all, the Imperial Treasury had become 'particularly pinched for money' during the middle of 1888, and, as White had predicted, the Sultan proved to be open to 'temptation by advances'.[3]

Indeed, it was a symptom of the extraordinary times that White listened to the advice of Vincent Caillard during the autumn of 1888. True to his motto, *Aide-toi, Dieu t'aidera*, Caillard had achieved success early in life. In 1879, when only twenty-three years of age, he had been appointed Assistant Commissioner for Great Britain on the Montenegrin

[1] Malet to Salisbury, No. 180 Confidential, 29 June 1888, F.O. 64/1187.
[2] H. Feis, *Europe, the World's Banker, 1870–1914*, p. 296.
[3] Cf. White's 'Remarks applying to different British Schemes for the construction of Turkish Railways in Asia', 25 July 1887, F.O. 78/3999.

Boundary Commission because of his exceptional knowledge of Near Eastern affairs. Four years later he had become so well established in financial circles at Constantinople that he was chosen to succeed Sir Edgar Vincent as President of the Council of the Ottoman Public Debt.[1] Unfortunately, Caillard was not content with his official position, and he often became involved in financial and political schemes which brought him into sharp conflict with White. 'Caillard complains that you do not regard with sufficient reverence the rights of the Bondholder', Salisbury informed White early in 1887, but he then went on to add that he himself was not prepared to offer the bondholder more than 'a tender, but perfectly platonic, expression of sympathy'.[2] 'The fact is', White replied, 'Mr. Caillard is deficient in tact, and at times takes the airs of a diplomatic Representative of some important class at home, and comes to me assuming a rather dictatorial tone. He is also fond of interfering like all people who have been thrust into positions for which they are not made.'[3] White continued to deplore Caillard's practice of 'extending his financial duties to other than financial schemes',[4] and it was well known at the German embassy that White and Caillard were not on speaking terms.[5]

In comparison, White's relations with Colonel Alt, the other British subject interested in the Anatolian concession, had been good. In August 1887 he had been pleased to hear that Alt's company had concluded a preliminary arrangement with the Turkish government for the extension of their line from Ismidt to Angora and Diarbekir, and ultimately to Bagdad.[6] It was not until the following July, when he learnt that Alt and his associates were co-operating with French financial groups, that White became cooler in his attitude towards Alt, and began to fear that any benefit which he might derive from the support of the British embassy would be 'turned to the advantage of interests which can hardly be

---

[1] *Dictionary of National Biography, 1922–1930*, pp. 151–2.
[2] Salisbury to White, Private, 5 Apr. 1887, Additional White Papers.
[3] White to Salisbury, Private, 15 Apr. 1887, Bound Volume No. 32, Salisbury Papers.
[4] White to Salisbury, Private, 14 July 1888, F.O. 364/1.
[5] Malet to Salisbury, No. 180 Confidential, 29 June 1888, F.O. 64/1187.
[6] White to Salisbury, No. 273 Confidential, 16 Aug. 1887, F.O. 195/1567.

called ours'.¹ On 10 August 1888 he informed Salisbury that as there were other British financiers interested in the concession, it would be inexpedient to act without sufficient knowledge of the value of the rival schemes.² Salisbury replied that the Foreign Office did not have the material to form a confident opinion, and left the advice to be given to the Porte on the subject to White's own judgement.³

On 23 September an Imperial *irade* was issued conferring the Anatolian railway concession upon the Kaulla group. Meanwhile Caillard had not been idle. He had learnt that the two French groups had combined to prevent the *irade* being put into force and to secure the concession for themselves—an action 'directly contrary to British interests'. He had originally intended to make a bid for the concession on behalf of 'a powerful British financial group', and at the same time he would have welcomed the participation of German and Italian financial houses to the exclusion of French and French-controlled Austrian houses. However, he had failed to persuade his friends in London of the urgent necessity for such co-operation. But since he had already secured the support of an Italian group, he had written to certain German houses on his own initiative, and had communicated with Radowitz through whom he had met Kaulla and come to terms with the Deutsche Bank: the British and German financial groups were to share the concession equally, the Italian group being a third party whose share was to be deducted equally from the shares of the other two; no French or Austrian houses were to be allowed to participate, and the fusion of the British and German groups was to be kept a secret until the *irade* had been confirmed. 'It was agreed between M. Kaulla and myself', Caillard explained to White, 'that *I* should appear to hang back without withdrawing my proposal, and that *he* should go entirely forward with a combined proposal for a loan and for the Ismidt-Angora Railway, upon which we had both previously agreed.'⁴

Caillard's scheme seemed to solve most of White's

[1] White to Salisbury, No. 283 Secret, 21 July 1888, F.O. 78/4264.
[2] White to Salisbury, Tel. No. 63, 10 Aug. 1888, F.O. 78/4264.
[3] Salisbury to White, Tel. No. 97, 13 Aug. 1888, F.O. 78/4264.
[4] Caillard to White, Private, 24 Sept. 1888, F.O. 78/4103.

problems. There were obvious arguments against the formation of an exclusively British syndicate to undertake the construction of this important railway system in Asia Minor: such a syndicate would have aroused the Sultan's suspicions and called into existence a large number of powerful opponents; it would also have committed both the British embassy and the British government to 'an attitude in their support which it was most undesirable for them to assume', and have forced them into the impossible position of having to compete with the other Powers in the use of baksheesh and the advancing of loans to the Ottoman exchequer. But Caillard's idea of an equal financial partnership with Germany would smooth away all these difficulties. For example, the German syndicate had been able to offer the Turks a loan of £T1,500,000 as an inducement to accept its project: White strongly doubted that a British syndicate would have been willing, or able, to enter into a transaction of that kind. 'That', White concluded, 'is why I consider the success of the German scheme, especially with the participation of English capital, as one of the most desirable things for British Interests, and for the Ottoman Empire, that could have happened.'[1]

White's behaviour during the critical days between 23 September, when the Imperial *irade* was issued to the Kaulla group, and 4 October, when it was finally confirmed, closely resembled that of Caillard: during that short period the diplomat was merely shadowing the financier. Thus White carefully abstained from showing any interest in the scheme, avoided the embarrassment of choosing between the rival claims of Alt and Caillard, and stood by while the Germans used all their influence at the Palace to establish their hold on the concession. Salisbury approved of this policy. When Caillard had asked him to cancel all instructions to White which advocated the support of Alt's claims, Salisbury had refused his request. He was confident, however, that White would 'not move with inconvenient vigour on behalf of Alt'.[2] On 15 October—when the German concession was secure—he went through the formality of reminding White that

[1] White to Salisbury, No. 377, 29 Sept. 1888, F.O. 78/4103.
[2] Caillard to Salisbury, Private, 25 Sept. 1888 (with minute by Salisbury), F.O. 78/4264.

'whatever may be the advantages offered by the new combination, the legal rights of the British subjects interested in the Haidar Pasha-Ismidt Line must not be ignored', but he went on to congratulate his ambassador upon his 'abstention from all interference with the negotiations'.[1]

Anglo-German co-operation in the working of the Kaulla concession was to help to restore Great Britain's financial influence at Constantinople; even more important, it was to serve as the basis for a political partnership between the two Powers which would have far greater ramifications; it was to be White's answer to the Franco-Russian partnership which had wrecked the Drummond Wolff Convention in the summer of 1887. At a banquet given in honour of the settlement of the concession upon the German group, White declared that event to be of great significance because it meant that Great Britain had gained a partner who would help to relieve her of the burden which she had hitherto been condemned to bear alone in the Near East.[2] 'This business', he confided to Salisbury on 16 October, 'is the commencement of a split between Radowitz and Nelidoff, and bids fair to become a new departure for Germany at Constantinople which it will be most interesting to watch.'[3] The bulwark of Bulgarian nationalism in the Balkans, and the German economic 'scarecrow' in Asia Minor, were to keep the Ottoman Empire secure from any further Russian incursions.

But disillusionment was soon to follow. White, who had always scorned the financial speculator, had ironically been drawn into one of the most unsound schemes ever hatched on the Bosphorus. Caillard believed that once he had won the support of the Deutsche Bank he would be able to overcome 'that exasperating slowness which seems so often to seize city-men'.[4] But when he visited London during the October and November of 1888 he discovered that his high-handed methods had lost him support in the City, and that none would be forthcoming unless the claims of Alt were in some

---

[1] Salisbury to White, No. 315, 15 Oct. 1888, F.O. 78/4264.
[2] R. von Kühlmann, *Erinnerungen*, pp. 364–5.
[3] White to Salisbury, Private, 16 Oct. 1888, F.O. 364/1.
[4] Caillard to Sanderson, Private, 25 Sept. 1888, F.O. 78/4264.

way settled.¹ Meanwhile, White had also become anxious about the success of Caillard's scheme, for in the middle of November there was still no sign of the expected transfer of half of the Kaulla group's interests to Caillard and his associates.²

On 26 November, when he returned to Constantinople from London, Caillard calmly announced that he wanted the embassy to support the claims of Alt, his former opponent. The news of this volte-face prompted the Assistant Under-Secretary at the Foreign Office to comment: 'Of all crooked negotiations, this is the crookedest.'³ But the concession remained exclusively German, and by December all hopes of Anglo-Italian participation were becoming 'more and more of the kind of shadows disappearing in the distance',⁴ and White was making a humiliating return to his original belief that Great Britain's financial interests on the Bosphorus were too diverse and divided to be reconciled with her political interests there. Looking back upon the struggle for the concession, he complained to Sanderson:

Alt and Caillard have both committed the same error here, instead of putting forward their strongest financiers at once, and showing their best cards—they cancelled these and played alone—of course, success would have been attended with glory and profit in which they would have profited almost alone. But the Turks would not believe there was anything behind them and would not hear either of Alt or C[aillard] for the concession.

Had those two men not put themselves forward in this way and muddled the thing, English capital, and what is better, English Industry would have the construction of these Asiatic lines.⁵

On 7 January 1889 the line from Haidar Pasha to Ismidt was seized by the Turkish government in spite of protests from Alt and his associates, and the German group announced that it was ready to take over the line and make the agreed extensions.⁶ Alt called at the Foreign Office on 19 January and

¹ White to Sanderson, Private, 12 Dec. 1888, F.O. 78/4264.
² White to Salisbury, No. 448 Confidential, 10 Nov. 1888, F.O. 78/4105.
³ White to Sanderson, Private, 26 Nov. 1888 (with minute by Sanderson), F.O. 78/4264.
⁴ White to Sanderson, Private, 12 Dec. 1888, F.O. 78/4264.
⁵ White to Sanderson, Private, 9 Dec. 1888, F.O. 78/4264.
⁶ White to Salisbury, Tel. No. 1, 7 Jan. 1889, F.O. 78/4265.

informed Sanderson that since the Caillard scheme had come to grief, he himself would try to come to some arrangement with the Deutsche Bank.[1] However Alt met with little success in Berlin, and the concession remained virtually under German control.[2] When the Anatolian Railway Company was formed, early in 1889, the British were given three seats on its board of directors and at first subscribed part of the capital, but the Italians, who feared French reprisals upon their securities, took no part. But even this pale shadow of Caillard's original scheme only lasted until 1890 when the British sold out their shares.[3] Not until January 1895 was £T130,000 paid to Alt and his group by the Turkish government as compensation for the seizure of the line.[4]

The experiences of the autumn and winter of 1888 confirmed White in his original belief that an ambassador should keep aloof from the financiers who flourished at Constantinople. His relations with Caillard, which had never been cordial, rapidly deteriorated. By the middle of 1889 they had become so bad that Salisbury himself pleaded with White and asked him to become reconciled with Caillard. He pointed out that it would be better to bring Caillard under embassy guidance than allow him to remain independent and able to influence opinion in Great Britain on Turkish affairs.[5] But even Salisbury failed to make White renew his acquaintance with Caillard: 'This Gentleman', White explained, 'is fond of pursuing a variety of schemes quite independent of his own duties here: and I must avoid every knowledge of these so as to keep myself free from all suspicion—like Caesar's wife.'[6] Once bitten, White was more than twice shy.

White has often been criticized for encouraging the economic aspirations of the Germans in the autumn of 1888;

[1] Sanderson to Salisbury, minute dated 19 Jan. 1889, F.O. 78/4265.
[2] Beauclerk (chargé d'affaires at Berlin) to Salisbury, No. 82, 2 Mar. 1889 (Copy), F.O. 78/4265; Wolf, p. 15; Helfferich, iii. 40-42.
[3] Helfferich, iii. 40-41, 51; Holborn, p. 105.
[4] Currie to Kimberly, Tel. No. 40, 30 Jan. 1895, F.O. 78/4681.
[5] Salisbury to White, Private, 11 June 1889, F.O. 364/1.
[6] White to Salisbury, Private and Confidential, 29 June 1889, Bound Volume No. 33, Salisbury Papers.

he has often been accused of paving the way for their political predominance at Constantinople.[1] But such criticisms spring from a serious misunderstanding of the situation at that capital during the period of White's embassy: they fail to take account of the important fact that the growth of German influence on the Bosphorus was once welcomed by Great Britain, not feared.

There was no widespread anxiety about the threat of German predominance during the period of White's embassy at Constantinople. There were occasional alarms, but these attracted little serious attention: all too often the unsuccessful speculator equated Great Britain's ruin with his own. But as the result of an official inquiry it was stated in 1886 that 'the condition of trade in general, and of British trade in particular, cannot be considered as depressed in the Ottoman Empire generally at the present time as compared with the last twenty years'.[2] In November 1887 Colonel Swaine, the British military attaché at Berlin, expressed the opinion that Germany might outstrip Great Britain both commercially and politically in Turkey and the Far East. It is significant, however, that although his warnings were forwarded to Tokyo and Peking, the Foreign Office did not think it necessary to make them known at Constantinople.[3] The British government was not unduly apprehensive about the successes of German business men in Turkey: an official report of 1888 concluded that 'Germany has not been gaining in common markets in late years at the expense of English trade. Its gains have been special and in certain directions. Our preponderance remains substantially what it was ten years ago.'[4] Nor was this report too optimistic as far as trade with Turkey was concerned: Great Britain was still in the first rank of her suppliers with a considerable lead over Germany, and there seemed to be no cause for alarm at the

---

[1] Cf. Holborn, p. 103; G. Gaulis, *La Ruine d'un Empire*, p. 114; Sir W. M. Ramsay, *The Revolution in Constantinople and Turkey*, pp. 142–3, 303–4; G. Young, *Constantinople*, p. 229; Lord Hardinge of Penshurst, *Old Diplomacy*, p. 47; M. Moukhtar Pacha, *La Turquie, l'Allemagne et L'Europe*, pp. 71–72.

[2] *P.P.* (1886), xxiii [C–4893], 715.

[3] Malet to Salisbury, No. 419, 5 Nov. 1887 (encloses Swaine to Malet, No. 70 Confidential, 1 Nov. 1887), F.O. 64/1160.

[4] *P.P.* (1888), xciii [C–5297], 266.

distribution of German products in the Ottoman Empire;[1] British shipowners even found the carrying of German merchandise a new and profitable freight, and the foundation of the German Levant Line in 1889, with a direct service from Hamburg, Bremen, and Antwerp, passed almost unnoticed.[2] Dilke, who gleaned much of his information on Near Eastern affairs from his friend White, has perhaps given the best summing up of the British attitude to the part being played by Germany at Constantinople during the late 'eighties: 'England ought to view with pleasure the permanent character of German influence at Constantinople, which is always the second influence there . . . is friendly to England, and it is the only influence that never wanes.'[3]

In the autumn of 1888 White had hoped to achieve two things: to strengthen British finance at Constantinople by directing its energies towards participation in a single comprehensive scheme for the economic development of Asia Minor, and to enlist German support for such a scheme and so ensure that the German government took a greater interest in the fate of the Ottoman Empire. White did not achieve his first aim, but he was all too successful in his second. However, it would be wrong to hold him responsible for either of these results, for by the end of the 'eighties the future of Asiatic Turkey was largely being decided not by diplomats, but by financiers. Having missed earlier opportunities, British finance at Constantinople was holding its own against foreign competitors with increasing difficulty, while German finance at that capital was experiencing the beginnings of a period of rapid expansion; speculators such as Alt and Caillard were no match for financiers of the calibre of Siemens and Kaulla whose sound schemes and vigorous methods were slowly forcing a reluctant German government to increase and extend its interest in Turkey. White had not failed the British financier: on the contrary, the British financier had failed him in the autumn and winter of 1888.

[1] R. J. Sontag, *Germany and England, Background of Conflict*, p. 217.
[2] L. Ragey, *La Question du chemin de fer de Bagdad*, p. 16.
[3] Sir C. Dilke, *The Present Position of European Politics*, p. 25.

VI

THE END OF AN EMBASSY, 1888-91

SIR WILLIAM WHITE took his final leave of absence from the embassy at Constantinople on 24 December 1891. He had planned to break his journey at Berlin and spend the Christmas there with his wife and married daughter. But as a result of the long trip and the rapid change of climate he caught a severe chill, and when he arrived at the German capital he was immediately ordered to bed. He died suddenly and unexpectedly on 28 December. His body was buried at Berlin with full military honours, being given the funeral escort of a full general; Queen Victoria sent a bronze wreath of oak and laurel leaves, the German emperor hastened to express his deep sympathy and sorrow, and the Sultan sent a wreath decked with the Imperial Ottoman colours.[1]

There were rumours, however, that White's death had not seriously curtailed his career as a diplomat, that ill health had gradually forced him to take a less active part in Near Eastern politics, and that the purpose of his last journey to London had been 'to receive the thanks of his Queen and claim a well earned pension'.[2] But the correspondence which passed between Salisbury and White on the eve of the latter's departure from Constantinople fails to substantiate this view; although it reveals that White was anxious to consult his chief during his stay in London, it contains no explicit mention of his permanent recall and retirement. But what does stand out —after a close examination of the final years of his embassy— is that White's ideas about the conduct of British affairs in the Near East were becoming increasingly different from those of Salisbury, and it is possible to suggest, therefore, that it was only by the sudden tragedy of his death that an open rift was avoided.

White had always taken two things for granted: that the main aim of Great Britain's Near Eastern policy was to protect the Straits, and that this object could only be achieved by

---

[1] *The Times*, 29 Dec. 1891; 2 Jan. 1892.
[2] The *Daily Telegraph*, 29 Dec. 1891; cf. *G.P.* ix, No. 2111.

working in partnership with Germany and her Triple Alliance allies. These, according to White, were the two simple and unalterable rules to be remembered when grappling with the complexities of the Eastern question. These were the views which he upheld in 1885 in a spirited correspondence with his friend Morier, and which, a year later, Salisbury himself defended against the bitter attacks of Randolph Churchill. Indeed, there is no evidence that White was ever prepared to abandon them, but by the end of 1891 there were already signs that Salisbury, in certain circumstances, was prepared to do so.

Between 1885 and 1891 Salisbury's views upon the Straits question underwent a series of gradual changes. In 1885 he had risked the humiliation of a diplomatic defeat at the hands of the Three Emperors' Alliance, and had accepted the creation of a 'big Bulgaria' as a *pis aller*, in order to halt Russia's steady advance down the Balkans towards Constantinople. And, a year later, when Randolph Churchill suggested that the protection of India and Egypt was far more important than the defence of the Straits, Salisbury firmly reminded him that there could be no question of allowing Constantinople to fall into Russian hands. Yet he argued that it was for party rather than strategic reasons that he was compelled to 'draw the line' at Constantinople: 'I pity the English party that has this item on their record', he wrote to Churchill on 28 September 1886. 'They will share the fate of Lord North's party.'[1] A few days later he confided to the same correspondent: 'I consider the loss of Constantinople would be the ruin of our party and a heavy blow to the country.'[2]

Great Britain's ability to defend the Straits was becoming increasingly questionable. Until 1888 the naval strength of France, her great rival in the Mediterranean, had been distributed fairly evenly between Brest, Cherbourg, and Toulon, but from then onwards France's most powerful battleships were concentrated at Toulon, and the British fleet therefore ceased to be the undisputed master of the Mediterranean. Worse still, should the Russian Black Sea fleet force its way

---

[1] Winston S. Churchill, *Lord Randolph Churchill*, p. 519; cf. also pp. 515–32.
[2] Ibid., p. 520.

through the Straits and join forces with the French in the Mediterranean, the situation there would be one of grave peril for the British Navy. It was therefore decided, in May 1890, that the British Mediterranean fleet should be divided into two squadrons: one to be based upon Gibraltar, and the other upon Malta; one to keep the French fleet in the western Mediterranean, and the other to prevent any Russian attempt to sail through the Bosphorus and the Dardanelles.[1] But in spite of these precautions Salisbury became convinced that once Russia gained control of the Straits little could be done to dislodge her. Yet at the same time he had become less concerned about the consequences of a successful Russian blow against Constantinople. In July 1891, when Joseph Chamberlain asked him if he considered that a Russian occupation of Constantinople would be as injurious to British interests as was supposed at the time of the Crimean war, Salisbury replied that it would not, and went on to explain that Palmerston had made a great mistake in not accepting Tsar Nicholas's proposals since Russia with Constantinople would be far more vulnerable than Russia in the Black Sea. He added, however, that the policy since adopted by the British government, and the rise of the Balkan states, had completely altered the situation.[2] Two months later, after seeking the expert advice of Sir John Lintorn Simmons, he expressed the view that: 'If Russia does once get hold of the Dardanelles, I doubt whether any effort which it will be worth our while to make will shake her off.'[3] And by October 1891 he had added a new doctrine to his Straits policy by officially informing White that 'any privilege in respect of the Straits granted to any one Power should *ipso facto* be granted to all'.[4] All this was very remote from the position which he had taken up in 1885 when White was first placed in charge of the embassy at Constantinople.

The change in Salisbury's attitude towards Germany was equally marked. Since 1885, when they had first worked to-

[1] A. J. Marder, *British Naval Policy, 1880–1905*, chapter ix, passim.
[2] Joseph Chamberlain, *A Political Memoir, 1880–92* (edit. C. H. D. Howard), pp. 295–7; J. L. Garvin, *Life of Joseph Chamberlain*, ii. 457–61.
[3] Salisbury to Simmons, Private, 21 Sept. 1891, F.O. 358/6.
[4] H. W. V. Temperley and L. M. Penson, *Foundations of British Foreign Policy, 1792–1902*, pp. 466–9.

gether in their respective roles as main planner and prime executor of British policy in the Near East, both he and White had sought to put an end to the Three Emperors' Alliance by coming to terms with Bismarck—a policy which had reached its zenith with the conclusion of the Second Mediterranean Agreement. Even in 1887, however, Salisbury could not feel completely at ease about Anglo-German relations: during that spring the 'Holmwood incident' had shown how, without any warning, German policy could be subjected to Bismarck's personal whims; and during that same summer, again without any warning, Germany's enthusiastic support of the Drummond Wolff Convention had become mysteriously half-hearted.[1] But greater shocks were yet to come. In the spring of 1888, for instance, there were two important developments at Berlin which deeply impressed Salisbury.

The first of these developments was the death of the Emperor William I. Although Crown Prince Frederick's succession to the throne appeared to guarantee cordial relations between Germany and Great Britain, and although Malet assured Salisbury that Bismarck was 'most true, loyal and attached to the Crown Prince',[2] it was well known, long before the old Emperor's death, that his eldest son would outlive him only by a few months.[3] Prince William was next in line for the throne, and his attitude towards Great Britain, whether friendly or hostile, was too uncertain a factor to be relied upon in the formulation of British policy.[4]

Secondly, there was the Battenberg marriage question. Bismarck's sharp and sudden refusal to allow young Princess Victoria to become betrothed to Prince Alexander of Battenberg at one time threatened to have serious repercussions upon Anglo-German relations. Besides using the occasion to pursue a personal vendetta, and to demonstrate his authority over the Court at the outset of the new reign, Bismarck attempted to put pressure upon Salisbury by implicating

[1] *Supra*, pp. 76–78.
[2] Malet to Salisbury, Private, 14 Jan. 1888, F.O. 343/9.
[3] Sir F. Ponsonby, *Letters of the Empress Frederick*, pp. 224–316; G. E. Buckle, *The Letters of Queen Victoria*, 3rd ser., i. 244, 311; Lady G. Cecil, *The Life of Robert, Marquis of Salisbury*, iv. 71, 95.
[4] Cecil, iv. 101–2; Buckle, 3rd ser., i. 397–9.

Queen Victoria and threatening to withdraw German support in Egypt.[1] But Salisbury was not to be intimidated: he contended that if German support was only to be bought at such a price, he would prefer to do without it.[2] He was both puzzled and disgusted at Bismarck's conduct throughout the entire proceedings, and could only suggest that 'alcohol by day and narcotics at night' had affected the Chancellor's brain.[3] 'This incident', he remarked to Malet, 'joined to the Holmwood incident of last year shows that friendship with Germany is a more uncertain staff to lean upon than friendship with France. The Chancellor's humours are as changeable as those of the French Assembly.'[4] It was not surprising, therefore, that Salisbury refused to entertain Bismarck's offer of an alliance in the spring of 1889.[5] Long before the Cronstadt visit threatened to make the Franco-Russian Alliance a reality, and even before Bismarck was forced to retire from the political scene, Salisbury had grown weary of German 'blackmail', and had become anxious to ensure that Great Britain should not be completely dependent upon the goodwill of Germany and her Triple Alliance partners.

Meanwhile, at Constantinople, White discovered that co-operation with Germany was becoming increasingly difficult. For a brief spell during the autumn of 1888 he had high hopes of the political ties between the two governments being strengthened by the formation of a close partnership between British and German finance on the Bosphorus. But nothing came of this scheme.[6] Like Salisbury, he found that it was not easy to work with Germany; but, unlike his chief, he seems to have been neither prepared to suggest, nor eager to accept, any alternative policy. He still assumed that the strength of Great Britain's position in the Near East was to be measured by the extent of her influence at Constantinople. He could never forget how, in 1885, that influence had had two narrow escapes from complete destruction at

---

[1] Malet to Salisbury, Tel. Private and Secret, 7 Apr. 1888, F.O. 343/2; Cecil, iv. 99–100.
[2] Salisbury to Malet, Private and Personal, 8 Apr. 1888, F.O. 343/2.
[3] Salisbury to Malet, Private, 2 May 1888, F.O. 343/2.
[4] Salisbury to Malet, Secret, 11 Apr. 1888, F.O. 343/2 (printed in Cecil, iv. 100).
[5] Cf. W. L. Langer, *European Alliances and Alignments, 1871–1890*, pp. 493–4.
[6] *Supra*, pp. 122–33.

the hands of Germany and her two Eastern allies. But Salisbury viewed the situation differently. He was ceasing to look upon the Near Eastern problem as being primarily a question of guarding the Straits against Russia, and becoming increasingly aware that Great Britain's main interest in the Near East ought not to be the Straits, but Egypt and the Suez Canal.

How was it that these fundamental differences in outlook did not become immediately obvious? How was it that White was not recalled from Constantinople, and replaced by an ambassador who shared Salisbury's views?

The main clue to the answer to such questions lies in the fact that the years 1888–91 were not marked by any major diplomatic activity on the Bosphorus. Between 1885 and 1887 Constantinople had vied with Berlin and London for the distinction of being in the diplomatic limelight, but between 1888 and 1891 its importance in this respect was rapidly waning. At first the death of two emperors and the dismissal of Bismarck gave Berlin an undisputed predominance, but later on the protracted negotiations for the Franco-Russian Alliance drew attention to the claims of Paris and St. Petersburg. Meanwhile, in contrast to the prominent position which it had occupied during the earlier years of White's embassy, Constantinople had retired into the background of European politics. Writing to his friend Morier at the beginning of 1889, White made the significant comment: 'My political work here is now reduced, I am glad to say, to that of a passive observer.'[1]

It had been for his expert handling of Balkan problems, and more especially the Bulgarian question, that White had earned a European reputation as a first-class diplomat. But during his last years at Constantinople the Balkans played a much less conspicuous part in European affairs, and, partly owing to the skilful policy which he himself had pursued in the past, their ultimate fate had become an Austro-Russian rather than an Anglo-Russian issue. In 1889, for example, it was Kalnoky, not Salisbury, who attempted to re-open the Bulgarian question: it was Kalnoky, alarmed by a steady increase of Russian influence in Serbia, Roumania, and Greece,

[1] White to Morier, Private, 5 Jan. 1889, Morier Papers.

who hinted to the Turkish ambassador at Vienna that the Porte would do well to legalize Prince Ferdinand's position in Bulgaria.[1] Salisbury, on the other hand, refused to make himself conspicuous either as an ardent champion or as a bitter opponent of that Prince's recognition.[2] Both Bismarck and Crispi adopted similar attitudes,[3] and Kalnoky was therefore forced to drop the subject.[4] Meanwhile there was no evidence of any eagerness at St. Petersburg to raise the Bulgarian question. 'The affairs of the Balkan peninsula have begun to pall', Morier reported to his chief from that capital, and he went on to explain that public interest in Russia was becoming more and more absorbed in problems which concerned Central Asia and eastern Siberia.[5] Events were soon to prove the accuracy of his observations. As early as 1885 there had been plans to build a railway which was to link Russia's European homeland with Vladivostok, her most southerly Pacific port, and in 1891 work was started on the first section of the famous Trans-Siberian Railway.[6]

The Egyptian question, another source of constant embarrassment to White between 1885 and 1887, also slumbered uneasily during these years. In Egypt itself, Sir Evelyn Baring finally won the race against national bankruptcy; by 1888 financial equilibrium was achieved and the prospect of a small surplus realized, and by 1891 Baring could proudly announce that he had been able to remit taxation to the extent of £E53,000 a year.[7] But Egypt was still loaded with international fetters, and the Turkish and French governments pressed for the ending of the British occupation with mono-

---

[1] Phipps (chargé d'affaires at Vienna) to Salisbury, No. 239 Confidential, 20 Aug. F.O. 7/1147; Tel. No. 21 Secret, 25 Sept. 1889, F.O. 7/1150; cf. Sir E. Pears, *Life of Abdul Hamid*, p. 102.

[2] Salisbury to Dering (chargé d'affaires at Rome), No. 213, 3 Oct.; No. 223A Very Confidential, 15 Oct. 1889, F.O. 45/622.

[3] Ibid., F.O. 45/622; Beauclerk (chargé d'affaires at Berlin) to Salisbury, No. 262 Secret, 28 Sept. 1889, F.O. 64/1214.

[4] Paget to Salisbury, No. 281 Confidential, 16 Oct. F.O. 7/1149; Tel. (no number) Very Secret, 8 Nov. 1889, F.O. 7/1150.

[5] Morier to Salisbury, No. 165, 15 May, F.O. 65/1361; No. 239 Secret and Confidential, 6 Aug. F.O. 65/1362; No. 299 Most Secret, 2 Oct. 1889, F.O. 65/1363.

[6] W. L. Langer, *The Diplomacy of Imperialism*, pp. 171-2; G. F. Hudson, *The Far East in World Politics*, pp. 71-76.

[7] The Marquess of Zetland, *Lord Cromer*, pp. 168-78; The Earl of Cromer, *Modern Egypt*, ii. 443-55.

tonous regularity. From the spring until the autumn of 1888 the Turks made several attempts, both at London and Constantinople, to re-open the negotiations which they had forced Sir Henry Drummond Wolff to abandon in the July of the previous year.[1] During the summer of 1889 the French government took the lead, and tried to put pressure upon Salisbury by refusing to give its consent to the conversion of the Privileged Debt.[2] But neither this threat, nor the offer of French support for Great Britain in all Eastern matters, persuaded Salisbury to resume negotiations for the evacuation of Egypt.[3] Renewed overtures on the part of Turkey were similarly unsuccessful. Thus in the spring of the following year, when the Turkish ambassador in London approached Salisbury with yet another project for the amendment of the Drummond Wolff Convention, the Prime Minister informed him that he would neither consider such a project, nor express an opinion upon its contents, until he was satisfied that the obstacles upon which the previous convention had been wrecked no longer existed; he added that he would have to be assured that the Sultan would give Great Britain the right of re-entry into Egypt, and that the Powers would consent to such an arrangement, before entering into another period of laborious negotiation.[4] There the matter rested until June 1890, when the conclusion of an Anglo-German agreement concerning Zanzibar and Heligoland convinced the French government that Great Britain and Germany had reached a general understanding about European as well as colonial affairs, and prompted it to retaliate by making renewed efforts to force the British out of Egypt.[5] Once more the

[1] White to Salisbury, Tel. No. 27 Very Secret, 22 Mar. F.O. 78/4107; Salisbury to White, No. 100, 3 Apr. 1888, F.O. 78/4095; *D.D.F.*, 1st ser., vii, Nos. 93–94. Cf. also White to Salisbury, No. 280 Confidential, 19 July; No. 292 Confidential, 1 Aug. F.O. 78/4102; No. 361, 18 Sept. F.O. 78/4103; No. 399 Confidential, 11 Oct. 1888, F.O. 78/4104; *D.D.F.*, 1st ser., vii, Nos. 171–2, 196–7.
[2] Salisbury to Egerton (chargé d'affaires at Paris), No. 257, 4 June 1889, F.O. 27/2950.
[3] Salisbury to Egerton, No. 264 Most Confidential, 18 June; No. 292 Confidential, 24 June, F.O. 27/2950; No. 297, 1 July 1889, F.O. 27/2951; *D.D.F.*, 1st ser., viii, No. 413.
[4] Salisbury to White, No. 125, 29 Apr. F.O. 78/4273; Tel. No. 25, 29 Apr. 1890, F.O. 78/4280; *D.D.F.*, 1st ser., viii, No. 49.
[5] Lytton to Salisbury, No. 246 Confidential, 28 June 1890, F.O. 27/2998; *D.D.F.*, 1st ser., viii, Nos. 83, 85, 87; *G.P.* viii, No. 1690.

Quai d'Orsay fell back upon the use of obstructive tactics. Early in July, for instance, Ribot refused to support a British scheme for effecting economies in the Egyptian *corvée*: he pointed out to Lytton that the irritation created in France by the continued British occupation of Egypt had been inflamed by the Anglo-German agreement about Zanzibar and Heligoland, and insisted that, as far as his government was concerned, it was impossible to separate the question of the Egyptian *corvée* from that of Zanzibar. Lytton, on the other hand, considered that it was 'preposterous' to demand that two such wholly independent questions should be tied together.[1]

There appeared to be no way out of the Egyptian deadlock: in contrast to the steady improvement in the internal condition of that country, no progress was made towards settling the international difficulties involved in the Egyptian problem. Few disputed Baring's administrative genius, but whether the success of his reforms called for the continuance or the ending of the British occupation was fiercely contested: on the British side, Salisbury argued that a man did not dismiss his gardener because his flowers were good; for the French, Waddington replied that it was not necessary to keep a gardener for ever.[2] Although the Egyptian question had retired into the second line of European politics since 1887, there was no guaranteeing how long it was likely to remain there.

There was a similarly uneasy calm in the Asiatic provinces of the Ottoman Empire. There, just as in Egypt, White had always preferred to let well alone. He had always been convinced that if Russia were to aim a sudden blow at Constantinople it was far more likely that she would strike through Asia Minor than through the Balkans; and he was also aware that little could be done to defend Asiatic Turkey: whereas Balkan nationalism had served, and was serving, as a useful weapon to protect what remained of 'Turkey in Europe' against Russia, Armenian nationalism was a spurious

---

[1] Salisbury to Lytton, Tel. No. 16, 4 July; Lytton to Salisbury, Tel. No. 53, 5 July, F.O. 27/3001; No. 257 Confidential, 6 July 1890, F.O. 27/2999; *D.D.F.*, 1st ser., viii, No. 104; *G.P.* viii, No. 1691.

[2] Salisbury to Lytton, No. 226, 21 June 1890, F.O. 27/2995.

movement which threatened to hasten the final collapse of the Ottoman Empire. Only once—during the autumn of 1888—did White pride himself upon having found a way out of that dilemma. He had hoped, during that brief spell, that the fostering of an ambitious Anglo-German scheme to cover Asia Minor with a network of railways would act as a panacea for both the economic and political ills of that area, giving it greater prosperity, better government, and a more effective defence against invasion. Although nothing came of this projected partnership between British and German finance at Constantinople, Germany's increasing interest in the economic penetration of Asia Minor served as a 'scarecrow' against a Russian invasion there.[1]

It was not until the summer of 1891 that important developments in Europe began to have a marked effect upon the situation at Constantinople. The fall of Bismarck in March 1890, followed three months later by the suspicious coincidence between the dropping of the Re-insurance Treaty with Russia and the signing of the Zanzibar-Heligoland Treaty with Great Britain, had caused considerable anxiety at St. Petersburg and made it more and more difficult for Giers to adhere to his policy of close co-operation with Germany.[2] Meanwhile the French government, wrongly assuming that the Anglo-German Agreement about Zanzibar and Heligoland pointed to the existence of a secret and more general understanding between those two Powers, more than ever felt the need to find an ally on the Continent.[3] Prompted by the fall of Crispi in January 1891, it made its first bid to escape from isolation by attempting to lure Italy away from the Triple Alliance. But the renewal of the Triple Alliance that May—a year before the existing treaty was due to expire—soon made it obvious that these manœuvres had failed.[4] This, combined with Germany's dedication to the cause of friendship with Great Britain, so exuberantly expressed by the German emperor during his state visit to London early in July, made the French government increasingly

[1] *Supra*, pp. 122-33.
[2] W. L. Langer, *The Franco-Russian Alliance, 1890-1894*, pp. 26-81; R. W. Seton-Watson, *Britain in Europe, 1789-1914*, pp. 567-70.
[3] *Supra*, p. 141.
[4] A. F. Pribram, *The Secret Treaties of Austria-Hungary, 1879-1914*, ii, chap. iii.

conscious of its isolation, and forced it to renew its search for a powerful ally.[1]

The Cronstadt visit was an ostentatious announcement of the success of that search: the two ugly ducklings of European politics had at last found consolation in each other's company. But in spite of the displays of fraternal affection which took place during the visit of the French fleet to Cronstadt at the end of July, and in spite of the Tsar's unprecedented gesture of standing bareheaded to the salute while the *Marseillaise*, the battle hymn of the French Revolution, was being played, the contents of the document signed by the French and Russian governments were limited to vague promises to 'concert measures' if the peace of Europe were in danger. Nevertheless, the Cronstadt visit and the *entente* of 1891 constituted a significant step towards the formation of a closer and more effective alliance between those two Powers. In the long run, the effect of the public demonstration was far more important than the terms of the private agreement.[2]

Great Britain alone, bound only loosely to the Triple Alliance by the Mediterranean agreements, remained outside the two great armed camps which were being formed on the Continent. But this enhanced rather than lessened the importance of her position in European politics, for her definite adherence either to one side or the other was certain to tip the delicate balance between the Triple Alliance Powers and the Franco-Russian grouping. Formerly she had been left with no alternative to submitting herself to periodic German 'blackmail' and working with the Triple Alliance, but from now onwards she was to be confronted with the equally difficult and embarrassing task of deciding whether the Triple Alliance or the Franco-Russian grouping was to receive her casting vote.

White's ability to adapt himself to this changing set of circumstances was soon to be tested, for in the late summer and early autumn of 1891 he was suddenly faced with a triple crisis: a revival of the Straits problem, the fall of a grand vizier, and a further attempt to re-open the Egyptian question. None of these problems was sufficient in itself to

[1] Langer, pp. 172–84.
[2] Ibid., pp. 184–90; B. Nolde, *L'Alliance franco-russe*, pp. 616–45.

disturb the comparative calm which had prevailed at Constantinople since the first few months of 1888: the Straits question had last been raised in the spring of 1891, but it had not caused a serious crisis; grand viziers, like French governments, were expected to fall every other day; and familiarity with numerous French and Turkish attempts to resume negotiations about Egypt had bred a certain amount of contempt at the Foreign Office. What really mattered was that these three crises coincided, and that they occurred at a time when the Cronstadt visit had increased diplomatic tension all over Europe.

Two incidents—one early in August, and the other in the middle of September—suddenly re-awakened European interest in the Straits problem: one seemed to confirm widespread rumours that a Russian *coup de main* against Constantinople was imminent, and the other appeared to indicate that Great Britain would not hesitate to resist such a move with force. The first of these suppositions was completely false, and the second was highly questionable.

On 4 August 1891 the transport steamer *Moskva* of the Russian Volunteer Fleet was detained by the Turkish authorities as it passed through the Straits with discharged troops from the Far East. From 1856 onwards it had been possible, in certain circumstances, to apply to the Porte for the relaxation of the rule which forbade the passage of foreign warships through the Straits. In the case of the *Moskva* this formality had been overlooked. But in spite of this, Nelidov, acting presumably on his own initiative, vehemently criticized the action of the Turkish government, and the vigour of his protests convinced uninformed observers that his government was using the whole incident as an excuse for taking drastic action against Turkey;[1] following the lead given by the Stamboul correspondent of the *Standard*, both the British and the continental press announced excitedly that Turkey and Russia had come to an agreement whereby Russian warships were to be allowed through the Straits.[2]

[1] Langer, p. 202; H. W. V. Temperley and L. M. Penson, *Foundations of British Foreign Policy, 1792–1902*, p. 466.
[2] White to Salisbury, No. 377 Confidential, 6 Sept. 1891, F.O. 195/1708; *D.D.F.*, 1st ser., ix, No. 10; the *Standard*, 31 Aug. 1891; *The Times*, 4 Sept. 1891 (cited in Langer, p. 202).

On 19 September the Porte helped to dispel such wild alarms by issuing a circular to those Powers who were signatories of the international instruments concerning the Straits. It recounted the history of the arrangements made for the passage of transports belonging to the Russian Volunteer Fleet, and drew a distinction between vessels carrying a merchant flag, which were defined as commercial ships and therefore allowed to pass freely through the Straits, and ships carrying soldiers, for whose passage a special *irade* would be needed.[1] While Germany remained aloof, Great Britain, Austria-Hungary, and Italy acknowledged the Turkish circular, expressed their determination to forbid any change in the treaty provisions without the consent of the signatory Powers, and, at the instigation of Salisbury, laid down the new doctrine that 'any privilege in respect to the Straits granted to any one Power is *ipso facto* granted to all'.[2]

The *Moskva* incident had been magnified out of all proportion by the 'Sigri landing scare'. On 13 September Europe had been startled by the news that a British force had landed on the island of Sigri, a deserted rock a little to the west of Mytilene.[3] In a report which he later made to the Admiralty, Rear-Admiral Kerr, the officer responsible for the 'invasion', admitted that he had ordered a landing to be made on the island without obtaining the permission of the Turkish authorities. He explained that he had carried out exercises in submarine mining combined with a sham night attack, and that during the course of these operations some unarmed parties had been landed upon Sigri with searchlights, and with one or two cannons from which blank charges had been fired. He claimed, however, that these manœuvres had neither alarmed nor inconvenienced the local Turkish authorities.[4] 'The trouble has come', Sanderson sharply commented, 'not from objections by the local authorities,

---

[1] White to Salisbury, No. 420, 24 Sept. 1891, F.O. 195/1708 (encloses copy of the Turkish circular).

[2] Temperley and Penson, pp. 466–7.

[3] Langer, p. 204.

[4] Salisbury to White, No. 224 Confidential, 13 Oct. 1891, F.O. 195/1705 (contains copy of Rear-Admiral Kerr's report to the Secretary of the Admiralty, dated 18 Sept. 1891); Memorandum by T. H. Sanderson, Assistant Under-Secretary at the Foreign Office, dated 26 Sept. 1891, F.O. 78/4372.

but from reports from foreign consular agents and press correspondents.'[1] At a time when the Straits question had become a subject for lively discussion in diplomatic circles, and when the European press had become obsessed with the idea that Russia was preparing to strike a sudden blow at Constantinople, it seemed unlikely that any explanation by the British government would be taken seriously either at home or abroad; it would be difficult to convince anyone that such a landing, so near to the entrance of the Dardanelles, was the result of a naval officer's blunder—not a government's decision to stage a naval demonstration.[2]

In fact, Salisbury was singularly unperturbed at the prospect of a Russian *coup de main* against Constantinople. Discussing the subject with Sir John Lintorn Simmons, he wrote:[3]

I have some doubt of Russia venturing upon the bold *coup de main* of which you speak until she has made Bulgaria tolerably safe. Otherwise, in what position would her expeditionary force be if we were to get into the Sea of Marmora? . . . If Russia does once get hold of the Dardanelles I doubt whether any effort which it will be worth our while to make will shake her off.

Salisbury therefore had two reasons for refusing to get excited about the Straits: he did not share the popular belief in Russia's preparedness to strike a sudden blow against Constantinople, but at the same time he had resigned himself to the fact that once Russia had gained control of the Dardanelles any attempt to dislodge her would be futile.

White's approach to this problem was entirely different. Having spent over six years in the embassy at Pera, he found it impossible to view the inevitable decline of British influence on the Bosphorus with such detachment. Although he was confident that the particular question concerning the status of the Russian Volunteer Fleet could easily be solved, he was deeply concerned about the Straits problem as a whole.[4] He agreed with Kalnoky that 'Russia's attention was not attracted now so much to Bulgaria as to the question of the

[1] Minute by T. H. Sanderson, dated 5 Oct. 1891, F.O. 78/4372.
[2] Cf. Langer, pp. 204–5.
[3] Salisbury to Simmons, Private, 21 Sept. 1891, F.O. 358/6.
[4] White to Salisbury, No. 377 Confidential, 6 Sept. 1891, F.O. 195/1708.

Straits',[1] and he therefore looked upon the defence of the Bosphorus and the Dardanelles as being a problem of 'immense importance'.[2]

No doubt the fall of the grand vizier, on 3 September, helped to add to the alarm with which White viewed the situation at Constantinople. In an empire in which constant ministerial changes were the rule rather than the exception, Kiamil Pasha, appointed grand vizier a few days after the Eastern Roumelian outbreak in 1885, had achieved the rare distinction of remaining in office for just under six years. During that period he had used what little influence he possessed at the Palace to counteract the repeated attempts of Montebello and Nelidov to intimidate the Sultan, and he had built up a reputation for being the main Turkish advocate of a policy of close co-operation with Great Britain and the Triple Alliance.[3] Several theories, some plausible and some fantastic, were advanced to explain the grand vizier's fall. It was put down to the Sultan's alarm at the Cronstadt visit and the growing strength of the Franco-Russian *entente*, to his frustration at the failure of repeated attempts to re-open negotiations with Great Britain about Egypt, and even to his annoyance at the Palace being suddenly plunged into darkness because of a failure in the gas supply at Yildiz![4] White's own view was that the Sultan, deeply impressed by the dropping of the Bismarckian pilot, was emulating the German emperor's example.[5] But although the reasons for Kiamil's dismissal were obscure, its effect was obvious: Great Britain and the Triple Alliance Powers had lost the services of one of the few powerful Turks who was likely to influence the Sultan in their favour, and that in itself was to the advantage of the Franco-Russian *entente*.[6]

However, it was the Egyptian question which was White's greatest source of embarrassment during the last few months

---

[1] White to Salisbury, No. 365 Secret, 28 Aug. 1891, F.O. 195/1708.
[2] White to Salisbury, No. 397 Confidential, 12 Sept. 1891, F.O. 78/4347.
[3] White to Salisbury, No. 379 Secret, 7 Sept. 1891, F.O. 78/4347; *D.D.F.*, 1st ser., ix, No. 3 (Montebello to Ribot, 5 Sept. 1891).
[4] White to Salisbury, No. 390 Confidential, 9 Sept. 1891, F.O. 78/4347.
[5] White to Salisbury, No. 379 Secret, 7 Sept. 1891, F.O. 78/4347.
[6] Malet to Salisbury, No. 164 Confidential, 4 Sept. F.O. 64/1254; Paget to Salisbury, No. 181 Confidential, 11 Sept. 1891, F.O. 7/1171; *D.D.F.*, 1st ser., ix, No. 3.

of his embassy. Throughout the summer of 1891 there had been rumours that the Sultan was anxious to resume discussions with the British government about Egypt, but he made no serious move in this direction until after the Cronstadt visit.[1] On 3 August Rustem Pasha, who had been rushed back to London from a rest cure at Kissingen, approached Salisbury with yet another project for the evacuation of Egypt, but Salisbury fobbed him off with the excuse that he could do nothing about such matters without consulting his colleagues, and that this was impossible since Parliament was about to be prorogued.[2] However, this was only a temporary expedient for silencing the Turks, and once Parliament had met again they made fresh soundings both at London and Constantinople: on 20 October Rustem Pasha reminded Salisbury of the Sultan's desire to reach a settlement with the British government about Egypt,[3] and a fortnight later Djevad Pasha, the new grand vizier, had a heated argument with White about the same subject.[4]

France, strengthened by her recent understanding with Russia, appeared to be the Power most likely to support the Sultan in the stand he was taking about Egypt. But there was a paradoxical division in French opinion upon this issue: those who pressed most eagerly for an early settlement of the Egyptian question were the most bitter opponents of the connexion with Russia, whereas those who were reluctant to do so were the most ardent enthusiasts for a more formal and definite alliance with Russia. Clemenceau, who visited Joseph Chamberlain in England a fortnight before the Cronstadt visit, sought the solution of the Egyptian question by means of an Anglo-French agreement. Unofficial proposals made to Chamberlain by the leader of the French Radicals included the suggestion that if Great Britain dissociated herself entirely from the Triple Alliance and gave France her moral support, France would reciprocate by giving her, amongst other things, a free hand in Egypt—even to the extent of

---

[1] White to Salisbury, Tel. No. 35 Secret, 24 June 1891, F.O. 78/4350; *D.D.F*, 1st ser., viii, No. 383.
[2] Salisbury to Fane (chargé d'affaires at Constantinople), No. 176, 4 Aug. 1891, F.O. 78/4341; *D.D.F.*, 1st ser., viii, Nos. 447, 464.
[3] Salisbury to White, No. 227, 20 Oct. 1891, F.O. 78/4341.
[4] White to Salisbury, No. 462 Secret, 5 Nov. 1891, F.O. 78/4348.

allowing her to set up a protectorate.¹ Paul Cambon, soon to succeed Montebello as French ambassador at Constantinople, held similar views. He considered the idea of a Franco-Russian alliance to be not only a dream, but a danger, since it would only serve to bind Great Britain closer to the Triple Alliance. This would be disastrous because Great Britain was the traditional ally of France, and her assistance would always be needed against Germany who was the real enemy. But an Anglo-French alliance presupposed French recognition of Great Britain's position in Egypt '. . . Quand le vin est tiré', he concluded, 'il faut le boire.' And, in criticism of the attitude which his government persisted in adopting, he added: 'Il y a des gens et même des peuples qui préfèrent mourir de soif.'²

At the Quai d'Orsay Ribot confined himself to stating that he agreed in principle with the Sultan's project for an Egyptian settlement, and remained silent when Salisbury refused to listen to the proposals put forward by Rustem Pasha at the beginning of August.³ In November, when Giers travelled to Paris and discussed the Eastern question with Ribot and Freycinet, all three were agreed that no action should be taken about Egypt which went beyond the bounds of prudence. In spite of their protests against the continued occupation of Egypt by British troops, neither the French nor the Russian government was particularly anxious to free Great Britain from her Egyptian entanglements and drive her into the arms of the Triple Alliance Powers.⁴

Meanwhile Germany, whose past attitude towards Great Britain and her Egyptian difficulties had so often been that of a *tertius gaudens*, had become suddenly interested in her being released from their grip. Germany was sharing Great Britain's misfortunes at Constantinople, and her influence there was rapidly declining. It was vital, therefore, that their two governments should pursue a common policy in regard to Egypt—a policy directed towards an understanding be-

1 Joseph Chamberlain, *A Political Memoir, 1880–92* (edit. C. H. D. Howard), pp. 295–7; J. L. Garvin, *The Life of Joseph Chamberlain*, ii. 458–62.
2 Paul Cambon, *Correspondence, 1870–1924*, i. 342–3; cf. also pp. 343–5.
3 *D.D.F.*, 1st ser., viii, No. 433; W. L. Langer, *The Franco-Russian Alliance, 1890–94*, p. 201.
4 B. Nolde, *L'Alliance franco-russe*, pp. 646–50.

tween Great Britain and Turkey, a policy which would dispel the Sultan's suspicions of Great Britain and those Powers which co-operated with her in the Near East. Such was the argument put forward by Marschall von Bieberstein, the German foreign minister, in a long conversation with Salisbury early in July 1891,[1] and at the same time the German emperor, on his first state visit to London, assured those who had gathered to welcome him at the Guildhall that he would do everything in his power to maintain the 'historical friendship' that existed between Germany and Great Britain.[2]

Nor did the Sultan's latest manœuvres pass unobserved in Great Britain itself. One of the results of the Cronstadt visit was that the British Liberals, who had been reserved in their attitude towards the Egyptian question since the failure of the Drummond Wolff mission, renewed their agitation for the withdrawal of British troops from Egypt. Harcourt feared that the Franco-Russian *entente* of August 1891 would be followed by some demand 'on the part of Turkey *nominally*, and France and Russia *really*' for the evacuation of that country.[3] The radical wing of the party, which had always insisted that Great Britain should get out of Egypt as soon as possible, was quick to seize upon any opportunity to justify its views: John Morley spoke strongly against the British occupation in September, and Dilke warmly supported him both in a long and lively correspondence with Joseph Chamberlain,[4] and in a private interview with a French newspaper reporter.[5] Gladstone, in a speech at Newcastle on 2 October, made a cryptic reference to the 'burdensome and embarrassing' occupation of Egypt—'escape from which it was to be feared the Tory Government would hand over to its successors to deal with'.[6] And this pronouncement, made at a time when government defeats at by-elections indicated that the Liberals would soon return to office, was regarded both in Paris and Berlin as a pledge of

---

[1] *G.P.* ix, No. 2111 (Memorandum by Baron Marschall von Bieberstein, written at Windsor Castle, 6 July 1891).
[2] Sir Sidney Lee, *King Edward VII*, i. 666–7; *G.P.* viii, No. 1727.
[3] A. G. Gardiner, *The Life of Sir William Harcourt*, ii. 130.
[4] S. Gwynn and G. M. Tuckwell, *The Life of the Rt. Hon. Sir Charles W. Dilke*, ii. 253–5.
[5] *D.D.F.*, 1st ser., ix, No. 7.   [6] *The Times*, 3 Oct. 1891.

early evacuation.¹ It seems far more likely, however, that Gladstone shared Harcourt's sentiments: 'Let us pray that this plague may not break out in our time, Oh Lord, but in that of Salisbury.'²

Salisbury answered his critics in his Guildhall speech on 9 November. After pointing out that the decision to occupy Egypt had not been made by a Conservative government, he stressed that it was, nevertheless, Great Britain's duty to abide by that decision, and to prevent Egypt from relapsing into its former state of anarchy—the great work which she had achieved there at the cost of much blood and treasure should not 'be swept away as if it were last year's almanac'. 'Whatever party may be in power', he concluded, 'the English people will never withdraw its hand from the steady and vigorous prosecution and the benefit of the humane undertaking with which now it is their pride and honour to be connected.'³ These statements silenced the Liberals. Far from challenging them, both Gladstone and Morley claimed that their speeches had been misunderstood, and neither they nor their followers made any further use of the Egyptian problem in the great electoral struggle which took place during the next few months.⁴

But the fact that the Liberals had forced Salisbury to refer to Egypt in his Guildhall speech had had an unfortunate effect in other quarters. It had not helped to improve Salisbury's relations with the French. Throughout the summer of 1891 he had been anxious to impress upon the French government that Great Britain was not bound hand and foot to the Triple Alliance Powers: in May he had readily accepted a French suggestion that the French fleet should call either at some Scottish port or at Plymouth after its return from Russia,⁵ and two months later, when it had been decided that it should visit Portsmouth, he had encouraged Queen Victoria to review the French fleet in person.⁶ 'Though in the

---

¹ D.D.F., 1st ser., ix, No. 27; G.P. viii, No. 1808.
² Gardiner, ii. 130.
³ Lady G. Cecil, *The Life of Robert, Marquis of Salisbury*, iv. 394; D.D.F., 1st ser., ix, No. 62. ⁴ Cecil, loc. cit.
⁵ W. L. Langer, *The Franco-Russian Alliance, 1890–1894*, p. 199.
⁶ G. E. Buckle, *The Letters of Queen Victoria*, 3rd ser., ii. 50–53; D.D.F., 1st ser., viii, Nos. 431, 523.

present state of Europe', he afterwards explained to her, 'our interests lie on the side of the Triple Alliance, it is most important to persuade the French, if we can, that England has no antipathy to France nor any partisanship against her.'[1] Moreover, there was a personal as well as a political basis to Salisbury's reluctance to abandon France: he had always been an admirer of French culture and civilization, and French literature was almost as familiar to him as that of his own country; from the very beginning he had taken the side of the French in the Franco-Prussian war,[2] and he had been deeply impressed by the consistent support which he had received from Waddington at the Congress of Berlin.[3] Thus, in spite of the fact that he often found himself in the opposite diplomatic camp to France, a strong tradition of personal sympathy towards her, and an instinctive distrust of her eastern neighbour, made him unwilling to desert France altogether and identify himself completely with Germany and her Triple Alliance partners.[4]

White, in contrast to his chief, classed France with Russia as an inveterate foe. Throughout his embassy he looked upon Germany as being Great Britain's main supporter at Constantinople, and the dominant theme in both his private and official correspondence during those years was the need to counteract 'French and Russian intrigues' at the Porte and the Palace. And, as with Salisbury, personal prejudices helped to crystallize political ideas. White was an expert on eastern, not western, Europe; his leaves on the Continent were spent at Berlin and Bad Gastein, not Paris; in general his sympathies were with Germany, and together with those sympathies he seems to have inherited a hostility towards France which was almost German. This hatred and suspicion was mutual. Paul Cambon, one of the warmest advocates of an Anglo-French *rapprochement*, regarded White's death as the removal of a most formidable obstacle to improved relations between Great Britain and France.[5] The French press

[1] Salisbury to Queen Victoria, 22 Aug. 1891 (printed in Buckle, 3rd ser., ii. 64–65); cf. Sir Sidney Lee, *King Edward VII*, i. 668.
[2] Cecil, ii. 32–37.
[3] W. N. Medlicott, *The Congress of Berlin and After*, pp. 34–35; 141–2.
[4] Cecil, ii. 32–37.
[5] Paul Cambon, *Correspondence, 1870–1924*, i. 359.

was even more outspoken. Announcing his death, *Le Gaulois* observed that Great Britain had lost one of her most clever diplomats—'un de ceux qui personnifient le mieux sa politique perfide et égoïste'.[1] Other Paris newspapers insisted that he was not British, but Polish by birth, and went so far as to hint that he was not legitimate.[2] Some, however, confined themselves to more accurate, more relevant, and less scurrilous comments. *L'Eclair* confused cause with effect and attributed White's bitter opposition to any further negotiations about Egypt to his personal hostility towards France.[3] In fact, he was opposed to any re-opening of the Egyptian question not primarily because of his personal antipathy to France, but, as another French newspaper shrewdly pointed out, because he feared the consequences of a second Drummond Wolff fiasco, and was anxious to avoid the humiliation of a diplomatic defeat.[4]

The different attitudes adopted by Salisbury and White towards France accentuated the growing divergence in their views about Egypt. During the last few weeks of 1891 they frequently exchanged opinions about that question, and their ideas repeatedly clashed. The first signs of an open disagreement appeared early in November. Commenting upon the Sultan's avowed eagerness to re-open negotiations about Egypt at Constantinople, Salisbury assured White that any formal discussion of that problem at the Porte was bound to become 'a negotiation conducted publicly in the face of Europe', and that he was therefore opposed to it; he added, however, that he could see no harm in White having a private audience with the Sultan.[5] White argued in reply that such an audience, which could hardly be kept secret, would prove to be fruitless and even harmful: Great Britain would be playing into the hands of France and Russia if she attempted to re-open such negotiations at Yildiz where the influence of those two Powers was predominant; moreover, their renewal

---

[1] *Le Gaulois* (Paris), 29 Dec. 1891.
[2] *Le Radical* (Paris), 31 Dec. 1891; *L'Echo de Paris*, 31 Dec. 1891.
[3] *L'Eclair* (Paris), 30 Dec. 1891.
[4] *Le Soleil* (Paris), 31 Dec. 1891; cf. the *Standard*, 29 Dec. 1891 (gives an account of a conversation between White and its Vienna correspondent in which White himself made this point).
[5] Salisbury to White, Tel. No. 60, 6 Nov. 1891, F.O. 78/4349.

at Constantinople would remind the Sultan of the humiliating part which he had played in the struggle over the Wolff Convention, and that in itself was certain to increase his hostility towards Great Britain. He therefore suggested that it would be better, in the circumstances, if the negotiations took place in London.[1]

But there were several arguments against White's proposed alternative: it was rumoured, for instance, that the Turkish ambassador at London was about to retire from official life, and it was well known that Tewfik Pasha, his most likely successor, was notorious at Berlin for his muddleheadedness and inefficiency. 'I do not put down Tewfik Pasha as a fool,' observed Malet, 'but if he were sent to you, I think you would be obliged to be very painstaking with him to be sure of his not unintentionally misrepresenting you.'[2] But this was only a minor consideration. Explaining his reasons for complying with the Sultan's desire to re-open the Egyptian negotiations at Constantinople, Salisbury pointed out to White that such a step might improve Great Britain's relations both with Turkey and with France. He wished to discover whether a conspicuous acknowledgement of the Sultan's nominal suzerainty over Egypt, or his supremacy over the Islamic world, would silence his repeated demands for a British evacuation. He concluded:

In the eyes of France, too, it might under certain circumstances be preferable for them to have our troops at Alexandria instead of at Cairo. As far as the substance of power goes, our position would remain the same. It would be a question of shadows; but shadows go for a good deal in this matter both at Paris and at Constantinople.[3]

Thus, in spite of White's protests, Salisbury stuck to his original idea of a personal conference between White and the Sultan.[4]

The next move was left to the Sultan. In anticipation of an important announcement from the Palace, White delayed his

[1] White to Salisbury, Paraphrase of Tel. No. 61 Secret, 7 Nov.; F.O. 78/4350; Recorder of Private and Confidential Tel., 8 Nov. 1891, F.O. 195/1713.
[2] Malet to Salisbury, Private, 21 Nov. 1891, F.O. 343/12.
[3] Salisbury to White, Private, 9 Nov. 1891, Bound Volume No. 33, Salisbury Papers.
[4] Salisbury to White, No. 244 Confidential, 9 Nov.; No. 247 Confidential, 10 Nov. 1891, F.O. 78/4341; cf. *D.D.F.*, 1st ser., ix, No. 57.

leave for eleven days. But he waited in vain, and finally, on 24 December, he set out for London and a consultation with Salisbury.[1] He died five days later at Berlin.[2]

The attempt made to re-open the Egyptian question at the end of 1891 went the way of so many others—it came to nothing. But it would be wrong to assume that the final skirmish between White and Salisbury was therefore trivial and insignificant. Like the Straits incident of that same autumn, it indicated that White's ideas about the part which Great Britain should play in the Near East no longer tallied with Salisbury's, or rather that Salisbury's no longer tallied with White's. Six years at Constantinople had given White a parochial outlook upon the Near Eastern question: in 1885 he had possessed good health, tireless energy, and an approach to Near Eastern politics which had instilled new life into Great Britain's waning influence on the Bosphorus; but by the end of 1891 he was a sick man who could only look back upon past triumphs and cling to the tatters of outworn policies. He could never forget how isolated Great Britain had been at the time of the Pendjeh and Eastern Roumelian crises, and how severely his position had been compromised by the humiliating failure of the Wolff Convention. These were the experiences which coloured his ideas about Near Eastern politics; these were the lessons which he was never able to dismiss from his mind. They had taught him to regard the Straits question as the central problem in Near Eastern politics, and to avoid, if possible, the distracting embarrassments of the Egyptian question; they had convinced him that British influence on the Bosphorus must either perish or go into partnership with that of Germany and her Triple Alliance colleagues. But by 1891 this policy had become outdated. Salisbury, who had accepted and championed it during White's first few years at Constantinople, had begun to doubt and dispute its wisdom long before White's final departure from that capital. He had begun to ask himself whether it was either possible or necessary for Great Britain to defend the Straits; whether it was either possible or ad-

---

[1] White to Salisbury, Tel. No. 68, 17 Dec.; Tel. No. 69, 21 Dec. 1891, F.O. 78/4350.
[2] *The Times*, 29 Dec. 1891; 2 Jan. 1892.

visable for her to evacuate Egypt; and whether it was possible or desirable for her to associate herself too closely with the Triple Alliance and abandon France completely. Two years previously Salisbury had expressed concern at 'the various indications' he was getting about his ambassador at Constantinople, and had asked if White was 'quite the man he was'.[1] And perhaps, long before the news of White's death had reached him at London, he had already begun to weigh up the possibilities of recalling his representative on the Bosphorus.

[1] White to Salisbury, Private and Confidential, 29 June 1889 (with minute by Salisbury), Bound Volume No. 33, Salisbury Papers.

APPENDIX I

Two documents follow from the Salisbury Papers which are now being sorted at Christ Church, Oxford. These give an excellent picture of the situation at Constantinople as seen by White in the summer of 1885, that is, a few months after his arrival at that capital as a *locum tenens* for Sir Edward Thornton.

1. *Memorandum by Sir William White, dated 27 June 1885*[1]

The question of the probable meeting of the Three Emperors (next August) must not be overlooked. The one at Skiernievitze last autumn would never have been so intimate if we had accepted and taken to heart the warnings at the time. The Czar has certainly acquired some degree of popularity with his Army and People since General Komaroff's action, and he finds in this sufficient to go on. Should the meeting of the Emperors take place—as it probably will on Austrian soil if the Emperor William continues so far well in health—and should we fail until then in re-establishing a thorough understanding with Berlin—it would be a bad look out. Prince Bismarck can be reasoned with and spoken to sensibly—the great thing is to find the right man to speak to him and to gain his confidence. But this is a vast subject and cannot be touched upon lightly. The Egyptian Question will be the one which H.M.G. will have to take in hand first of all.

If the German Ambassador at Constantinople is right in his view, the time for deciding upon a course to be followed about Egypt does not depend on England any more, though it may have at one time. H.E. refuses to be drawn into speaking as to details but his meaning is clear. The idea is to internationalize Egypt as well as neutralize the Canal, and subsequently a similar plan may and will most likely be evolved for the Bosphorus and the Dardanelles.

In the present condition of Europe it is quite worth while examining such a plan—with impartiality—with a view to see how it could be worked, so as to protect and serve British interests and keep France out of Egypt, and Russia out of Constantinople.

Within the last few weeks we have seen that the Powers were anxious to keep the Dardanelles (the Straits) closed to our men of war, which would have had the effect of securing Russia in the Black Sea against us. If such a system is likely to be applied again, so as to deprive us of being able to take the aggressive in the Black Sea, it is as well to see what permanent arrangement could be made cutting both ways, and also whether a Railway in Asiatic Turkey cannot give us what we may require.

The Russians tell me that is what they want and seek in the cessation of all neutral zones—the disappearance of Afghanistan, and to become our neighbour they want to be *coterminous* with us in India—as they can they [? think] threaten our flank at all times.

The Turks, and especially the Sultan, are very sore about Egypt. He is ex-

[1] Bound Volume No. 43, Salisbury Papers.

tremely suspicious of everything we do and is almost inaccessible. The German Radowitz is going on leave and cannot get his audience. Count Corti had to go away without getting one, and in fact there is no intercourse whatever between Osmanlis and foreigners. All Embassies are treated alike—kept at a distance. All claims and demands are disregarded, and I have told a few of the Turks with whom I have come into contact that Foreign Powers may discontinue to keep Ambassadors if they find by experience so little use in having them.

The negotiations between Lord Granville and Hassan Fehmi were broken off by the latter's sudden departure from London and nothing has indicated a desire on our part to take them up since. Indeed I doubt anything further can be done until H.M.G. has felt the pulse of the Great German Chancellor and has settled its future policy with regard to Egypt.

2. *White to Salisbury, Private Letter, dated 4 July 1885*[1]

... The Porte has become a mere shadow of former authority and the Palace absorbs all. ... The order of transacting public business has been entirely altered, Ministers have been deprived of all power and authority, every decision after having passed from one office to another and after it has been even sanctioned by the Council of Ministers, is sent to the Palace, and is frequently relegated there 'in limbo' for months, years, or even for ever. ... But the Sultan is painstaking, and one who is not wanting in ability.

There are now three ruling ideas in his mind which have gradually become maxims of his Government, viz:

1. As the Khalife he exercises influence over all the Mohommedans, all over the world. As such the English are at his mercy in India and Afghanistan, he can help or injure them as he chooses, but he must preserve his dominion unimpaired in Egypt and Arabia, and must resent their encroachments there, and those of the Italians.

2. The Russians are paying him great attentions (their lost ground greatly regained by our friend Nelidoff) they evidently want and appreciate his friendship. So do the Germans, for why should they be so kind to him, and as for the English, he has only to wait and they will come apologising to him for their past negligences. Evidently from these premises H.I.M. concludes that his Alliance is a most precious one and much sought after. He thinks he has upset Mr. Gladstone and Mr. Mancini and is waiting to hear what their successors will come to offer.

3. The flights of the Mussulmans from provinces that have become Christian States has brought home the idea that everything Christian is injurious and destructive of a true-believing condition of Society, these Reforms, Railways, Schools on Christian models, are all to be deprecated and abhorred everywhere, but most of all in Asia.

These foregone conclusions, erroneous and even ridiculous though they may be, effect in a most injurious manner the relations of the Foreign Embassies at Constantinople to the Porte. I say Embassies for I presume the

[1] Bound Volume No. 43, Salisbury Papers.

Governments at London, Paris and Vienna hardly perceive the great change that has come over the influence formerly possessed by their Representatives to the Sultan.

Their former influence here is completely gone. They were too much consulted formerly, now their advice is unheeded and even heard with ill-humour, if not with disdain. Their notes and applications receive evasive replies, or none at all. The claims they bring forward for their countrymen are seldom attended to, after much coaxing, begging, pressing, etc., etc.

The other Embassies feel all this much less than we do, for they have adapted themselves much earlier to this new state of things. They have entirely ceased giving advice when not asked, or making useless representations, they entirely abstain from interference except in cases which demand immediate redress. Germany gave the example of this new system, and combined with her general policy, this has helped her to reap the full benefit by gaining considerable moral influence. Russia, by assuming a friendly tone and her artful way of always pointing out with irony to the others and saying 'Behold your allies', has gained much ground, France and Italy are not thought much of here, but Noailles is extremely delicate and reserved in his dealings. We alone of the Great Powers adhere to the old system of acting *School-master*. I have certainly confined myself only to speaking or advising when I had actual instructions to do so, but the carrying out of these embarrasses me frequently, and it is imperative on me to place this novel view of the situation as early as possible before Your Lordship. . . .

APPENDIX II

THE two letters which follow deal with the outbreak of the Eastern Roumelian crisis in September 1885. The first letter, taken from the Salisbury Papers, shows how White responded to the news of that outbreak, and the second, taken from the correspondence of Sir William White which was in the possession of his grandson, the late Captain William de Geijer, neatly sums up Salisbury's first reaction to the situation created by the union of the two Bulgarias. A comparison of these two documents reveals that there was a striking similarity between the attitudes adopted, quite independently, by White and Salisbury: both regretted that the Sultan had failed to act quickly and put down the insurrection, and neither mentioned the cause of Bulgarian nationalism or the wishes of the Bulgarian people.

1. *White to Salisbury, Private and Confidential Letter, dated 22 September 1885*[1]

... Here the Ambassadors Calice and Nelidoff are protesting their innocence and those of their chiefs at Kremsier, of having had any part in fostering the Unionist movement in Bulgaria. A union now an accomplished fact—unless Turkey draws the sword.

But then she is hardly prepared for such an effort. Her military strength is being quietly dried up: and secondly, the German Chargé d'Affaires tells me—'Let Turkey gain a battle and Macedonia is lost to her.' What does this mean? —These ominous words—probably that a rising in Macedonia will bring Austrian troops as a sequel. So that a shot fired by the Turks would bring on a new partition. The two Ambassadors did not speak so plainly as one could read the same thing between the lines. As for the rest, they were full of protestations of their innocence and I thought of the French proverb: 'Qui s'excuse, s'accuse.'

I still think however that Russia had planned the deposition of Prince Alexander as the first step, and that the Union was to follow, how these two became inverted we cannot tell yet, but we shall see bye and bye.

It is evident someone struck the lucifer match too soon, and that this happened to give Prince Alexander a chance. I do not blame him. You may not endorse this opinion of mine, but I should be glad if it could reach the Queen as my humble opinion.

Corti said most amusingly: 'Les Turcs sont furieux—ils vont—ils vont envoyer une *Circulaire télégraphique* aux Puissances.' This I believe they have done, and *is all they will do*—for the present.

I am more and more inclined to think that the reconciliation of Austria and Russia at Kremsier, and the revived affection of these two Emperors, goes even further than Bismarck likes. If so, he will play them some very nice little tricks, and this Union may be the first of his tricks. He has so many cards in his hand that he can play off one against the other at his leisure....

[1] Bound Volume No. 43, Salisbury Papers.

2. *Salisbury to White, Private Letter, dated 24 September 1885*[1]

As far as your post is concerned, it seems as though all questions had settled themselves. If the Turks had had a spark of vitality left they would have marched in all the force at their command and stamped out this insurrection at once. I do not say they would have been successful. Very likely they would have roused the Russians and we should have had another war. But still, no state with any life in it would have allowed a province to be snatched from under its eyes, and stretched out no hand to save it.

That Turkey has not done this spontaneously, proves that Turkey is dead. But it was not a course for any of the Powers to advise: for such advice would have amounted to a promise of some sort of help if the advice failed; and England, alone, has certainly no motive to undertake any such responsibility. Our language must be to condemn Alexander's enterprise, to adhere to the Treaty, and not to commit ourselves to the abandonment of any right or claim of the Sultan's. But at present it is an internal matter exclusively. The Sultan has a rebellious subject to settle with: and it is not for us to advise him how to do it. If others try to coerce him, it may then be our business to interfere. Or if Austria takes measures herself to prevent the conflagration spreading, we may take joint action with her. But until the question reaches one of those two phases, we are not called upon for action: and our opinion must simply be a condemnation of those who have broken a great law of Europe.

I have not much hope myself that a big Bulgaria will be avoided. It is an evil, and a danger to Turkey. But there seems to me nowhere the will to stop it: and stopping it would require measures of considerable stringency. The next best thing to hope for is a personal union of the two Bulgarias in Prince Alexander, each retaining otherwise its present institutions. The institutions of Bulgaria are detestable: it would be hard that E. Roumelia should be subjected to them. It is to be hoped that the conflagration will not spread. If it does, we are at the beginning of the end.

[1] Additional White Papers.

APPENDIX III

In the private letter which follows Salisbury gives White a brief description of the terms and significance of the First Mediterranean Agreement. This letter, taken from the private papers of Sir William White which remain in the possession of his family, is especially interesting because it is the only piece of direct evidence which we possess of White's being informed of that important and highly secret agreement.

Salisbury to White, Private and Secret Letter, dated 20 April 1887[1]

I hope my telegram did not seem unintelligible to you.[2] The explanation was this. England has been recently exchanging despatches with Italy and Austria, pledging the three Powers to maintain in their diplomacy the *status quo* in the Mediterranean and neighbouring seas: and if unhappily it should be broken, pledging them in the same way to resist any other Great Power increasing its coastline. The question of material co-operation is carefully put aside. These agreements have been adopted to a great extent by the advice of Germany which has evidently attached a very great—and to my eyes inexplicable—importance to them. Her object I presume is to provide either Austria or Turkey with backers, supposing that Russia should by any means whatever become entangled with either Power.

Now Hatzfeldt wants the agreement to be extended by the admission of Turkey. I asked your advice upon that point and am much obliged for the answer that has just been received. I am myself rather doubtful upon the point. In the first place, it is well the agreement should remain secret: and nothing in Constantinople is secret. Secondly, Turkey could not be expected to assent to the second part of it which contemplates a possible change in the *status quo* which could only take place at her expense. Thirdly, Turkey will never be satisfied with the platonic form to which our parliamentary exigencies compelled us to reduce our stipulations. Still, as Hatzfeldt pressed it so earnestly, I promised to obtain your opinion. If it be Germany's intention to embroil Russia with the Balkan States, it is obviously her policy to make them as strong and hard to overcome as she possibly can. But the difficulty is to appease her fears of Russia. . . .

[1] Additional White Papers.
[2] Cf. Salisbury to White, Tel. No. 67 Most Secret, 19 Apr. 1887, F.O. 78/4002.

'German Ambassador is very anxious that the Porte should come to some understanding with the East Mediterranean Powers, Italy, Austria, England, as to the maintenance of the *status quo* of the shores of that sea and the seas communicating with it, the Aegean and the Euxine. The three Powers are in clear agreement on the question of policy, though they have abstained from any material engagements.

'I wish to ask your opinion whether it would be possible to induce the Sultan to associate himself quite confidentially with any such assurance of policy. It would add strength to the bulwark against war, and it would give him confidence.'

APPENDIX IV

THESE two documents throw new light upon the attitude of the British government towards early schemes for a railway network in the Asiatic provinces of the Ottoman Empire—the beginnings of the famous Berlin–Baghdad Railway. The first document, White's 'Remarks applying to different British schemes for the construction of Turkish Railways in Asia', is to be found in the unpublished official correspondence of the Foreign Office. It is interesting to note that Alwyn Parker's article on the Berlin–Baghdad Railway, long considered to be the best account of British policy towards that project, owes much to White's memorandum. In fact, the first few pages of Parker's article are almost *verbatim* borrowings from White. The second document, a letter from White to Salisbury taken from the private papers of Sir William White which have been deposited at the Public Record Office, has been included because it helps to explain White's support of the first Kaulla concession in October 1888.

1. *Memorandum by Sir William White entitled: 'Remarks applying to different British schemes for the construction of Turkish Railways in Asia', dated 25 July 1887*[1]

Lord Salisbury has sent me a copy of a communication made by Mr. Pender to H.I.M. the Sultan on the subject of railways, and I have seen Mr. Vere who is the Agent of the Eastern Telegraph Co. and I have ascertained from him that he has spoken to the Grand Vizier on this question, but I do not see any immediate prospect of the attention of the Porte being given just now to any Asiatic Railway Scheme.

Every few weeks some scheme of this kind is talked of at Pera, and some foreign Ambassador is credited with giving it an immense amount of support whilst an active and energetic agent is supposed to be on the eve of success, after which he takes his departure and the entire scheme which was to be successful drifts into obscurity and is forgotten. . . .

As Lord Salisbury has expressed a wish to hear what I have to say on the subject of the various Asiatic Railway schemes, I propose speaking my mind openly in this Memorandum with that freedom to which His Lordship has accustomed me for some years past.

The Turkish railways in Asia are a subject of primary importance to us not only commercially, but also politically and strategically, and on that account we should be bound to give any scheme which embraced all these different interests a very considerable amount of support.

Indeed, in the year 1872 a Parliamentary Committee sat on the Euphrates Valley Railway and the advisability of giving material support or even a guarantee to such a railway had already been advocated at that time.

More than 30 years have now elapsed since the Treaty of Paris, and

[1] F.O. 78/3999.

APPENDIX IV 165

8 British Ambassadors have been here since. The importance of this question has been felt all along without obtaining any practical result. Future historians will no doubt wonder how so few important results were accomplished after the conclusion of the Crimean War when British Interest in the East was still fresh and our influence paramount and shared only with France.

But without any digression, I think no argument is needed to prove the truth of the following 4 propositions:

1. It is an essentially British interest that there should be railway communications established throughout Asiatic Turkey.
2. It is desirable that this should be a British Enterprise and should not fall into French or Franco-Russian hands.
3. It is essential that it should be a sound financial undertaking, and should not require or expect any material support whatever from H.M.G.
4. The great difficulties for obtaining a concession must not be overlooked, and the alleged propitious disposition of the Sultan, knowing his irresolute and suspicious character, must not be counted for too much in its favour.

Lord Salisbury has been told that the Sultan himself has suggested the desirability of a British proposal being put forward and his surprise at none being forthcoming whilst 'agents of various nationalities: French, German, etc., supported by their diplomatic representatives were pressing for extensive concessions and commercial advantages.'

In this form the above assertions appear to me to be strongly open to doubt.

It is true that H.I.M. has spoken to me myself occasionally and to the Rt. Hon. J. Chamberlain 9 months ago, at an audience he gave him, at greater length on the subject of Asiatic Railways, but it was always in general terms and asking for assistance and advice, but never in the precise form which is now reported.

As to foreigners pressing for a concession, there has been for some months only one, namely Mr. Donou, whose chances are reported as being at rather a low ebb at this moment.

There is no foreign company in existence in the Turkish provinces in Asia, and the four short lines there are every one held by British Capitalists as may be seen with other particulars in Mr. Bax-Ironside's report which accompanied my despatch No. 48 Commercial of April 2nd last.

What happens generally is that some enterprising stranger arrives at Constantinople (I am not speaking of our countrymen alone), hears railway schemes favourably spoken of and is assured by local friends that if he can secure powerful diplomatic support an advantageous concession is sure to repay his troubles. He sets to work directly to ensure this quite regardless of the numerous other difficulties which have to be surmounted, and it is only then that he finds out that the real support which is of any value must be got at the Palace and that for money, being under such circumstances, the price is enhanced by increasing competition. An unsuccessful contractor goes away disappointed after months of fruitless exertions and makes his own Embassy responsible for his failure.

Both in Servia and in Roumania (in the former not so very long ago) foreign support had been instrumental in obtaining railway concessions which were

APPENDIX IV

ultimately the cause, by failing to perform their obligations, of much internal trouble and considerable pecuniary loss to those young kingdoms, whilst the countries which gave these companies diplomatic support and patronage suffered for a long time afterwards in loss of influence.

The proceedings of Baron Hirsch in Turkey are well known and gave a fatal blow to the confidence formerly felt by the Turks in foreign promoters.

It is not easy to judge from a distance the difficulties in obtaining railway concessions in Turkey, and the greatest of these is the Sultan himself as no one can say positively whether H.M. is really desirous to have an extensive network of railways constructed in Asia or whether he is not. The Sultan always speaks as if he were, but very well informed persons doubt his sincerity in the matter and affirm the contrary.

At any rate to overcome H.M.'s hesitation a novel mode of proceeding has lately been introduced in pressing a project of this kind on his attention as they have to be accompanied with an offer of a ready sum to be advanced to the Imperial Treasury as an equivalent for real or ideal advantages to be secured by the concession.

If such an offer comes at a moment when the Treasury is particularly pinched for money it may help to carry the point though even this is not always certain.

A similar method was followed by the Smyrna-Cassaba Railway Co. for the purpose of obtaining an extension in 1885 and is again being tried by the Haidar Pasha Co. for a similar object.

This method of temptation by advances in cash to the Imperial Government does not exclude however the extensive use of baksheesh for the purpose of gaining the support of influential persons and in this lies, in my opinion, the chief and almost insurmountable impediment which militates against a British Embassy coming forward as the patron and active supporter of railway or any other concessions in which money has to be spent in this way in the Ottoman Empire.

But whenever the Asiatic lines come to be spoken of, I cannot help feeling that we have no single adequate general scheme which we could recommend conscientiously without pledging ourselves for this or that concession but only on political grounds. By this omission there is a danger that minor lines may be adopted or even constructed which will either not tally with such an extensive scheme of real practical utility or that even foreign competition may step in to modify its purpose disadvantageously for our political or strategical interest.

Our main interest lies in a railway line joining the port of Alexandretta with some place on the Persian Gulf and taking in the points of most importance in Asia.

In one sense even the Ismidt-Haidar Pasha is considered by some persons as not properly coming within the framework which it is our interest to see constructed, but H.M. Embassy has been told repeatedly by the F.O. to support its extension.

Our present system of supporting concessions without any regard to our general interests appears to me objectionable and would be called by a German 'planlos'.

It was to obviate the encouragement of such partial and possibly contradictory schemes that Mr. Chamberlain advised the Sultan to appoint a Commission of foreign engineers to be recommended by their Governments who would work out a regular practical scheme of a network for Asiatic Turkey with accurate statistical tables of the income which might be derived from such lines after which it would be possible to seek the support of a sound financial syndicate for their construction.

In my humble opinion, it is highly desirable that H.M.G. should call for such a preparatory scheme from our own Intelligence Department who would no doubt be able to give valuable confidential advice as to what it is desirable for us to support and what to eschew with regard to these railways after which the F.O. would have a basis enabling it to give specific instructions to this Embassy as the occasion might arise.

2. *White to Salisbury, Private Letter, dated 16 October 1888*[1]

... By far the most important event I have seen happening here since my return as Ambassador, just two years ago—is in my opinion the Railway Concession [? for] Ismidt-Angora with proposed continuation across Asia.

The Russians and French are furious to see this important Railway going into Anglo-German hands and finding out that, whilst we were keeping in the background, Radowitz was working for a South German syndicate, and that Prince Bismarck is for the first time pushing Bavarian and Würtemburg capital into Turkish investments—a highly significant fact. Although everything has been signed and has the Sultan's approbation, intrigues are going on against this Asiatic concession. These are led by the French capitalists, the Ottoman Bank and even Bleichröder: the latter finds himself for the first time in his life opposed by his all-powerful Patron. It is even mentioned that Baring Brothers have promised their support to the French action. I really do hope that this is not the case. Radowitz tells me that English capitalists will share these works with the Germans, and I am quite satisfied that, if Her Majesty's Embassy had come more to the front—as was desired by some parties, the Sultan's suspiciousness would have been too strong, and the Russo-French intrigues even bolder than they are at present. But both Russians and French, seeing Radowitz to the front, dare not act more openly which they would no doubt have done, if they had seen us, and us alone.

They are directing now all their shafts against Blanc, who was the first originator of a scheme for counteracting the preponderance of French capitalists by the joint efforts of England, Germany and Italy, and by whose initiative and zeal the Franco-Russian combination, it can now be fairly hoped, will be successfully ousted: a result which I hardly ventured to anticipate or hope until a few weeks ago.

This business is the commencement of a split between Radowitz and Nelidov, and bids fair to become a new departure for Germany at Constantinople which it will be most interesting to watch.

[1] F.O. 364/1.

BIBLIOGRAPHY

I. UNPUBLISHED MATERIAL

A. *Foreign Office Papers and Embassy Archives in the Public Record Office*

1. *Foreign Office Papers: Turkey*
   F.O. 78   Dispatches and Telegrams to and from the British Embassy at Constantinople, 1885–91.
   Dispatches to and from Sir Henry Drummond Wolff, 1885–7.
   Domestic and various:
   Correspondence with the Turkish Embassy in London; correspondence with other Government Departments; and correspondence with private persons, 1885–91.
   Case volumes:
   3863, 3978–80, 4170–1: Blue Book permissions from foreign governments, 1885–8.
   4264–5: The Haidar Pasha to Ismidt Railway, 1885–9.
   4272: The Passage of the Bosphorus and the Dardanelles, 1882–90.
   4332–4: The Trial of Moussa Bey, 1889–90.
2. *Archives of the British Embassy at Constantinople*
   F.O. 195 Dispatches to and from the Foreign Office, 1885–91.
   Correspondence to and from the Sublime Porte, 1885–91.
   Communications with Dragomans and the Military Attaché, 1885–91.
3. *Foreign Office Papers: Austria-Hungary*
   F.O. 7   Dispatches and Telegrams to and from the British Embassy at Vienna, 1885–91.
4. *Archives of the British Embassy at Vienna*
   F.O. 120 Dispatches and Telegrams to and from the Foreign Office, 1885–91.
5. *Foreign Office Papers: France*
   F.O. 27   Dispatches and Telegrams to and from the British Embassy at Paris, 1885–91.
6. *Archives of the British Embassy at Paris*
   F.O. 146 Dispatches and Telegrams to and from the Foreign Office, 1885–91.
7. *Foreign Office Papers: Italy*
   F.O. 45   Dispatches and Telegrams to and from the British Embassy at Rome, 1885–91.
8. *Archives of the British Embassy at Rome*
   F.O. 165 Dispatches and Telegrams to and from the Foreign Office, 1885–91.

BIBLIOGRAPHY 169

9. *Foreign Office Papers: Germany*
    F.O. 64   Dispatches and Telegrams to and from the British Embassy at Berlin, 1885–91.
10. *Archives of the British Embassy at Berlin*
    F.O. 244 Dispatches and Telegrams to and from the Foreign Office, 1885–91.
11. *Foreign Office Papers: Russia*
    F.O. 65   Dispatches and Telegrams to and from the British Embassy at St. Petersburg, 1885–91.
12. *Archives of the British Embassy at St. Petersburg*
    F.O. 181 Dispatches and Telegrams to and from the Foreign Office, 1885–91.
13. *Foreign Office Papers: Denmark*
    F.O. 22   Dispatches and Telegrams to and from the British Legation at Copenhagen, 1885.
14. *Foreign Office Papers: Greece*
    F.O. 32   Dispatches and Telegrams to and from the British Legation at Athens, 1885–6.
15. *Foreign Office Papers: Roumania*
    F.O. 104 Dispatches and Telegrams to and from the British Legation at Bucharest, 1886.
16. *Foreign Office Papers: Servia*
    F.O. 105 Dispatches and Telegrams to and from the British Legation at Belgrade, 1885.
17. *Foreign Office Papers: General*
    F.O. 83   Treaties, Circulars, and Foreign Embassies, 1885–91.

B. *Private Papers in the Public Record Office*

1. F.O. 364/1–6   Private Papers of Sir William White, 1857–90. Correspondence with Salisbury, Rosebery, and Iddesleigh.
2. F.O. 343/1–13 Private Papers of Sir Edward Malet, 1885–95. Correspondence with Granville, Salisbury, Rosebery, Iddesleigh, and Kimberley; letters to and from the Queen, the Emperor William II, and other members of the Royal Families.
3. F.O. 358/6   Private Papers of General Sir John Lintorn Simmons. General, 1857–96; letters to and from Salisbury, 1891.
4. P.R.O. 30/29   Private Papers of Lord Granville, 1885. Correspondence with Embassies abroad; with Lord Dufferin, 1882–5; with Members of the Cabinet; and with the Queen.

5. P.R.O. 30/6　　　　　Private Papers of Lord Carnarvon, 1885–7. Correspondence with Members of the Cabinet; Confidential Prints.

C. *Private Papers in the British Museum*

1. *The Private Papers of W. E. Gladstone*
   Add. MS. 44149　　　Correspondence with Dilke, 1870–94, vol. lxiv.
   Add. MSS. 44178–80　Correspondence with Granville, 1885, 1886, 1887–91; vols. xciii–xcv.
   Add. MS. 44268　　　Correspondence with Madame Olga Novikoff, 1873–96; vol. clxxxiii.
   Add. MSS. 44288–9　Correspondence with Rosebery, 1872–85, 1886–92; vols. cciii–cciv.
2. *The Private Papers of Sir A. H. Layard*
   Add. MSS. 39038–48　General Correspondence, 1884–91, vols. cviii–cxviii.
3. *The Private Papers of Sir Charles Dilke*
   Add. MSS. 43895–9　General Correspondence, 1885–91; (unbound).

D. *The Private Papers of Lord Salisbury in the Library of Christ Church, Oxford*

Volume 36　Private Letters to Austria, Belgium, China, Egypt, France, Germany, Greece, Holland, Italy, Russia, Turkey; Sir H. D. Wolff, 1885 and 1886.
Volume 43　Private Letters from Bulgaria, Egypt, Greece, Russia, Turkey; Sir H. D. Wolff's Mission, 1885 and 1886.
Volume 45　The Queen, Private, 1886–92.
Volume 75　Turkey, Private, 1887 and 1888.
Volume 76　From Turkey, Private, 1889–92; to Turkey, Private, 1887–92.
Unbound　Private Letters from Sir William White and Sir H. D. Wolff.

E. *The Private Papers of Sir William White in the possession of his family*

After White's sudden death, an attempt was made by the staff of the embassy at Constantinople to send all his private correspondence to the Foreign Office. That which they succeeded in collecting can now be seen at the Public Record Office, but the greater part of the correspondence eluded them and was retained by Lady White. H. Sutherland Edwards was allowed to use some of these papers when he wrote his biography of White at the turn of the century, but as many of White's correspondents were still living at that time most of the papers remained unseen. During the Second World War, a German bomb fell

BIBLIOGRAPHY

on a water-main in the bank-vaults in which the papers were stored, and only two small volumes escaped being turned into pulp.

These volumes, referred to throughout this work as the 'Additional White Papers', contain some letters from Salisbury which provide some interesting material on his policy towards Bulgaria and his attitude towards the Mediterranean agreements. They also include some letters from Iddesleigh which help to throw some light upon Great Britain's Near Eastern policy during the autumn and winter of 1886.

Correspondence from Dilke shows that he often consulted White about Near Eastern politics, and that much of the material and many of the opinions which he gathered on this subject for his famous book *The Present Position of European Politics* were derived from White. A series of letters to White from Lady Jane Ely, Lady of the Queen's Bedchamber, helps to explain how White first became known and admired by Queen Victoria.

The remainder of the correspondence is mainly composed of letters from Sir Henry Elliot and Sir Austen Layard which deal with White's career at Belgrade and Bucharest during the late 'seventies and early 'eighties. There are also a few letters from Morier, but the most important of these have already been published in H. Sutherland Edwards' biography of White.

F. *The Private Letters of Sir Robert Morier in the possession of his granddaughter*

Transcripts of some of these papers have very kindly been shown to the author by Miss Agatha Ramm of Somerville College, Oxford, who has examined the Morier correspondence.

The correspondence between Morier and Salisbury reveals two different approaches to Eastern politics. It shows that Morier subscribed to the ideas of Randolph Churchill, and repeatedly asserted that the problem of Central Asia and the defence of India was far more important than the Near Eastern question and the defence of the Straits. Unfortunately, the private correspondence between Morier and White was irregular and seldom contained any real political discussion.

II. PARLIAMENTARY PAPERS AND COLLECTIONS OF DOCUMENTS

A. *Accounts and Papers*

The following work has been used as a guide to the Parliamentary Papers:

H. W. V. TEMPERLEY and L. M. PENSON, *A Century of Diplomatic Blue Books, 1814–1914* (Cambridge, 1938).

1886   Correspondence respecting the Port of Batoum: (1886), lxxiii [C–4857], 153.
Correspondence respecting Sir H. Drummond Wolff's Special Mission to Constantinople: (1886), lxxiv [C–4604], 1.

Further Correspondence respecting the Affairs of Egypt: (1886), lxxiv [C–4611], 49.
Correspondence respecting the Reorganization of the Egyptian Army: (1886), lxxiv [C–4740], 159.
Correspondence respecting the Affairs of Eastern Roumelia and Bulgaria: (1886), lxxv [C–4612], 1.
Further Correspondence respecting the Affairs of Eastern Roumelia and Bulgaria: (1886), lxxv [C–4767], 455.

1887 Further Correspondence respecting the Affairs of Bulgaria and Eastern Roumelia: (1887), xci [C–4933], 317.
Further Correspondence respecting the Affairs of Bulgaria and Eastern Roumelia: (1887), xci [C–4934], 627.
Reports by Sir Henry Drummond Wolff on the Administration of Egypt: (1887), xcii [C–4996], 431.
Further Correspondence respecting Sir H. Drummond Wolff's Mission (November 1886–June 1887): (1887), xcii [C–5050], 481.
Further Correspondence respecting Sir H. Drummond Wolff's Mission (May–August 1887): (1887), xcii [C–5110], 557.

1888 Further Correspondence respecting the Affairs of Bulgaria and Eastern Roumelia: (1888), cix [C–5370], 397.

1889 Correspondence respecting the Condition of the Populations in Asiatic Turkey: (1889), lxxxvii [C–5723], 143.
Further Correspondence respecting Affairs in the East: (1889), lxxxvii [C–5824], 241.

1890 Correspondence respecting the Condition of the Populations in Asiatic Turkey and the Trial of Moussa Bey: (1890), lxxxii [C–5912], 1.

1890–1 Correspondence respecting the Condition of the Populations in Asiatic Turkey and the Proceedings in the case of Moussa Bey: (1890–1), xcvi [C–6214], 455.

1891 Further Correspondence respecting Affairs in the East: (1891), xcvi [C–6259], 563.
Further Correspondence respecting Affairs in the East (June–December 1890): (1891) xcvi [C–6319], 665.
Further Correspondence respecting Affairs in the East (January–June 1891): (1891), xcvi [C–6493], 761.

1892 Further Correspondence respecting the Condition of the Populations in Asiatic Turkey: (1892), xcvi [C–6632], 1.

B. *Ministère des Affaires Etrangères (Paris)*

Affaires de Roumélie et de Grèce, 1885–1886 (Paris, 1886).
Affaires d'Egypte, 1884–1893 (Paris, 1893).

BIBLIOGRAPHY

C. Collections of Documents

1. Belgium — *Zur Europäischen Politik, 1897–1914*, 5 vols. (Berlin, 1919), Wilhelm Köhler, general editor. Vol. 5, *Revancheidee und Panslawismus*, edited by Bernard Schwertfeger. (Documents taken by the Germans from the Belgian Archives during the First World War.)

2. France — *Documents Diplomatiques Français, 1871–1914* (Paris, 1933–9), Ministère des Affaires Etrangères, 1st series, v–vi, vi *bis*, vii–ix.

3. Germany — *Die Grosse Politik der europäischen Kabinette, 1871–1914*, 40 vols. (Berlin, 1922–7), edited by J. Lepsius, A. M. Bartholdy, and F. Thimme. Vols. iii–ix, xiv. 2.

4. Great Britain — *British Documents on the Origins of the War, 1898–1914*, 11 vols. (London, 1926–38), edited by G. P. Gooch and H. W. V. Temperley. (Vol. viii (1932) contains documents relating to the Mediterranean agreements of 1887.)
Letters from the Berlin Embassy, edited by Paul Knaplund, Annual Report of the American Historical Association, vol. ii (Washington, 1942).

5. Russia — *Correspondance diplomatique de M. de Staal, 1884–1900*, 2 vols. (Paris, 1929), edited by Baron Alexandre Meyendorff.
Documents secrets de la politique russe en Orient, 1881–1890, published by R. Léonoff (Berlin, 1893).

6. Other Collections

HERTSLET, SIR EDWARD, *The Map of Europe by Treaty*, vols. ii–iv (1828–91), (London, 1875–91). (For all the relevant treaties.)

TEMPERLEY, H. W. V., and PENSON, L. M., *Foundations of British Foreign Policy from Pitt to Salisbury (1792–1902)* (Cambridge, 1938).

NORADOUNGIANG, G., *Racueil d'actes internationaux de l'Empire Ottoman*, 4 vols. (Paris, 1878–1902).

YOUNG, G., *Corps de Droit Ottoman*, 7 vols. (Oxford, 1905–6).

Hansard's Parliamentary Debates, 1885–91.

D. Newspapers

I am very grateful to the late Captain William de Geijer for kindly allowing me to examine a volume of cuttings about his grandfather taken both from British and foreign newspapers. Besides drawing upon *The Times* for the years 1885–91, I have therefore been able to make use of newspaper sources which would not normally be available in Great Britain.

III. BIOGRAPHIES, MEMOIRS, AND LETTERS

BUCKLE, G. E. (editor), *The Letters of Queen Victoria*, 2nd series, vol. iii (London, 1928); 3rd series, vols. i–ii (London, 1930).

BIBLIOGRAPHY

Busch, M., *Bismarck, Some Secret Pages of his History*, vol. iii (London, 1898), 3 vols.

Cambon, Paul, *Correspondence, 1870–1924*, vol. i (Paris, 1940), 3 vols.

Cecil, Lady Gwendolen, *The Life of Robert, Marquis of Salisbury*, vols. iii–iv (London, 1921–31), 4 vols.

—— *Biographical Studies of the Life and Political Character of Robert, Third Marquis of Salisbury* (London, 1948), privately printed.

Chamberlain, Joseph, *A Political Memoir, 1880–1892*, edited from the original manuscript by C. D. H. Howard (London, 1953).

Churchill, Winston S., *Lord Randolph Churchill* (London, 1951), new edition.

Corbett, Sir Vincent, *Reminiscences, Autobiographical and Diplomatic* (London, 1928).

Corti, Count Egon C., *Alexander von Battenberg: Sein Kampf mit den Zaren und Bismarck* (Vienna, 1920).

Crewe, Marquis of, *Lord Rosebery*, vol. i (London, 1931), 2 vols.

Dugdale, E. T. S., *Maurice de Bunsen. Diplomat and Friend* (London, 1934).

Edwards, H. Sutherland, *The Career and Correspondence of Sir William White* (London, 1902).

Elliot, The Hon. Arthur J., *The Life of George Joachim Goschen, First Viscount Goschen* (London, 1911), 2 vols.

Fitzmaurice, Lord Edmond, *The Life of Granville George Leveson Gower, Second Earl of Granville*, vol. ii (London, 1905), 2 vols.

Freycinet, Charles de, *Souvenirs, 1878–1893* (Paris, 1913).

Gardiner, A. G., *The Life of Sir William Harcourt*, vol. ii (London, 1923), 2 vols.

Garvin, J. L., *The Life of Joseph Chamberlain*, vol. ii (London, 1932–4), 3 vols.

Gathorne-Hardy, A. E., *Gathorne-Hardy, First Earl Cranbrook*, vol. ii (London, 1910), 2 vols.

Goltz, Colmar von der, *Denkwürdigkeiten* (Berlin, 1929).

Graves, Sir Robert, *Storm Centres of the Near East: Personal Memories, 1879–1929* (London, 1933).

Gwynn, Stephen, and Tuckwell, Gertrude M., *The Life of the Rt. Hon. Sir Charles Dilke Bart., M.P.*, vol. ii (London, 1917), 2 vols.

Hamilton, Lord George, *Parliamentary Reminiscences and Reflections, 1886–1906* (London, 1922).

Hardinge, Sir Arthur, *A Diplomatist in Europe* (London, 1927).

—— *A Diplomatist in the East* (London, 1928).

Hardinge of Penshurst, Lord, *Old Diplomacy* (London, 1947).

Helfferich, Karl, *Georg von Siemens. Ein Lebensbild aus Deutschlands grosser Zeit*, vol. iii (Berlin, 1921–3), 3 vols.

Holenlohe-Schillingfürst, Prince Clovis Carl von, *Memoirs of Prince Chlodwig of Hohenlohe-Schillingfürst*, vol. ii (London, 1906), 2 vols.

Kennedy, A. L., *Salisbury, 1830–1903. Portrait of a Statesman* (London, 1953).

Koch, Adolf, *Prince Alexander of Battenberg: reminiscences of his reign in Bulgaria* (London, 1887).

BIBLIOGRAPHY 175

KÜHLMANN, RICHARD VON, *Erinnerungen* (Heidelberg, 1948).
LANG, A., *The Life, Letters and Diaries of Sir Stafford Northcote, First Earl of Iddesleigh* (London, 1891).
LEE, SIR SIDNEY, *King Edward VII. A Biography*, vol. i (London, 1925–7), 2 vols.
LUCIUS VON BALLHAUSEN, R., *Bismarck-Erinnerungen* (Stuttgart, 1920).
LYALL, SIR ALFRED, *The Life of the Marquis of Dufferin and Ava*, vol. ii (London, 1905), 2 vols.
MAXWELL, SIR HERBERT, *The Life and Times of the Rt. Hon. William Henry Smith, M.P.*, vol. ii (London, 1893), 2 vols.
MIJATOVICH, COUNT C., *Memoirs of a Balkan Diplomatist* (London, 1917).
MITIS, OSKAR, *Das Leben des Kronprinzen Rudolf* (Leipzig, 1928).
MORLEY, JOHN, *The Life of William Ewart Gladstone*, vols. ii–iii (London, 1903), 3 vols.
MOÜY, COMPTE CHARLES DE, *Souvenirs et causeries d'un diplomate* (Paris, 1909).
MOWAT, R. B., *The Life of Lord Pauncefote* (London, 1929).
NEWTON, LORD A. P., *Lord Lyons*, vol. ii (London, 1913), 2 vols.
NICOLSON, HAROLD, *Lord Carnock* (London, 1930).
—— *Helen's Tower* (London, 1937).
OPPER DE BLOWITZ, H. G., *Une Course à Constantinople*, 3rd edition (Paris, 1884).
PALAMENGHI-CRISPI (editor), *The Memoirs of Francesco Crispi*, vol. ii (London, 1912), 3 vols.
PEARS, SIR EDWIN, *Forty Years in Constantinople, 1873–1915* (London, 1916).
PONSONBY, ARTHUR, *Henry Ponsonby, Queen Victoria's Private Secretary: His Life from his Letters* (London, 1942).
PONSONBY, SIR FREDERICK (editor), *Letters of the Empress Frederick* (London, 1928).
RADOWITZ, JOSEF MARIA VON, *Aufzeichnungen und Erinnerungen*, vol. ii (Berlin, 1925), 2 vols.
RODD, SIR JAMES RENNELL, *Social and Diplomatic Memoirs, 1884–1893* (London, 1922).
RONALDSHAY, EARL OF, *The Life of Lord Curzon*, vol. i (London, 1928), 3 vols.
RUMBOLD, SIR HORACE, *Final Recollections of a Diplomatist* (London, 1905).
SCHWEINITZ, GENERAL VON, *Denkwürdigkeiten des Botschafters*, vol. ii (Berlin, 1927), 2 vols.
STEAD, W. T., *The M.P. for Russia. Reminiscences of Madame Olga Novikoff*, vol. ii (London, 1909), 2 vols.
SYKES, SIR PERCY, *The Rt. Hon. Sir Mortimer Durand: a biography* (London, 1926).
VAMBÉRY, ARMINIUS, *The Story of My Struggles: the Memoirs of Arminius Vambéry*, vol. ii (London, 1904), 2 vols.
WALDERSEE, ALFRED GRAF VON, *Denkwürdigkeiten*, vol. ii (Berlin and Stuttgart, 1922–5), 3 vols.
—— *Aus dem Briefwechsel des General-Feldmarschalls Alfred Grafen von Waldersee* (Berlin and Leipzig, 1928).

WASHBURN, GEORGE, *Fifty Years in Constantinople, and Recollections of Robert College* (Boston and New York, 1909).
WHYTE, FREDERIC, *The Life of W. T. Stead*, vol. ii (London, 1925), 2 vols.
WOLFF, SIR HENRY DRUMMOND, *Rambling Recollections*, vol. ii (London, 1908), 2 vols.
WRATISLAW, A. C., *A Consul in the East* (London, 1924).
ZETLAND, MARQUESS OF, *Lord Cromer* (London, 1932).

IV. SECONDARY WORKS

ALBERTINI, LUIGI, *The Origins of the War of 1914* (translated and edited by I. M. Massey), vol. i: *European Relations from the Congress of Berlin to the eve of the Sarajevo Murder* (Oxford, 1952).
ALBIN, PIERRE, *La Paix armée. L'Allemagne et la France en Europe, 1885–1894* (Paris, 1913).
ANDRASSY, COUNT JULIUS, *Bismarck, Andrassy and their Successors* (London, 1927).
ANONYMOUS, *Les Causes occultes de la question bulgare* (Paris, 1887).
—— 'Who Shall Inherit Constantinople?', *National Review*, December 1890.
—— *L'Alliance franco-russe devant la Crise orientale* (Paris, 1891).
—— 'German Methods in Turkey', *Quarterly Review*, ccxxviii, October 1917.
—— 'Our Diplomatists', *Temple Bar*, vol. lxxxiv, No. 335, October 1888.
AYDELOTTE, W. O., *Bismarck and British Colonial Policy: South West Africa, 1883–1885* (London, 1937).
BEAMAN, A. G. H., *Stambuloff* (London, 1895).
BECKER, O., *Bismarcks Bundnispolitik* (Berlin, 1923).
BINDOFF, S. T., 'The Unreformed Diplomatic Service, 1812–60', *Transactions of the Royal Historical Society*, 4th series, xviii (1935).
BLACK, CYRIL E., *The Establishment of Constitutional Government in Bulgaria* (Princeton, 1943).
BLAISDELL, D. C., *European Financial Control in the Ottoman Empire* (New York, 1929).
BOURCHIER, JAMES D., 'Prince Alexander of Battenberg', *Fortnightly Review*, lxi, January 1894.
BOURGEOIS, ÉMILE and PAGÈS, GEORGES, *Les Origines et les responsabilités de la Grande Guerre* (Paris, 1921).
BRANDENBURG, ERICH, *From Bismarck to the World War* (London, 1927).
BUXTON, NOEL, *Europe and the Turks*, 2nd edition (London, 1912).
CARROLL, E. M., *French Public Opinion amd Foreign Affairs, 1870–1914* (New York, 1931).
CHÉRADAME, ANDRÉ, *The Baghdad Railway* (London, 1911).
CHIROL, SIR VALENTINE, *Fifty Years in a Changing World* (London, 1927).
COCHERIS, J., *La Situation internationale de l'Égypte et du Soudan, juridique et politique* (Paris, 1903).
COLVIN, SIR AUCKLAND, *The Making of Modern Egypt* (London, 1906).
CORTI, COUNT EGON C., *The Downfall of Three Dynasties* (London, 1934).
CROMER, LORD, *Modern Egypt* (London, 1908), 2 vols.

CROWE, S. E., *The Berlin West Africa Conference, 1884–5* (London, 1942).
CYON, E. DE, *Histoire de l'Entente franco-russe* (Lausanne, 1895).
DAUDET, ERNEST, *Histoire diplomatique de l'alliance franco-russe* (Paris, 1894).
DEBIDOUR, ANTONIN, *Histoire diplomatique de l'Europe depuis le Congrès de Berlin jusqu'à nos jours*, 2 vols. (Paris, 1916–17).
DILKE, SIR CHARLES, *The Present Position of European Politics* (London, 1887).
DORPALEN, ANDREAS, 'Tsar Alexander III and the Boulanger Crisis in France', *Journal of Modern History*, xxiii, No. 2, June 1951.
DRANDAR, A. G., *Les événements politiques en Bulgarie depuis 1876 jusqu'à nos jours* (Brussels, 1896).
DRIAULT, ÉDOUARD, and LHÉRITIER, MICHEL, *Histoire diplomatique de la Grèce*, vol. iv (Paris, 1926), 6 vols.
EARLE, EDWARD M., *Turkey, the Great Powers, and the Bagdad Railway* (New York, 1923).
EYCK, ERICH, *Bismarck: Leben und Werk*, vol. iii (Zürich, 1944), 3 vols.
FEIS, H., *Europe, the World's Banker, 1870–1914* (New Haven, 1930).
FILLION, GEORGES, *Entre Slaves* (Paris, 1894).
FLOURENS, ÉMILE, *Alexandre III, sa vie, son œuvre* (Paris, 1894).
FREYCINET, CHARLES DE, *La Question d'Égypte* (Paris, 1905).
FULLER, J. V., *Bismarck's Diplomacy at its Zenith* (Cambridge, Mass., 1922).
GAULIS, GEORGES, *La Ruine d'un Empire* (Paris, 1913).
GIGLIO, CARLO, 'L'Inghilterra e l'Impresa Italiana di Massaua', *Dalla Nuova Antologia*, No. 1823, November 1952.
GILLET, L., *Gabriel Hanotaux* (Paris, 1933).
GOOCH, G. P., *History of Modern Europe, 1878–1919* (London, 1923).
—— *Franco-German Relations, 1871–1918* (London, 1923).
—— *Studies in Diplomacy and Statecraft* (London, 1942).
—— *Studies in German History* (London, 1948).
GORIANOV, SERGE, 'The End of the Alliance of the Emperors', *American Historical Review*, xxiii, January 1918.
GOSSES, F., *The Management of British Foreign Policy before the First World War. Especially during the Period 1880–1914*, translated from the Dutch by Miss E. C. Van Der Gaaf (Leiden, 1948).
GROGAN, ELLINOR F. B., 'Bulgaria under Prince Alexander', *Slavonic Review*, i, March 1923.
GRÜNING, I., *Die russische öffentliche Meinung und ihre Stellung zu den Grossmächten, 1878–1894* (Berlin, 1929).
HAGEN, M. VON, *England und Agypten* (Bonn, 1915).
—— *Bismarcks Kolonialpolitik* (Berlin, 1923).
—— *Bismarck und England* (Stuttgart, 1941).
HAMMANN, OTTO, *The World Policy of Germany, 1890–1912* (London, 1927).
HANOTAUX, GABRIEL, 'La Prétendue Conjuration Franco-Russe', *Revue des Deux Mondes*, 7th period, xliii, January 1928.
HANSEN, JULES, *L'Alliance franco-russe* (Paris, 1897).
—— *L'Ambassade à Paris du Baron de Mohrenheim, 1884–98* (Paris, 1907).
HAUSER, H., *Histoire diplomatique de L'Europe, 1871–1914. Manuel de Politique européenne* (Paris, 1929).

HEADLAM-MORLEY, SIR J., *Studies in Diplomatic History* (London, 1930).
HELFFERICH, KARL, *Die Deutsche Türkenpolitik* (Berlin, 1921).
HOBART PASHA, 'A Strategical View of Turkey', *Nineteenth Century*, cvi, December 1885.
HOLBORN, HAJO, *Deutschland und die Türkei, 1875–1890* (Berlin, 1926).
HORNIK, M. P., 'The Special Mission of Sir Henry Drummond Wolff to Constantinople, 1885–1887', *English Historical Review*, lv, October 1940.
—— *Baron Holstein. Studies in German Diplomacy* (Vienna, 1948).
HOSKINS, HALFORD L., *British Routes to India* (New York, 1928).
HUHN, A. VON, *The Struggle of the Bulgarians for National Independence under Prince Alexander* (London, 1886).
—— *The Kidnapping of Prince Alexander of Battenberg, his return to Bulgaria and subsequent abdication* (London, 1887).
HYDE, ARTHUR M., *A Diplomatic History of Bulgaria* (Urbana, 1928).
IMBERT, PAUL, 'Le Chemin de Fer de Bagdad', *Revue des Deux Mondes*, 5th period, xxxviii, April 1907.
JENKS, L. H., *The Migration of British Capital to 1875* (London, 1938).
KLEINE, MATHILDE, *Deutschland und die ägyptische Frage, 1875–1890* (Greifswald, 1927).
KLUKE, PAUL, 'Bismarck und Salisbury: ein Diplomatisches Duell', *Historische Zeitschrift*, 175/2, April 1953.
KNAPLUND, PAUL, *Gladstone's Foreign Policy* (New York, 1935).
KRAUSNICK, HELMUT, *Holsteins Geheimpolitik in der Ära Bismarck, 1886–1890* (Hamburg, 1942).
LANGER, WILLIAM L., *The Franco-Russian Alliance, 1890–1894* (Cambridge, Mass., 1929).
—— *European Alliances and Alignments, 1871–1890*, 2nd edition (New York, 1950).
—— *The Diplomacy of Imperialism, 1890–1902*, 2nd edition (New York, 1950).
MARRIOTT, SIR J. A. R., *The Eastern Question*, 4th edition (Oxford, 1940).
MARDER, A. J., *British Naval Policy, 1880–1905* (London, 1940).
MEDLICOTT, W. N., 'The Mediterranean Agreements of 1887', *Slavonic Review*, v, June 1926.
—— 'Corrections to the Dictionary of National Biography on Sir William White', *Bulletin of the Institute of Historical Research*, v (1927–8).
—— 'Lord Salisbury and Turkey', *History*, October 1927.
—— 'Austria-Hungary and the War Danger of 1887', *Slavonic Review*, vi, December 1927.
—— 'The Powers and the Unification of the Two Bulgarias', *English Historical Review*, liv, January–April 1939.
—— 'The Gladstone Government and the Cyprus Convention', *Journal of Modern History*, xii, No. 2, June 1940.
—— 'Bismarck and the Three Emperors' Alliance, 1881–1887', *Transactions of the Royal Historical Society*, 4th series, xxvii (1945).
MILLER, W., *The Ottoman Empire and its Successors* (Cambridge, 1934).
MILNER, SIR ALFRED, *England in Egypt*, 4th edition (London, 1893).
MOUKHTAR PACHA, M., *La Turquie, L'Allemagne et L'Europe* (Paris, 1924).

BIBLIOGRAPHY

NOACK, V., *Bismarcks Friedenspolitik* (Leipzig, 1924).
NOLDE, BARON BORIS, *L'Alliance franco-russe* (Paris, 1936).
OSTRONOG, L., *The Turkish Problem* (London, 1919).
(PARKER, ALWYN), 'The Bagdad Railway Negotiations', *Quarterly Review*, ccxxviii, October 1917.
PEARS, SIR EDWIN, 'The Bagdad Railway', *Contemporary Review*, xciv, November 1908.
—— *The Life of Abdul Hamid* (London, 1917).
PENSON, LILLIAN M., 'The Principles and Methods of Lord Salisbury's Foreign Policy', *Cambridge Historical Journal*, v. ii, 1935.
—— 'The New Course in British Foreign Policy', *Transactions of the Royal Historical Society*, 4th series, xxv (1943).
PRESSEL, WILHELM VON, *Les Chemins de fer en Turquie d'Asie* (Zürich, 1902).
PRIBRAM, A. F., *The Secret Treaties of Austria-Hungary* (Cambridge, Mass., 1920–1), 2 vols.
RAGEY, LOUIS, *La Question du Chemin de fer de Bagdad, 1893–1914* (Paris, 1936).
RAMM, A., 'Great Britain and the Planting of Italian Power in the Red Sea, 1868–1885', *English Historical Review*, lix, May 1944.
RAMSAY, SIR WILLIAM M., *The Revolution in Constantinople and Turkey* (London, 1909).
RAWLINSON, SIR HENRY, 'The Russian Advance in Central Asia', *Nineteenth Century*, xcviii, April 1885.
RENOUVIN, P., PRECLIN, E., and HARDY, G., *La Paix armée et la grande Guerre, 1871–1919* (Paris, 1914).
RITTER, GERHARD, *Bismarcks Verhältnis zu England und die Politik des 'Neuen Kurses'* (Berlin, 1924).
ROTHSTEIN, T., *Egypt's Ruin* (London, 1910).
ROY, GILLES, *Abdul Hamid, le Sultan rouge* (Paris, 1936).
SALVATORELLI, L., *La Triplice Alleanza, 1877–1912* (Milan, 1939).
SCHÄFER, C. A., *Deutsch-Türkische Freundschaft* (Berlin, 1914).
—— *Die Entwicklung der Bagdadbahn-politik* (Berlin, 1916).
SETON-WATSON, R. W., 'Pan-German Aspirations in the Near East', *Journal of the Royal Society of Arts*, March 1916.
—— *Britain in Europe, 1789–1914. A Survey of Foreign Policy* (Cambridge, 1937).
SONTAG, RAYMOND J., *Germany and England, Background of Conflict, 1848–1894* (New York, 1938).
SPENDER, J. A., *Fifty Years of Europe* (London, 1933).
STEAD, W. T., *The Truth about Russia* (London, 1888).
SUMNER, B. H., *Russia and the Balkans, 1870–1880* (Oxford, 1937).
—— 'Tsardom and Imperialism in the Far East and Middle East, 1880–1914', *Proceedings of the British Academy*, xxvii (1942).
TAYLOR, A. J. P., *Germany's First Bid for Colonies, 1884–1885* (London, 1938).
TEMPERLEY, H. W. V., 'British Policy towards Parliamentary Rule and Constitutionalism in Turkey, 1830–1914', *Cambridge Historical Journal*, iv. ii, 1933.
—— 'British Secret Diplomacy from Canning to Grey', ibid., vi. i, 1938.

BIBLIOGRAPHY

TOUTAIN, EDMUND, *Alexandre III et la République française* (Paris, 1929).
TOWNSEND, MARY E., *The Origins of Modern German Colonialism* (New York, 1921).
—— *The Rise and Fall of Germany's Colonial Empire, 1884–1914* (New York, 1930).
TRÜTZSCHLER VON FALKENSTEIN, HEINZ, *Bismarck und die Kriegsgefahr des Jahres 1887* (Berlin, 1924).
WEEKS, D. C., *The Egyptian Question in British Foreign Policy with special reference to 1885–1887*, typescript thesis (Ph.D. (London), 1952).
WINDELBAND, W., *Bismarck und die europäischen Grossmachte, 1879–1885* (Essen, 1940).
WITTLIN, ALMA, *Abdul Hamid* (London, 1940).
WOLF, J. B. *The Diplomatic History of the Bagdad Railroad* (Columbia, 1936).
WREN, M. C., 'Pobedonostov and Russian Influence in the Balkans, 1881–1888', *Journal of Modern History*, xix, June 1947.
YOUNG, GEORGE, *Constantinople* (London, 1926).

INDEX

Abdul Hamid II, Sultan of Turkey: hatred of British ambassadors, 1; opposition to White's appointment, 49–50; and Bulgaria, 56, 91–92; and Egypt, 88, 150–1; and Asia Minor, 106; attitude towards railway enterprises, 110–11, 115–16, 125–8; and death of White, 134; and dismissal of Kiamil Pasha, 148.
Aksakov, Ivan, 18.
Alexander of Battenberg, Prince of Bulgaria, 14–18, 32–37, 47–48, 60, 77, 90–91, 104, 137–8.
Alexander III, Emperor of Russia, 13–14, 17–18, 48, 69, 93–94.
Alt, Colonel, 112, 124, 126–33.
Anatolian Railway Company, 131.
Andrassy, Count Julius, 69.

Bad Gastein, 58, 62, 67, 89, 153.
Baring, Sir Evelyn (afterwards Earl of Cromer), 81, 140, 142.
Bashford, 71.
Batum crisis, 42, 56.
Bax-Ironside, 111.
Bieberstein, Baron Marschall von, 151.
Bismarck, Herbert, Count von, 36, 69, 98, 123, 125.
Bismarck-Schönhausen, Prince Otto von: Pendjeh crisis and, 11–12; Bulgarian policy of, 15–16, 88–89, 92–95, 140; meeting with White, 58–60, 67; First Mediterranean Agreement and, 67–72; the German Army Bill and, 70, 94; Egyptian policy of, 75–80, 84; the Holmwood incident and, 76–77, 137–8; Reinsurance Treaty and, 77–78, 94; Anglo-Russian rapprochement and, 86–87; financial war against Russia and, 93–94; 1879 Austro-German Alliance and, 94; Second Mediterranean Agreement and, 94–95, 122; Battenberg marriage project and, 137–8; dismissal of, 143.
Blanc, Baron, 79–80, 89, 95, 97, 100, 119–21, 125.
Bleichröder, 124.
Boulanger, General Georges, 69.
Boutenev, 72–73.
Brackenbury, Major-General, 104, 117.

Bryce, James (afterwards Viscount), 106.
Busch, Dr., 121.

Caillard, Sir Vincent, 124–33.
Calice, Baron H. von, 95, 97, 100.
Cambon, Paul, 150, 153.
Carnarvon, 4th Earl of, 106.
Catalini, 118.
Chamberlain, Joseph, 109, 136, 149, 151.
Churchill, Lord Randolph, 26–27, 51–55, 135.
Clemenceau, Georges, 149.
Collas, 124.
Corti, Count, 66.
Council of the Ottoman Public Debt Administration, 120–1.
Cranbrook, Viscount, 51.
Crispi, Francesco, 89–90, 95, 99, 118–19, 121, 140, 143.
Cronstadt visit, 144–5, 149, 151.
Currie, Sir Philip, 107.
Cyprus Convention (1878), 104–5.

Depretis, Agostino, 20, 89.
Derby, 15th Earl of, 2, 7.
Deutsche Bank, 124, 127, 129, 131.
Dilke, Sir Charles W., 5–6, 53–54, 65, 133, 151.
Djevad Pasha, 149.
Dolgoruki, Prince, 60.
Dufferin and Ava, 1st Marquis of, 1, 6, 43.

Elliot, Sir Henry, 1, 6.
Ely, Lady Jane, 7.
Ernroth, General, 83, 89, 92–93, 95.
Erzeroum, 105, 107.
Euphrates Valley Railway Company, 112.

Ferdinand of Saxe-Coburg-Kohary, Prince, 83, 88, 91, 101–3, 116.
Forster, W. E., 5.
Flourens, Émile, 84, 102.
Freycinet, Charles de, 20, 150.
Friedrichsruh, 92, 95, 118.

Gardiner, General William Neville, 2.
German-Italian Military Agreement, 119.
German Levant Line, 133.

INDEX

Giers, Nicholas: Bulgaria and, 17–18, 101; Germany and, 69; Great Britain and, 85–87; attitude towards the Armenian question, 108.
Gladstone, William Ewart: Russia and, 8–9; Bulgaria and, 23–24; Egypt and, 66, 151–2; Moussa Bey and, 106–7.
Goschen, G. J. (afterwards Viscount), 1, 105.
Gosling, Sir A., 107.
Granville, 2nd Earl, 2–3, 4, 8–11, 23–24, 113.
Graves, Sir Robert, 4, 26–27.

Hamilton, Lord George, 52.
Hammond, Edmund, 4.
Hanson, 112.
Harcourt, Sir William V., 151–2.
Hatzfeldt-Wildenburg, Count Paul, 44–45, 54–55, 87.
Hengelmüller, Baron, 63.
'Holmwood incident', 76–77, 137–8.
Holstein, Baron Friedrich von, 70–71.

Iddesleigh, 1st Earl of (formerly Sir Stafford Northcote), 44–45, 51–57, 63–66, 68.
Imperial Ottoman Bank, 124.

Jones, Consul, 26.

Kalnoky, Count Gustav, Bulgaria and, 18–19, 139–40, 147; Germany and, 19, 89, 93, 95; Russia and, 19, 37, 64–65, 139–40; meeting with White, 59–60; Great Britain and, 62–66, 99, 120.
Katkov, Michael, 18, 69.
Kaulbars, General Nicholas, 48, 64.
Kaulla, Alfred, 123–4, 127–33.
Kennedy, Sir Arthur, 102, 120.
Kiamil Pasha, 148.
Kissingen, 58, 62, 149.
Kynock, 114.

Laboulaye, Antoine de, 69.
Lansdowne, 5th Marquis of, 52.
Lascelles, Sir Frank, 51.
Layard, Sir Henry, 1, 6, 105.
Loftus, Lord Augustus, 3.
Lyons, Lord, 51, 81.
Lytton, 1st Earl of, 102, 120, 142.

Malet, Sir Edward, 36, 60–61, 68, 76, 92, 98, 125, 137–8, 155.

Mediterranean Agreements: First Agreement, 62, 66, 72, 88; Second Agreement, 78, 94–104, 119.
Monson, Sir Edmund, 33.
Montebello, Count: Egypt and, 67, 77, 80, 84, 88, 150; Asia Minor and, 121.
Morier, Sir Robert, 6, 25–26, 52–53, 55, 83, 101–3, 120, 135, 139.
Morley, John (afterwards Viscount), 115.
'*Moskva* incident', 145–6.
Moussa Bey, 106.

Nelidov, Alexander: Bulgaria and, 17–18, 39; opposition to White's appointment, 49–50; Egypt and, 67, 75, 77–78, 80, 84, 88; Asia Minor and, 108, 129; the 'Moskva' incident and, 145–6.

Paget, Sir Augustus, 62–63, 89.
Portsmouth visit, 152.
Pressel, Wilhelm von, 112, 124.

Radolinsky, Count, 70.
Radowitz, Joseph Maria von: opposition to White, 39, 70; Egypt and, 75–77; Asia Minor and, 115, 119; split with Nelidov, 129.
Reinsurance Treaty, 77–78, 88, 94, 102, 122, 143.
Reuss, Prince Henry VII of, 89.
Ribot, 142, 150.
Rosebery, 5th Earl of, 39–42, 114.
Russell, Lord John, 7.
Russell, Lord Odo (afterwards Lord Ampthill), 6.
Rustem Pasha, 105, 149–50.

Salisbury, 3rd Marquis of: and White, 2, 4, 6, 38–39, 134–5, 153–7; Bulgarian policy of, 20–25, 72–73, 89–92; differences with Churchill, 51–55; and the First Mediterranean Agreement, 68; Egyptian policy of, 76–85, 87–88, 141–2; and the Second Mediterranean Agreement, 95–104; and Asia Minor, 103–8, 116–17, 121–2, 128–31; and Germany, 76–77, 87–88, 136–8; and Italy, 89–90; and Russia, 22–25, 87; and Austria-Hungary, 68, 99–100; and France, 152–3; general views on the Straits question, 51–55, 136, 145–7.

INDEX

Sanderson, Sir T. H., 76, 146–7.
Schweinitz, General H. L. von, 19.
Seefelder, 112, 124.
Shuvalov, Count Paul, 69–70, 77.
Siemens, Dr. Georg, 124, 133.
'Sigri landing scare', 146–7.
Simmons, Sir John Lintorn, 136, 147.
Smith, W. H., 52.
Stambulov, Stephen, 47, 102.
Stead, W. T., 9.
Stratford de Redcliffe, Lord, 109, 114.
Suez Canal Agreement, 84–85.
Swaine, Colonel, 72, 132.

Tewfik Pasha, 155.
Thornton, Sir Edward, 1, 8, 14, 39, 43–46, 56, 105–6.
Trans-Siberian Railway, 140.
Trotter, Major, 28, 117–18.

Victoria, Queen of England: White and, 7, 134; Bulgaria and, 23, 51; the Portsmouth visit and, 152–3.
Vincent, Sir Edgar, 126.

Waddington, William H., 142.
Waldemar, Prince of Denmark, 48.
Waldersee, Count Alfred von, 72.
Washburn, Dr. George, 27.
White, Sir William Arthur: early life, 2–8; Pendjeh crisis and, 8–13; at the 1885 Ambassadors' Conference, 29–40; Bulgaria and, 25–29, 91–92, 101–3; Sir Edward Thornton and, 43–46; opposition to his appointment as ambassador, 49–50; attitude towards Germany and Austria-Hungary, 57–58, 61–62; meetings with Bismarck and Kalnoky, 58–60, 67; Egypt and, 75–76, 80–81, 83–84, 86–88, 148–57; Asia Minor and, 103–33, 142–3; memorandum on Turkish railways, 111–13; general views on the Near East, 134–5, 138–9, 147–8, 156; France and, 153–4; death of, 134, 155–6.
William I, Emperor of Germany, 103, 137.
William II, Emperor of Germany: visit to Constantinople, 122–3; Great Britain and, 137; visit to London, 143.
Wolff, Sir Henry Drummond: criticism of Iddesleigh, 51–52; special mission to Constantinople and Egypt, 73–86, 88, 111, 129, 137, 141, 151, 155–6.
Wolkenstein, Count, 19, 64.
Würtembergische Vereinsbank, 124.

Zafiropoulo, 112.
Zankov, Dragan, 47.
Zanzibar-Heligoland Treaty, 141–3.

PRINTED IN
GREAT BRITAIN
AT THE
UNIVERSITY PRESS
OXFORD
BY
CHARLES BATEY
PRINTER
TO THE
UNIVERSITY

DATE DUE